IN PERSON: WORLD POETS

Dear Jessica
I hope you enjoy
this cornucopia of
poetry!   Pamela

Many thanks for coming.
with all good wishes

PAMELA ROBERTSON-PEARCE is an artist, filmmaker and translator. Her films include *IMAGO: Meret Oppenheim* (1988/1996), on the artist who made the fur-lined teacup, and *Gifted Beauty* (2000), about Surrealist women artists including Leonora Carrington and Remedios Varo. *IMAGO: Meret Oppenheim* won several awards, including the Swiss Film Board's Prize for Outstanding Quality and the Gold Apple Award at the National Educational Film and Video Festival in America. She has shown her work in solo exhibitions in New York and Provincetown (Cape Cod), and in various group shows in the US and Europe. Born in Stockholm, she grew up in Sweden, Spain and England, and then for over 20 years lived mostly in America – also working in Switzerland and Norway – before moving to Northumberland. She co-edited the anthology *Soul Food: nourishing poems for starved minds* (2007) with Neil Astley and was the filmmaker on *In Person: 30 Poets* (2008). For more information see www.pamelarobertsonpearce.com

NEIL ASTLEY is editor of Bloodaxe Books, which he founded in 1978, and was given a D.Litt by Newcastle University in 1995 for his pioneering work. He has edited over a thousand poetry books and published more than twenty anthologies with Bloodaxe, most notably the *Staying Alive* trilogy of *Staying Alive* (2002), *Being Alive* (2004) and *Being Human* (2011) – and *Essential Poems from the 'Staying Alive' Trilogy* (2012) – as well as *Passionfood: 100 Love Poems* (2005), *Soul Food: nourishing poems for starved minds* [with Pamela Robertson-Pearce] (2007), *Earth Shattering: ecopoems* (2007), *In Person: 30 Poets* [filmed by Pamela Robertson-Pearce] (2008), *The Hundred Years' War: modern war poems* (2014) and *Funny Ha-Ha, Funny Peculiar: a book of strange & comic poems* (2015). His other books include two poetry collections, *Darwin Survivor* (1988) and *Biting My Tongue* (1995), and two eco-novels, *The End of My Tether* (2002) (shortlisted for the Whitbread First Novel Award), and *The Sheep Who Changed the World* (2005).

IN PERSON: WORLD POETS

FILMED BY
PAMELA ROBERTSON-PEARCE
& NEIL ASTLEY

EDITED BY NEIL ASTLEY

BLOODAXE BOOKS

ISBN: 978 1 85224 985 4

First published 2017 by
Bloodaxe Books Ltd,
Eastburn,
South Park,
Hexham,
Northumberland NE46 1BS.

www.bloodaxebooks.com
For further information about Bloodaxe titles
please visit our website or write to
the above address for a catalogue.

Supported by
ARTS COUNCIL
ENGLAND

Cover design by Neil Astley & Pamela Robertson-Pearce

DVDs manufactured by TV Productions Ltd, Newcastle upon Tyne.

Book printed in Great Britain by Bell & Bain Limited, Glasgow, Scotland, on
acid-free paper sourced from mills with FSC chain of custody certification.

CONTENTS

NOTE ON THE TEXTS

Collections cited after each poem title in the anthology are the books (some not published by Bloodaxe) in which these poems were first published, in many cases followed by details of the books in which the poems can now be found. In the case of books published in other languages, a translation of the book title appears under the title of the poem translated into English, but this does not indicate publication of that book in English.

ACKNOWLEDGEMENTS

In Person: World Poets is dedicated to all the poets and translators who have been willing to let us film them reading and talking about their work, in many cases in their own homes. We also dedicate it to the memory of those poets we were fortunate to be able to meet and film while they were still with us: Roy Fisher, Thomas Lux, Samuel Menashe, Ruth Stone and Tomas Tranströmer.

Many other people and organisations helped the project in a variety of ways. As well as the poets who gave generously of their time and hospitality, we would like to thank in particular Ian and Angela Beer in Ledbury and Ledbury Poetry Festival (Chloe Garner), as well as Robert Adamson and Juno Gemes, Aldeburgh Poetry Festival and the Poetry Trust (Naomi Jaffa, Michael Laskey, Dean Parkin, Judy Braggins), the Arvon Foundation at Totleigh Barton, Peter and Terry Born, Peter and Diana Carter, Cove Park (Polly Clark and Julian Forrester), Marcia Croll and Nora Swan Croll, Cúirt International Festival of Literature (Dani Gill, Maura Kennedy), DLR Poetry Now, Dún Laoghaire (Belinda McKeon), Anil Dharker, Imtiaz Dharker, Katie Donovan, Finnish Literature Information Centre [FILI] (Iris Schwank), Francis A. Jones, Chris Gillooly, Selina Guinness, Ivor Indyk, Helen Ivory and Martin Figura, Lithuanian Cultural Institute (Kotryna Pranckūnaitė), Jack and Mercy Angela Mapanje, William and Cynthia Morrison-Bell, Newcastle University and NCLA (Linda Anderson, Pete Hebden), Renaissance One (Melanie Abrahams), Tom Pickard, the Romanian Cultural Institute, London (Gabriela Mocan), Barbara Russell and Brad Foster, Anna Selby, K. Sridhar and Gita Chadha, Lydia Towsey, Monica Tranströmer, Chase Twichell and Russell Banks, Tatiana Venclova, Venclovas' House-Museum (Justina Juozėnaitė), Petras Vyšniauskas, and the Wordsworth Trust (Andrew Forster, Michael McGregor).

INTRODUCTION

In Person: World Poets is the sequel to *In Person: 30 Poets*, published by Bloodaxe in 2008. This was a new concept in publishing: readings by 30 poets published by Bloodaxe in its first 30 years captured on film, with all the poems included in the footage printed in the book of the films. No other publisher has attempted anything like this in Britain or anywhere else for that matter. No one else has originated and produced short films of poets reading and discussing their work and made these available on DVDs with an anthology including all the texts.

'Such is its impact that it is impossible to imagine that it has never been done before,' wrote Fiona McCann in *The Irish Times*, reviewing the Dublin launch event for *In Person: 30 Poets*. 'What Astley and Robertson-Pearce have created for poetry readers is an opportunity to witness some of the most important poets in the English language giving voice to their own work.'

Four of the poets in *In Person: 30 Poets* wrote in other languages, with their work presented in English translation as well as in the original. Our even more international sequel features a dozen out of nearly twice as many poets reading in their own languages. The book includes their poems in the original as well as the English translations, providing readers with the opportunity to study how some of our most skilful translators try to recreate the particular music of the poem in its first language in their English versions while carrying over the meaning as accurately as possible.

This is quite a revelation in the case of poets working with translators such as Robin Fulton, David McDuff, Jamie McKendrick and Francis R. Jones, who seem almost literally to have the ear of the poet, working on their collections over many years, with questions and revisions passing back and forth between them until both are as happy as they can be with the final text. Pia Tafdrup, Esther Jansma and Piotr Sommer all stress the importance of this process in our films of them reading and discussing their work.

The greater international scope of *In Person: World Poets* also involves representing poets from many more parts of the world, including Albania, Australia, Brazil, Canada, Denmark, Estonia, Finland, India, Italy, Jamaica, Korea, Lithuania, Macedonia, Malawi, the Netherlands, Pakistan, Poland, Romania, Sweden and the USA, as well as from Britain and Ireland. Here we also show the cultural importance of Bloodaxe's poetry publishing, in contrast with the insularity – and indeed provincialism – of the few London-based commercial imprints which still publish poetry, which mostly offer readers only work by poets from these islands plus the odd token figure from elsewhere.

It has long been the case that in poetry, international publishing happens away from London, with most of the major figures in world poetry outside the UK – as well as the most diverse range of poets from different ethnic backgrounds within Britain – published by Arc, Bloodaxe, Carcanet and Peepal Tree in the north of England.

In Person: World Poets thus performs another service, that of enabling readers to see and hear poets from around the world, many of whom they might never have an opportunity to encounter at a literature festival in Britain, nor will they come across much notice of their work in the British media. We no longer have any poets of world standing with the moral stature of writers such as Ana Blandiana, Carolyn Forché, Robert Hass, Jaan Kaplinski, Tomas Tranströmer, Tomas Venclova and Ko Un, poets whose work addresses the fundamental questions of human existence and how we live our lives, certainly not since the passing of Seamus Heaney and Geoffrey Hill, and yet when their books are published here, even collected editions of their work are ignored by the mainstream cultural media.

It takes a Nobel Prize for such poets to be noticed, even by the broadsheet press, and even then, a truly great European poet like Tranströmer, his work translated into over 60 different languages, can be dismissed out of ignorance, with the *Observer* referring to him condescendingly as 'fairly obscure' and the *Telegraph* offering readers a snide guide to 'ten things you never knew about the poet you never knew'. But given that what little space is afforded to poetry in the press tends to be focussed on a small number of currently fashionable English poets, in many cases writers whose work has little or no significance outside our country, or even outside particular social groups, it's not surprising that the general public served by the media is unaware that poetry of any importance relies on a profound and radical engagement with language, form, tradition and thought, and that the major figures in world poetry are writers they probably won't have heard of.

Like the first *In Person* compilation, this new package is your own personal interactive poetry festival packaged into a book. As an educational resource for the oral art of poetry, whether writing it or reading and appreciating it, both compilations are without parallel. They also offer festival organisers and journalists the means of acquainting themselves with writers other than the "usual suspects", those known "names" continually recycled in festival programmes and newspaper features as if there weren't any other poets worth seeing or reading.

In Person: World Poets differs from its predecessor in several respects. It has taken eight years to bring this new project to fruition, with almost twice as many poets included this time round. The films are mostly longer, enabling the poet to present a wider range of their work in more depth or to read an extended sequence on a theme. There's more discussion of their work, sometimes in the form of interview responses, giving readers more context to the poems. In some cases we've been able to produce longer films showing the relationship between the poet and the place where they live, most notably in the films of Robert Adamson and Ruth Stone on the first DVD, which includes several other longer pieces.

Where possible we film the poets in their own homes, as we did with *In Person: 30 Poets*. With visiting writers caught on the hoof, we try find a quiet place somewhere else. Because the writer isn't invaded by a whole film crew, the dynamic is generally quite relaxed. I've usually met the poets a few times in course of publishing their work, and in many cases we've known each other for many years, so the way the writer reads and introduces their work feels much more open, their welcome to us as friends and supporters of their work extending to the reader/viewer, unlike the separateness felt by writer and viewer when the poet is taken to a studio and filmed against a black background.

Likewise, our approach to filmmaking is informal and straightforward, involving no visual trickery. Not unlike an alternative documentary filmmaker, Pamela puts the viewer inside the room with the person being filmed. Our camera becomes your eyes and ears as the poet reads to us, but there's no pretending that the film frame is the total world. Sometimes the poet may speak to us between poems, offstage as it were, or one of us may say something in response to what's just been said or read, and if that engagement connects with comments we want to keep as part of the film, then what we say is included as well.

With this project, my frequent unaccompanied travels as a publisher or speaker to festivals – and my continuing involvement with Ledbury Poetry Festival in particular – have offered opportunities for filming poets where I've had to be the camera man. Here I've tried as much as possible to follow Pamela's style of filming while inevitably falling short as regards the finer points of the art where the more nuanced touches are down to her intuitive approach.

The project has been very much a collaboration between us,

combining Pamela's filmmaking expertise with my knowledge of the poet and the poetry along with my still evolving editing skills, which now extend to editing the film footage as well as the texts, something which can be quite challenging if you're having to add the English translation in visible subtitles timed to follow lines being spoken in an unfamiliar language in a way that keeps step with the rhythm and pace of the poet's reading.

As with *In Person: 30 Poets*, which included John Agard on stage at London's Soho Theatre, we also wanted to feature some poets whose work has a different kind of impact performed live in front of an audience, as is the case with Jean 'Binta' Breeze, Ko Un and Mark Waldron.

With time we've also recognised the extent to which our film compilations acquire even great archival value with the passing of the poets. When *In Person: 30 Poets* was produced in 2008, we were able include Ivor Bowen's footage of Ken Smith, the first poet published by Bloodaxe 30 years earlier (who died in 2003). Later that year, Adrian Mitchell died. And we have since lost six other poets we filmed for *In Person: 30 Poets*: Galway Kinnell, Philip Levine, Taha Muhammad Ali, Peter Reading, C.K. Williams and C.D. Wright. Sadly, we've already lost five poets we've filmed for *In Person: World Poets* since starting work on the project, Roy Fisher, Thomas Lux, Samuel Menashe, Ruth Stone and Tomas Tranströmer, two of whom died only this year. However, their work – and the work of all the poets included in *In Person: World Poets* – comes alive for us when we see these films. Nearly all of them are powerful readers of poetry, and seeing and listening to their readings, anyone should gain a much greater appreciation not just of their poetry but of how the best modern poetry is conceived, written and spoken; and how it *sounds*, how it leaps off the page when read aloud by the poets themselves.

NEIL ASTLEY

DVD 1

POETRY FEATURES

1 | ROBERT ADAMSON

Filmed at home on the Hawkesbury River, NSW, Australia,
by Pamela Robertson-Pearce, 20-21 February 2010

Robert Adamson has been nourished for much of his life by Australia's Hawkesbury River. His poetry praises nature – red in tooth and claw – and celebrates existence as a mythological quest. His early poems trace his own journey through a difficult childhood, prison and exile in the city, the source of a hard-won scepticism undercutting the highly personal Romanticism and daring lyricism of his later work.

His grandfather was a fisherman on the Hawkesbury, where Bob has lived, on and off, for most of his life, and for the past three decades with photographer Juno Gemes. A series of juvenile misdemeanours resulted in him being sent to various detention centres. It was during this period that he began writing poetry, as he recounts in a memoir covering his early years, *Inside Out* (2004).

He was born in Sydney in 1943. From 1970 to 1985 he was the driving force behind Australia's *New Poetry* magazine, and in 1986, with Juno, he established Paper Bark Press, for two decades one of Australia's leading poetry publishers. He was the inaugural CAL chair of poetry at UTS (University of Technology, Sydney) in 2011-14. He has published over 20 books of poetry, including three with Bloodaxe in Britain, *Reading the River* (2004), *The Kingfisher's Soul* (2009) and *Net Needle* (2016), and *The Language of Oysters* (1997), a celebration of the Hawkesbury River combining his poems with Juno's photographs.

Our film's narrative covers some of the key aspects of his life and work: his early obsession with fishing, birds and nature; his discussions with American poets Robert Duncan and Robert Creeley during their visits to Australia (with Duncan's outing to the Hawkesbury inspiring one of the poems he reads); and the ways in which his poetry was transformed with their encouragement, and in particular by Duncan's insistence on the primacy of myth in poetry and Creeley's urging that he should write from his own life.

The selection of poems is directed by the stories he tells over the course of two days on and around the river. Their house on the point looks out over Mooney Creek and its old oysterbeds. On one trip downriver, he shows us his grandfather's old house on the shore, as a pelican takes flight across the water. The film starts with the boat moored at Jerusalem Bay, an inlet where he used to come fishing as a teenager on outings from Sydney.

The Gathering Light

BLACK WATER 1987 | READING THE RIVER 2004

Morning shines on the cowling of the Yamaha
locked onto the stern of the boat
spears of light shoot away
from the gun-metal grey enamel.
Now I wait for God to show
instead of calling him a liar.

I've just killed a mulloway –
it's eighty-five pounds, fifty years old –
the huge mauve-silver body trembles in the hull.

Time whistles round us, an invisible
flood tide that I let go
while I take in what I have done.
It wasn't a fight, I was drawn to this moment.
The physical world drains away
into a golden calm.

The sun is a hole in the sky, a porthole –
you can see turbulence out there,
the old wheeling colours and their dark forces –
but here on the surface of the river
where I cradle the great fish in my arms
and smell its pungent death, a peace
I have never known before –
a luminous absence of time, pain,
sex, thought – of everything but light.

Thinking of Eurydice at midnight

READING THE RIVER 2004

> where the light struck
>
> HD

My Siamese cat's left a brown
snake, its back broken, on my desk.
The underground throbs outside my window.
The black highway of the river's crinkled by a light
westerly on its last legs. I want to give praise
to the coming winter, but the problem
of belief flares and buckles under
the lumpy syntax. The Unelected
President's on the radio again,
laying waste to the world.

Faith – that old myth. I drag up
impossible meanings and double divisions
of love and betrayal, light and dark. Eurydice.
Where on earth am I after all these years?
A possum eats crusts on the verandah,
standing up on its hind legs.
My weakness can't be measured.
My head contains thousands of images –
slimy mackerel splashing about in the murk.
My failures slip through fingers pointed
at the best night of my life. This one.

The cold mist falls, my head floats in the stream
of thinking. Eurydice. Did I fumble? Maybe
I was meant to be the moon's reflection,
and sing darkness like the nightjar.
Why wouldn't I detest this place, where the
sun shines on settlers and their heirs
and these heirlooms I weave
from blond silk?

Black water

BLACK WATER 1987 | READING THE RIVER 2004

I took Robert Duncan in my grandfather's skiff
rowing across Mooney Creek
words hummed around our heads

The trees are speaking on the far shore
we'll never get there in time
the pages of books swim upstream

we study words growing on them
The time will come and you will turn
the present a breeze that passes

sweeps up carrying the odor
The Mower is creating as he moves through
the rushes looking for glowworms

Words little warm animals of air
words growing and teaming over the mudflats
This river has no bends

this river is not an actual river yet
this water has burnt its right of way into sandstone
Great sheets of it slide by on either side

parting and taking the flotsam
The Mower creates 'for she my mind hath so displaced
that I shall never find my home'

Marvell was calling from the mangroves
our souls crows gliding down to eat the words
time created endless bends

the river was never the same
that night Duncan gathered the southern stars
into his being the black water plopping with fat mullet

My granny

WHERE I COME FROM 1979 | READING THE RIVER 2004

When my granny was dying
I'd go into her bedroom
and look at her

she'd tell me to get out of it
leave this foul river

it will wear you out too

she was very sick
and her red curly hair
was matted and smelt of gin

sometimes I sat there all day
listening to the races
and put bets on for her at the shop

and I sat there the afternoon
she died and heard her say her last words
I sat there not telling

maybe three hours
beside the first dead person I'd seen

I tried to drink some of her gin
it made me throw up on the bed
then I left her

she said the prawns will eat you
when you die on the Hawkesbury River

The Southern Skua

BLACK WATER 1987 | THE KINGFISHER'S SOUL 2009

The skua flew into our heads in 1968 –
a new kind of poetry, a scavenging predator
frequently attacking humans,
flying through the streets of seaside towns,
foraging with seagulls. This bird
has few predators. One was found
in Tasmania, its beak embedded in the skull
of a spotted quoll, dragged
into a clearing by devils. They form clubs
and proclaim their territory
by various displays and loud aggressive calls;
they are agile metaphysicians,
sweeping along lines of projective verse,
echoing each other's songs.
Although the skua breeds on Black Mountain
it is migratory and dispersive, its call
a series of low quacks and thin whinnying squeals.
They are omnivorous and critical creatures;
animal liberationists never mention
the habits of skua. If you read skua poetry, beware:
one could fly out from the page
and change the expression on your face.

The Stone Curlew

BLACK WATER 1987 | THE KINGFISHER'S SOUL 2009

I am writing this inside the head
of a bush stone curlew,
we have been travelling for days

moving over the earth
flying when necessary.
I am not the bird itself, only its passenger

looking through its eyes.
The world rocks slightly as we move
over the stubble grass of the dunes,

at night shooting stars draw lines
across the velvet dark
as I hang in a sling of light

between the bird's nocturnal eyes.
The heavens make sense, seeing this way
makes me want to believe

words have meanings,
that Australia is no longer a wound
in the side of the earth.

I think of the white settlers
who compared the curlew's song
to the cries of women being strangled,

and remember the poets who wrote
anthropomorphically as I sing softly
from the jelly of the stone curlew's brain.

Juno & Eurydice

MULBERRY LEAVES 2001 | READING THE RIVER 2004

Our boat hits the warm air sitting in Mooney Creek
as the first light of dawn begins to trace dark mountains.
We come in from the night, leaving behind
our particular hells. Back up the creek
the mist rises in great white banks –
ahead of us, our house on the point.

Each year we make it through and time brings
images and poems to map the journey –
each year we find this place holding us back
from going, the river country taking us in.
We claim it just by being here, on the brink
of darkness. A crimson rosella draws a line

of colour across the white bay: we are drenched in light
and the rich smell of the river rising from mangroves.
A welcome swallow skims the fresh water in our pool.
I couldn't live without you now, though in dreams I've
betrayed Eurydice. Death has become
a part of what the river's taught me –

this world is created for us above ground,
where even lyre birds walk slowly through your
garden holding their lyres high. We move in and out of
the myths, becoming figures from them – maybe the longer
we live here the less they matter, as we tell ourselves
stories that were here before myth.

2 | RUTH STONE

(1915-2011)

Filmed by Pamela Robertson-Pearce in Vermont, at Ripton
on 18 September 2008 and Goshen on 7 September 2009

Ruth Stone was born in Virginia in 1915, and lived in rural Vermont
for much of her life, at Goshen near Middlebury. From 1959, after
her husband Walter committed suicide during a stay in London,
she had to raise her family alone, all the time writing what she
called her 'love poems, all written to a dead man' who forced her
to 'reside in limbo' with her three daughters. For 20 years she
travelled the US, teaching creative writing at many universities. A
greatly loved teacher, she was still working into her 80s, and still
writing poetry well into her 90s.

She was 87 when she received the National Book Award for *In
the Next Galaxy* (2002). Her retrospective, *What Love Comes To:
New & Selected Poems*, was published in the US in 2008 and by
Bloodaxe in Britain in 2009. She once said, 'I decided very early on
not to write like other people.' Her book shows the fruits of this
resolve in the lifetime's work of a true American original, from early
formal lyrics, fierce feminist and political poems, through medita-
tions on her husband's suicide, on love, loss, blindness and age-
ing. The poems she speaks – and embodies – in our film draw us
into her own particular world of serious laughter; of uncertainty
and insight; of mystery and acceptance.

By the time of our two visits, when she was 93 and 94, she had
almost lost her sight, but still knew many poems by heart, espe-
cially ones from earlier books, while declaring she had never learned
them, and that she never composed them either, she just had to
grab them when they came to her. Unable to live on her own by
then, she was staying with her daughter Marcia Croll in nearby
Ripton, where we filmed her on our first visit, but when we returned
the following September, we were able to film her sitting in her
favourite chair on the porch of the old house at Goshen. The film-
ing conditions were far from ideal, with sudden changes of light
and cars roaring past on the dirt road outside, but we think the
film's technical flaws are more than compensated for by Ruth's
extraordinary presence, her vitality, truth-telling and *being*.

The following account of Ruth's writing was collaged from her
interviews with J.F. Battaglia, Robert Bradley, Elizabeth Gilbert,
Sandra M. Gilbert and Mary Ann Wehler (a shorter version was
first published in the *PBS Bulletin*).

Poems through a life

My mother read poetry aloud when she was nursing me. She loved Tennyson deeply. She taught me all those poems by heart, so by the time I was two I knew many poems. What I absorbed from her was both a cadence of language and a music of poetry and patterns. Later on, when I was able, I wrote all these patterns of English poetry.

I started reading when I was three, and I've read all kinds of books all my life: a lot on science, nature and the universe. Women who love to write poetry are the hagfish of the world. We eat everything. We eat the language. We eat experience. We eat other people's poems.

I wrote my first poem without knowing I'd done it – and found that poems came with this mysterious feeling, a kind of peculiar ecstasy. I'd feel and hear a poem coming from a long way off, like a thunderous train of air. I'd feel it physically. I'd run like hell to the house, blindly groping for pencil and paper. And then the poem would write itself. I'd write it down from the inside out. The thing knew itself already. There were other times when I'd almost miss it, feeling it pass through me just as I was grabbing the pencil, but then I'd catch it by its tail and pull it backwards into my body. Then the poem came out backwards and I'd have to turn it round.

My father was a musician and played the drums all the time, so I learned a lot of rhythms just through my ear. Rhyme is automatic with me. I use a lot of internal rhyme. It's all in my ear, my own music. People are always talking to me about my sense of form but I think it's just built in. It's fun and challenging to work with form. It's a catalyst, it zips up your adrenaline. I don't know at what point I became more in control over what was so spontaneous, an uncontrollable process.

When I was younger there was a kind of singing in all my poetry, but after Walter died, that younger singing was subdued, not harsh enough. Of course I still have a lot of inner rhyme. But I needed to find a different way to write. Life altered me. Experience and suffering altered me. Having to endure and be strong for my daughters altered me. I couldn't cry, but I didn't talk for a year either. I couldn't even stand up straight, I shuffled: 'I shuffled and snuffled and whined for you' ['The Tree']. I couldn't live anywhere except in some sort of dreamlike state in which it seemed as though he'd never left me. And also the past kept intervening, and then it was as though there was no present, but only the past. And that kept going for a long long time.

Poems from filming at Ripton, VT:

In an Iridescent Time

IN AN IRIDESCENT TIME 1959

My mother, when young, scrubbed laundry in a tub,
She and her sisters on an old brick walk
Under the apple trees, sweet rub-a-dub.
The bees came round their heads, the wrens made talk.
Four young ladies each with a rainbow board
Honed their knuckles, wrung their wrists to red,
Tossed back their braids and wiped their aprons wet.
The Jersey calf beyond the back fence roared;
And all the soft day, swarms about their pet
Buzzed at his big brown eyes and bullish head.
Four times they rinsed, they said. Some things they starched,
Then shook them from the baskets two by two,
And pinned the fluttering intimacies of life
Between the lilac bushes and the yew:
Brown gingham, pink, and skirts of Alice blue.

Orchard

IN AN IRIDESCENT TIME 1959

The mare roamed soft about the slope,
Her rump was like a dancing girl's.
Gentle beneath the apple trees
She pulled the grass and shook the flies.
Her forelocks hung in tawny curls;
She had a woman's limpid eyes,
A woman's patient stare that grieves.
And when she moved among the trees,
The dappled trees, her look was shy,
She hid her nakedness in leaves.
A delicate though weighted dance
She stepped while flocks of finches flew
From tree to tree and shot the leaves
With songs of golden twittering;

How admirable her tender stance.
And then the apple trees were new,
And she was new, and we were new,
And in the barns the stallions stamped
And shook the hills with trumpeting.

The Talking Fish

TOPOGRAPHY 1971

My love's eyes are red as the sargasso
With lights behind the iris like a cephalopod's.
The weeds move slowly, November's diatoms
Stain the soft stagnant belly of the sea.
Mountains, atolls, coral reefs,
Do you desire me? Am I among the jellyfish of your griefs?
I comb my sorrows singing; any doomed sailor can hear
The rising and falling bell and begin to wish
For home. There is no choice among the voices
Of love. Even a carp sings.

The Excuse

TOPOGRAPHY 1971

Do they write poems when they have something to say,
Something to think about,
Rubbed from the world's hard rubbing in the excess of every day?
The summer I was twenty-four in San Francisco. You and I.
The whole summer seemed like a cable-car ride over the gold bay.
But once in a bistro, angry at one another,
We quarreled about a taxi fare. I doubt
That it was the fare we quarreled about,
But one excuse is as good as another
In the excess of passion, in the need to be worn away.

Do they know it is cleanness of skin, firmness of flesh that matters?
It is so difficult to look at the deprived, or smell their decay.
But now I am among them. I, too, am a leper, a warning.
I hold out my crippled fingers; my voice flatters
Everyone who comes this way. In the weeds of mourning,
Groaning and gnashing, I display
Myself in malodorous comic wrappings and tatters,
In the excess of passion, in the need to be worn away.

Advice

TOPOGRAPHY 1971

My hazard wouldn't be yours, not ever;
But every doom, like a hazelnut, comes down
To its own worm. So I am rocking here
Like any granny with her apron over her head
Saying, lordy me. It's my trouble.
There's nothing to be learned this way.
If I heard a girl crying help
I would go to save her;
But you hardly ever hear those words.
Dear children, you must try to say
Something when you are in need.
Don't confuse hunger with greed;
And don't wait until you are dead.

I Have Three Daughters

TOPOGRAPHY 1971

I have three daughters
Like greengage plums.
They sat all day
Sucking their thumbs.
And more's the pity,
They cried all day,
Why doesn't our mother's brown hair
Turn gray?

I have three daughters
Like three cherries.
They sat at the window
The boys to please.
And they couldn't wait
For their mother to grow old.
Why doesn't our mother's brown hair
Turn to snow?

I have three daughters
In the apple tree
Singing Mama send Daddy
With three young lovers
To take them away from me.

I have three daughters
Like greengage plums,
Sitting all day
And sighing all day
And sucking their thumbs;
Singing, Mama won't you fetch and carry,
And Daddy, won't you let us marry,
Singing, sprinkle snow down on Mama's hair
And lordy, give us our share.

Metamorphosis

TOPOGRAPHY 1971

Now I am old, all I want to do is try;
But when I was young, if it wasn't easy I let it lie,
Learning through my pores instead,
And it did neither of us any good.

For now she is gone who slept away my life,
And I am ignorant who inherited,
Though the head has grown so lively that I laugh,
'Come look, come stomp, come listen to the drum.'

I see more now than then; but she who had my eyes
Closed them in happiness, and wrapped the dark
In her arms and stole my life away,
Singing in dreams of what was sure to come.

I see it perfectly, except the beast
Fumbles and falters, until the others wince.
Everything shimmers and glitters and shakes with unbearable longing,
The dancers who cannot sleep, and the sleepers who cannot dance.

Bargain

CHEAP 1975

I was not ready for this world
Nor will I ever be.
But came an infant periled
By my mother sea,
And crying piteously.

Before my father's sword,
His heavy voice of thunder,
His cloud hung fiery eyes,
I ran, a living blunder.

After the hawker's cries,
Desiring to be shared
I hid among the flies.

Myself became the fruit and vendor.
I began to sing.
Mocking the caged birds
I made my offering.

'Sweet cream and curds...
Who will have me,
Who will have me?'
And close upon my words,
'I will,' said poverty.

The Widow's Song

WHO IS THE WIDOW'S MUSE? 1991

As I was a springbok,
I am a leper.
As my skirt lifted up as a veil,
so the shawl of a widow.
As the oxlip,
so the buffalo grass.
As the wall of a garden in winter,
so was I, hidden.
As the game of the keeper…
not counted.
So I am without number.
As the yellow star grass.

Mantra

IN THE NEXT GALAXY 2002

When I am sad
I sing, remembering
the redwing blackbird's clack.
Then I want no thing
except to turn time back
to what I had
before love made me sad.

When I forget to weep,
I hear the peeping tree toads
creeping up the bark.
Love lies asleep
and dreams that everything
is in its golden net;
and I am caught there, too,
when I forget.

The Season

WHO IS THE WIDOW'S MUSE? 1991

I know what calls the Devil from the pits,
With a thief's fingers there he slouches and sits;
I've seen him passing on a frenzied mare,
Bitter eyed on her haunches out to stare;
He rides her cruel and he rides her easy.
Come along spring, come along sun, come along field daisy.

Smell the foxy babies, smell the hunting dog;
The shes have whelped, the cocks and hens have lost their wits;
And cry, 'Why,' cry the spring peepers, 'Why,' each little frog.
He rides her cruel and he rides her easy;
Come along spring, come along sun, come along field daisy

Poems from filming at Goshen, VT:

Love's Relative

IN AN IRIDESCENT TIME 1959

The couple who remain in bed
Are not alike; he's tanned and hairy,
Has a fierce Egyptian head,
She's dimpled, brief; alas, contrary.

Rather defenseless on the sheet
When morning oozes in the cracks,
Her tiny toes, his monster feet,
Both of them upon their backs.

Her years are two and his are thirty.
He's long and bony, somewhat glum.
Her little peaceful feet are dirty.
She sucks a firmly calloused thumb.

At some point in the evil dawning
This oedipal arrangement grew,
The leap from crib to bed while yawning
Mother in disdain withdrew.

O man, whose waking breeds confusion,
Protect the comfort of her sleep.
Hers is the primal bright illusion
From which she makes the bridal leap.

Dream of Light in the Shade

TOPOGRAPHY 1971

Now that I am married I spend
My hours thinking about my husband.
I wind myself about his shelter.
I watch his sleep, dreaming of how to defend *
His inert form. At night
Leaning on my elbow I pretend
I am merely a lecherous friend.

And being the first to wake
Often wholly naked descend
To the dim first floor where the chairs
Hold the night before, and all says attend!
The light so coldly spells in innocence,
Attend! The cup is filled with light,
And on my skin the sun flashes
And fades as the shade trees bend.

* Ruth forgot the words 'I watch his sleep' in her reading of this poem.

Second-Hand Coat

SECOND-HAND COAT 1987

I feel
in her pockets; she wore nice cotton gloves,
kept a handkerchief box, washed her undies,
ate at the Holiday Inn, had a basement freezer,
belonged to a bridge club.
I think when I wake in the morning
that I have turned into her.
She hangs in the hall downstairs,
a shadow with pulled threads.
I slip her over my arms, skin of a matron.
Where are you? I say to myself, to the orphaned body,
and her coat says,
Get your purse, have you got your keys?

The Tree

CHEAP 1975

I was a child when you married me,
A child I was when I married you.
But I was a regular mid-west child,
And you were a Jew.

My mother needled my father cold,
My father gambled his weekly gold,
And I stayed young in my mind, though old,
As your regular children do.

I didn't rah and I hardly raved.
I loved my pa while my mother slaved,
And it rubbed me raw how she scrimped and saved
When I was so new.

Then you took me in with your bony knees,
And it wasn't them that I wanted to please –
It was Jesus Christ that I had to squeeze;
Oh, glorious you.

Life in the dead sprang up in me,
I walked the waves of the salty sea,
I wept for my mother in Galilee,
My ardent Jew.

Love and touch and unity.
Parting and joining; the trinity
Was flesh, the mind and the will to be.
The world grew through me like a tree.

Flesh was the citadel but Rome
Was right as rain. From my humble home
I walked to the scaffold of pain, and the dome
Of heaven wept for her sensual son
Whom the Romans slew.

Was it I who was old when you hung, my Jew?
I shuffled and snuffled and whined for you.
And the child climbed up where the dead tree grew
And slowly died while she wept for you.

Goyim wept for the beautiful Jew.

For My Dead Red-haired Mother

SIMPLICITY 1995

I loved a red-haired girl.
Freud knew it was a wicked thing to do.
This is how all poems begin.
Sometime after the age of two
I beat the Adam in me black and blue.
Infant, wicked infant!
I threw my love outside
and grew into a bride.

You and I reflecting in our bones
the sea and sky,
we dressed ourselves as flesh,
we learned to lie.

Dearly beloved,
forgive me for that mean and meager self,
that now would mingle
but must first die.

Women Laughing

SECOND-HAND COAT 1987

Laughter from women gathers like reeds in the river.
A silence of light below their rhythm glazes the water.
They are on a rim of silence looking into the river.
Their laughter traces the water as kingfishers dipping
circles within circles set the reeds clicking;
and an upward rush of herons lifts out of the nests of laughter,
their long stick-legs dangling, herons, rising out of the river.

Curtains

SECOND-HAND COAT 1987

Putting up new curtains,
other windows intrude.
As though it is that first winter in Cambridge
when you and I had just moved in.
Now cold borscht alone in a bare kitchen.

What does it mean if I say this years later?

Listen, last night
I am on a crying jag
with my landlord, Mr Tempesta.
I sneaked in two cats.
He screams 'No pets! No pets!'
I become my Aunt Virginia,
proud but weak in the head.
I remember Anna Magnani.
I throw a few books. I shout.
He wipes his eyes and opens his hands.
OK OK keep the dirty animals
but no nails in the walls.
We cry together.
I am so nervous, he says.

I want to dig you up and say, look,
it's like the time, remember,
when I ran into our living room naked
to get rid of that fire inspector.

See what you miss by being dead?

3 | TOMAS TRANSTRÖMER

(1931-2015)

Filmed by Pamela Robertson-Pearce in Stockholm, 18 August 2011, and on Runmarö, 20 June 2013; additional filming in Östergötland. Nobel Prize filming copyright © Nobel Media AB, 6 October 2011

Tomas Tranströmer was awarded the Nobel Prize in Literature in 2011. Born in 1931, he grew up in Stockholm, but spent many long summers on the island of Runmarö in the nearby archipelago. His grandfather was a maritime pilot based on the island. Swedish nature and landscape inspired much of his poetry, especially Runmarö, the Baltic coast and the country's lakes and forests. His poems are often explorations of the borderland between sleep and waking, between the conscious and unconscious states. Many use compressed description and concentrate on a single distinct image as a catalyst for psychological insight and metaphysical interpretation. This acts as a meeting-point or threshold between conflicting elements or forces: sea and land, man and nature, freedom and control.

Tranströmer was as much a poet of humanity as he was of nature, and worked as a psychologist for most of his life. He was married for over 50 years to Monica Tranströmer, who became his voice to the world after he suffered a stroke in 1990 which deprived him of most of his speech and left him unable to use his right arm. But he was also an accomplished classical pianist; unable to speak more than a few words for over 20 years, he could still express himself through music, despite only being able to play with his left hand. Swedish composers wrote several left-hand piano pieces especially for him to play.

Our film combines our own footage of Tranströmer (playing the piano at home in Stockholm and sitting in the garden on Runmarö) with archive film and audio recordings from a three-CD set of his readings, *Tomas Tranströmer läser 82 diker ur 10 böcker 1954–1996*, released by his Swedish publisher Bonnier in 2006. The subtitled English translations are by Robin Fulton, from *New Collected Poems* (Bloodaxe Books, 1997, 2011), which was expanded from the earlier *Collected Poems* (Bloodaxe Books, 1987) and later published in the US by New Directions under the title *The Great Enigma: New Collected Poems* (2006). The Swedish texts are from *Dikter och Prosa 1954-2004* (Albert Bonniers Förlag, 2011). Bloodaxe's ebook with audio of *New Collected Poems* includes all his audio recordings as well as the Swedish texts. The two left-hand piano pieces Tomas plays in the film are by Fibich and Mompou.

Efter någons död

KLANGER OCH SPÅR 1966

Det var en gång en chock
som lämnade efter sig en lång, blek, skimrande kometsvans.
Den hyser oss. Den gör TV-bilderna suddiga.
Den avsätter sig som kalla droppar på luftledningarna.

Man kan fortfarande hasa fram på skidor i vintersolen
mellan dungar där fjolårslöven hänger kvar.
De liknar blad rivna ur gamla telefonkataloger –
abonnenternas namn uppslukade av kölden.

Det är fortfarande skönt att känna sitt hjärta bulta.
Men ofta känns skuggan verkligare än kroppen.
Samurajen ser obetydlig ut
bredvid sin rustning av svarta drakfjäll.

från Galleriet

SANNINGSBARRIÄREN 1978

Det händer men sällan
att en av oss verkligen *ser* den andre:

ett ögonblick visar sig en människa
som på ett fotografi men klarare
och i bakgrunden
någonting som är större än hans skugga.

Han står i helfigur framför ett berg.
Det är mera ett snigelskal än ett berg.
Det är mera ett hus än ett snigelskal.
Det är inte ett hus men har många rum.
Det är otydligt men överväldigande.
Han växer fram ur det, och det ur honom.
Det är hans liv, det är hans labyrint.

After Someone's Death

BELLS AND TRACKS 1966

Once there was a shock
which left behind a long pale glimmering comet's tail.
It contains us. It makes TV pictures blurred.
It deposits itself as cold drops on the aerials.

You can still shuffle along on skis in the winter sun
among groves where last year's leaves still hang.
They are like pages torn from old telephone directories –
the subscribers' names are eaten up by the cold.

It is still beautiful to feel your heart throbbing.
But often the shadow feels more real than the body.
The samurai looks insignificant
beside his armour of black dragon-scales.

from The Gallery

THE TRUTH-BARRIER 1978

It happens rarely
that one of us really *sees* the other:

a person shows himself for an instant
as in a photograph but clearer
and in the background
something which is bigger than his shadow.

He's standing full-length before a mountain.
It's more a snail's shell than a mountain.
It's more a house than a snail's shell.
It's not a house but has many rooms.
It's indistinct but overwhelming.
He grows out of it, it out of him.
It's his life, it's his labyrinth.

[In the 1990 radio interview included in the film, Tranströmer reads Robert Bly's version of 'Efter någons död' and Robin Fulton's translation of the excerpt from 'Galleriet']

Näktergalen i Badelunda

FÖR LEVANDE OCH DÖDA 1966

I den gröna midnatten vid näktergalens nordgräns. Tunga löv hänger i trance, de döva bilarna rusar mot neonlinjen. Näktergalens röst stiger inte åt sidan, den är lika genomträngande som en tupps galande, men skön och utan fåfänga. Jag var i fängelse och den besökte mig. Jag var sjuk och den besökte mig. Jag märkte den inte då, men nu. Tiden strömmar ned från solen och månen och in i alla tick tack tick tacksamma klockor. Men just här finns ingen tid. Bara näktergalens röst, de råa klingande tonerna som slipar natthimlens ljusa lie.

Allegro

DEN HALVFÄRDIGA HIMLEN 1962

Jag spelar Haydn efter en svart dag
och känner en enkel värme i händerna.

Tangenterna vill. Milda hammare slår.
Klangen är grön, livlig och stilla.

Klangen säger att friheten finns
och att någon inte ger kejsaren skatt.

Jag kör ner händerna i mina haydnfickor
och härmar en som ser lugnt på världen.

Jag hissar haydnflaggan – det betyder:
»Vi ger oss inte. Men vill fred.«

Musiken är ett glashus på sluttningen
där stenarna flyger, stenarna rullar.

Och stenarna rullar tvärs igenom
men varje ruta förblir hel.

52

The Nightingale in Badelunda

FOR LIVING AND DEAD 1966

In the green midnight at the nightingale's northern limit. Heavy leaves hang in trance, the deaf cars race towards the neon-line. The nightingale's voice rises without wavering to the side, it is as penetrating as a cockcrow, but beautiful and free of vanity. I was in prison and it visited me. I was sick and it visited me. I didn't notice it then, but I do now. Time streams down from the sun and the moon and into all the tick-tock-thankful clocks. But right here there is no time. Only the nightingale's voice, the raw resonant notes that whet the night sky's gleaming scythe.

Allegro

THE HALF-FINISHED HEAVEN 1962

I play Haydn after a black day
and feel a simple warmth in my hands.

The keys are willing. Soft hammers strike.
The resonance green, lively and calm.

The music says freedom exists
and someone doesn't pay the emperor tax.

I push down my hands in my Haydnpockets
and imitate a person looking on the world calmly.

I hoist the Haydnflag – it signifies:
'We don't give in. But want peace.'

The music is a glass-house on the slope
where the stones fly, the stones roll.

And the stones roll right through
but each pane stays whole.

Från snösmältningen -66

STIGAR 1973

Störtande störtande vatten dån gammal hypnos.
An översvämmar bilkyrkogården, glittrar
bakom maskerna.
Jag griper hårt om broräcket.
Bron: en stor fågel av järn som seglar förbi döden.

Den halvfärdiga himlen

DEN HALVFÄRDIGA HIMLEN 1962

Modlösheten avbryter sitt lopp.
Ångesten avbryter sitt lopp.
Gamen avbryter sin flykt.

Det ivriga ljuset rinner fram,
även spökena tar sig en klunk.

Och våra målningar kommer i dagen,
våra istidsateljéers röda djur.

Allting börjar se sig omkring.
Vi går i solen hundratals.

Var människa en halvöppen dörr
som leder till ett rum för alla.

Den oändliga marken under oss.

Vattnet lyser mellan träden.

Insjön är ett fönster mot jorden.

From the Thaw of 1966

PATHS 1973

Headlong headlong waters; roaring; old hypnosis.
The river swamps the car-cemetery, glitters
behind the masks.
I hold tight to the bridge railing.
The bridge: a big iron bird sailing past death.

The Half-Finished Heaven

THE HALF-FINISHED HEAVEN 1962

Despondency breaks off its course.
Anguish breaks off its course.
The vulture breaks off its flight.

The eager light streams out,
even the ghosts take a draught.

And our paintings see daylight,
our red beasts of the ice-age studio;

Everything begins to look around.
We walk in the sun in hundreds.

Each man is a half-open door
leading to a room for everyone.

The endless ground under us.

The water is shining among the trees.

The lake is a window into the earth.

April och tystnad

SORGEGONDOLEN 1996

Våren ligger öde
Det sammetsmörka diket
krälar vid min sida
utan spegelbilder.

Det enda som lyser
är gula blommor.

Jag bärs i min skugga
som en fiol
i sin svarta låda.

Det enda jag vill säga
glimmar utom räckhåll
som silvret
hos pantlånaren.

Från mars -79

DET VILDA TORGET 1983

Trött på alla som kommer med ord, ord men inget språk
for jag till den snötäckta ön.
Det vilda har inga ord.
De oskrivna sidorna breder ut sig åt alla håll!
Jag stöter på spåren av rådjursklövar i snön.
Språk men inga ord.

April and Silence

THE SAD GONDOLA 1996

Spring lies desolate.
The velvet-dark ditch
crawls by my side
without reflections.

The only thing that shines
is yellow flowers.

I am carried in my shadow
like a violin
in its black box.

The only thing I want to say
glitters out of reach
like the silver
in a pawnbroker's.

From March 1979

THE WILD MARKET-SQUARE 1983

Weary of all who come with words, words but no language
I make my way to the snow-covered island.
The untamed has no words.
The unwritten pages spread out on every side!
I come upon the tracks of deer's hooves in the snow.
Language but no words.

Spår

HEMLIGHETER PÅ VÄGEN 1958

På natten klockan två: månsken. Tåget har stannat
mitt ute på slätten. Långt borta ljuspunkter i en stad,
flimrande kallt vid synranden.

Som när en människa gått in i en dröm så djupt
att hon aldrig ska minnas att hon var där
när hon återvänder till sitt rum.

Och som när någon gått in i en sjukdom så djupt
att allt som var hans dagar blir några flimrande punkter, en svärm,
kall och ringa vid synranden.

Tåget står fullkomligt stilla.
Klockan två: starkt månsken, få stjärnor.

Tracks

SECRETS ON THE WAY 1958

2 A.M.: moonlight. The train has stopped
out in the middle of the plain. Far away, points of light in a town,
flickering coldly at the horizon.

As when a man has gone into a dream so deep
he'll never remember having been there
when he comes back to his room.

As when someone has gone into an illness so deep
everything his days were becomes a few flickering points, a swarm,
cold and tiny at the horizon.

The train is standing quite still.
2 A.M.: bright moonlight, few stars.

All poems translated from the Swedish by Robin Fulton

4 | JACK MAPANJE

Filmed at home in York by Pamela Robertson-Pearce,
18 November 2014

Because he was a radical poet whose poems were thought to be
subversive, Malawi's Jack Mapanje was thrown into prison on the
orders of dictator Hastings Banda, who ruled the country with an
iron hand for three decades. The themes of his poetry range from
the search for a sense of dignity and integrity under a repressive
regime, incarceration, release from prison, exile and return to
Africa, and reconciliation with torturers, to the writer in Africa
and the continuing African liberation struggle in a hostile world.
While often deadly serious, Mapanje's poems are lifted by the
generosity of spirit and irrepressible humour which helped sustain
him through his prison ordeal.

He was head of the Department of English at the University of
Malawi where the Malawi authorities arrested him in 1987 after
his first book of poems, *Of Chameleons and Gods*, had been banned,
and he was released in 1991 after spending three years, seven
months and sixteen days in prison, following an international out-
cry against his incarceration. He has since published five poetry
books, *The Chattering Wagtails of Mikuyu Prison* (1993) from
Heinemann, and *Skipping Without Ropes* (1998), *The Last of the
Sweet Bananas: New & Selected Poems* (2004), *Beasts of Nalunga*
(2007) and *Greetings from Grandpa* (2016) from Bloodaxe, as well
as his prison memoir *And Crocodiles Are Hungry at Night* (Ayebia
Clarke Publishing, 2011).

After his release he was able to travel to Britain, where he has
since lived in exile with his family in York. In our film he reads
three poems relating to his arrest and incarceration in Mikuyu
Prison while recounting his prison experiences, telling how he and
his fellow political prisoners were completely cut off from the out-
side world, denied visitors for long periods, with their loved ones
knowing nothing of their fate. He describes the appalling condi-
tions they had to survive while maintaining their sanity, humanity,
self-belief and resolve not to be broken, and how much of that
was down to solidarity, singing and grim humour.

Scrubbing the Furious Walls of Mikuyu Prison

THE CHATTERING WAGTAILS OF MIKUYU PRISON 1993 |
THE LAST OF THE SWEET BANANAS 2004

Is this where they dump those rebels,
These haggard cells stinking of bucket
Shit and vomit and the acrid urine of
Yesteryears? Who would have thought I
Would be gazing at these dusty, cobweb
Ceilings of Mikuyu Prison, scrubbing
Briny walls and riddling out impetuous
Scratches of another dung-beetle locked
Up before me here? Violent human palms
Wounded these blood-bloated mosquitoes
And bugs (to survive), leaving these vicious
Red marks. Monstrous flying cockroaches
Crashed here. Up there the cobwebs trapped
Dead bumblebees. Where did black wasps
Get clay to build nests in this corner?

But here, scratches, insolent scratches!
I have marvelled at the rock paintings
Of Mphunzi Hills once but these grooves
And notches on the walls of Mikuyu Prison,
How furious, what barbarous squiggles!
How long did this anger languish without
Charge, without trial, without visit here, and
What justice committed? This is the moment
We dreaded; when we'd all descend into
The pit, alone, without a wife or a child –
Without mother; without paper or pencil
– Without a story (just three Bibles for
Ninety men), without charge without trial;
This is the moment I never needed to see.

Shall I scrub these brave squiggles out
Of human memory then or should I perhaps
Superimpose my own, less caustic; dare I
Overwrite this precious scrawl? Who'd
Have known I'd find another prey without
Charge, without trial (without bitterness)
In these otherwise blank walls of Mikuyu
Prison? No, I will throw my water and mop

61

Elsewhere. We have liquidated too many
Brave names out of the nation's memory.
I will not rub out another nor inscribe
My own, more ignoble, to consummate this
Moment of truth I have always feared!

Skipping Without Ropes

SKIPPING WITHOUT ROPES 1998 |
THE LAST OF THE SWEET BANANAS 2004

I will, I will skip without your rope
Since you say I should not, I cannot
Borrow your son's skipping rope to
Exercise my limbs, I will skip without

Your rope as you say even the lace
I want will hang my neck until I die;
I will create my own rope, my own
Hope and skip without your rope as

You insist I do not require to stretch
My limbs fixed by these fevers of your
Reeking sweat and your prison walls;
I will, will skip with my forged hope;

Watch, watch me skip without your
Rope watch me skip with my hope –
A-one, a-two, a-three, a-four, a-five
I will, a-seven, I do, will skip, a-ten,

Eleven, I will skip without, will skip
Within and skip I do without your
Rope but with my hope; and I will,
Will always skip you dull, will skip

Your silly rules, skip your filthy walls
Your weevil pigeon peas, skip your
Scorpions, skip your Excellency Life
Glory. I do, you don't, I can, you can't,

I will, you won't, I see, you don't, I
Sweat, you don't, I will, will wipe my

Gluey brow then wipe you at a stroke
I will, will wipe your horrid, stinking,

Vulgar prison rules, will wipe you all
Then hop about, hop about my cell, my
Home, the mountains, my globe as your
Sparrow hops about your prison yard

Without your hope, without your rope,
I swear, I will skip without your rope, I
Declare, I will have you take me to your
Showers to bathe me where I can resist

This singing child you want to shape me,
I'll fight your rope, your rules, your hope
As your sparrow does under your super-
vision! Guards! Take us for a shower!

Your Tears Still Burning at My Handcuffs, 1991

THE CHATTERING WAGTAILS OF MIKUYU PRISON 1993 |
THE LAST OF THE SWEET BANANAS 2004

After that millet beer you brewed, mother,
(In case Kadango Mission made something
Of another lake-son for the village to strut

About!), and after that fury with the Special
Branch when I was brought home handcuffed –
'How dare you scatter this peaceful house?

What has my son done? Take me instead, you
Insensitive men!' you challenged their threat
To imprison you too as you did not 'stop

Your gibberish!' After that constant care,
Mother, I expected you to show me the rites
Of homing in of this political prisoner,

Perhaps with ground herbal roots dug by
Your hand and hoe, poured in some clay pot
Of warm water for me to suffuse, perhaps

With your usual wry smile about the herbs
You wish your mother had told you about.
Today, as I invent my own cleansing rites

At this return of another fugitive, without
Even dead roots to lean on, promise to bless
These lit candles I place on your head and

Your feet, accept these bended knees, this
Lone prayer offered among these tall unknown
Graveyard trees, this strange requiem mustered

From the tattered Catholic Choir of Dembo
Village. You gave up too early, mother, two
More months and I'd have told you the story

Of some Nchinji upstart who tamed a frog at
Mikuyu Prison, how he gave it liberty to invite
Fellow frogs to its wet niche, dearly feeding

Them insects and things but how one day,
After demon bruises, his petulant inmate
Threw boiling water at the niche, killing

Frog and visitor. And I hoped you'd gather
Some tale for me too, one better than your
Granddaughter's about how you told her she

Would not find you on her return from school
That day. But we understand, after so many
Pointless sighs about your son's expected

Release, after the village ridicule of your
Rebellious breasts and sure fatigue of your
Fragile bones, your own minders, then your

Fear for us, when the release did finally come
You'd propose yet another exile without you –
We understand you had to go, to leave us space

To move. Though now, among the gentle friends
Of these Jorvik walls, I wonder why I still
Glare at your tears burning at my handcuffs.

5 | TOMAS VENCLOVA

Filmed by Pamela Robertson-Pearce in Grasmere, Cumbria,
22 April 2009, and in New Haven, USA, 17 September 2008,
with additional filming by Neil Astley in Vilnius, 12 October 2015

Lithuania's Tomas Venclova is one of Europe's major living poets. His work speaks with a moral depth exceptional in contemporary poetry. Venclova's poetry addresses the desolate landscape of the aftermath of totalitarianism, as well as the ethical constants that allow for hope and perseverance. His Bloodaxe retrospective *The Junction* (2008) brings together entirely new translations of later work as well as a selection of poems from his 1997 volume *Winter Dialogue*. The book's title and title-poem refers to a geographic junction where the borders of Lithuania, the Russian district of Kaliningrad (formerly East Prussia) and Poland meet.

Venclova was born in 1937 in Klaipeda, Lithuania. After graduating from Vilnius University, he travelled in the Eastern Bloc, where he met and translated Anna Akhmatova and Boris Pasternak into Lithuanian. In our film, after reading and introducing several poems, he recalls his first meeting with Akhmatova, and how an expert's endorsement of his translations led to his being allowed to see her on a number of occasions at a time when she was having to discourage visits by young poets seeking her approval.

Venclova took part in the Lithuanian and Soviet dissident movements and was one of the five founding members of the Lithuanian Helsinki Group. His activities led to a ban on publishing, exile and the stripping of his Soviet citizenship in 1977. From 1985 he taught Slavic languages and literature at Yale University, where we filmed him before a class in 2008, followed by a second filming session the following year after his reading for the Wordsworth Trust in Grasmere.

The subtitled English translations from *The Junction* are by Ellen Hinsey [EH] and Diana Senechal [DS]. The opening footage shows the setting of the first poem, 'Užupis', a district of the Lithuanian capital Vilnius popular with artists which declared itself an independent republic in 1997. The closing footage is from the Venclovas' House-Museum in Vilnius, the family home from 1945 to 1971, where Tomas grew up (his father Antonas Venclova was a well-known writer during the Soviet period). The Lithuanian texts are from *Visi eilėraščiai: 1956-2010* (Lietuvių literatūros ir tautosakos institutas, Vilnius, 2010).

Užupis

VISI EILERASCIAI: 1956-2010 (COLLECTED POEMS: 1956-2010) 2010

Liepų šurmuly, prieš akmens krantinę,
ties skubria srove, panašia į Tibrą,
su jaunais barzdočiais gurkšnoju „Gilbey's".
Sutema, stiklų skambesys ir dūmai.
Nepažįstu jų. Pažinau jų tėvus.

Ką gi, kartos keičiasi. Diktofonas
šlama ir užsikerta. Pašnekovams
rūpi lygiai tas, kas ir man kadaise:
ar kančia ir gailestis turi prasmę
ir ar menas tvers, jei nebus taisyklių.

Aš buvau kaip jie, kol patyriau keistą,
už kitas tikrai ne geresnę lemtį,
ir žinau, jog blogis nežūva niekad,
bet aklybę galima prasklaidyti,
ir eilės vertos daugiau nei sapnas.

Vasarą dažnai nubundu prieš aušrą
ir be baimės juntu, kad artėja laikas,
kai naujoms gentims pasiliks žodynas,
debesis, griuvėsiai, druska ir duona,
o man jau nieko, išskyrus laisvę.

* * *

TANKEJANTI SVIESA (THE CONDENSING LIGHT) 1990

Už pusmylio, kur kertas autostrados,
Įžiebia liepsną titnago grandis.
Atodrėkis. Paversmiuos krūpsi ledas
Ir netelpa uosyno atspindys.

Kol kas pradžia, kol kas ne pats kartumas.
Skaidrioj migloj suakmenės krantai,
Ir netgi Dievas, apsimetęs dūmais,
Išsisklaidys. Bet aš ne apie tai.

Užupis

THE JUNCTION 2008

Under an uproar of lindens, before the stone
embankment, by a fast current like the Tiber,
I am drinking Gilbey's with two bearded men.
In the twilight – the jingle of glasses, smoke.
But we have never met. I knew their parents.

Generations overtake another. The tape-recorder
warbles and crackles. My two interlocutors
want to know about questions I once pondered:
whether there is meaning to suffering and mercy –
whether art can survive if it obeys no rules.

I was the same as them, but destiny accorded
me a strange fate: this, of course, is no better
than any other. I know evil never disappears,
but one can at least strive to dispel blindness –
and poetry is more meaningful than dreams.

In summertime, I often wake before dawn,
sensing, without fear, the time is drawing
close when others will inherit the dictionary,
along with clouds, ruins, salt and bread.
And freedom is all that I will be granted.

[EH]

*   *   *

WINTER DIALOGUE 1997 | THE JUNCTION 2008

Half a mile away, where the highways cross,
A flame is struck up by a range of flint.
The ice, quivering above the springs, thaws,
And the reflection of the ash grove doesn't fit.

It's still too early for the bitterest stroke,
The banks will harden in transparent mist,
And even God, once simulating smoke,
Will dissipate. But that is not my point.

Tikėk žiema. Gerk palaimingą šaltį.
Didžiuokis tuo, kad netekai namų.
Nelyginant bėglys, prigludęs valty,
Alsuok tamsa ir druskos giedrumu.

Itakės kauburius apgaubia miegas,
Ir kūdikiai neatmena skriaudos,
Ir bus tiktai mirtis, ir drėgnas sniegas,
Ir muzika, ir nieko niekados.

[1987]

Ugnyje

TANKEJANTI SVIESA (THE CONDENSING LIGHT) 1990

ugnyje ugnyje ugnyje ugnyje ugnyje
kur erdvė pasitraukia į šalį ir lenkiasi laikui
mano sielą išbrauk sunaikink ne mane manyje
kad išaukštintas niekas patyręs nežemišką taiką
būtų žiežirba krislas brūkšnys ir spraga ugnyje

vandeny vandeny vandeny vandeny vandeny
po imperijos kupolu sklidinu šalčio ir aido
tu šiandieną mane dar gini ir kitiems dalini
tenegrįšiu namo nepažink neregėk mano veido
kur aštuonetas tiltų siūbuoja žvarbiam vandeny

po žeme po žeme po žeme po žeme po žeme
kur suyra akmuo ir begarsis upokšnis išlieka
kur subręsta žiema ir netenka spalvos žaluma
kūnas traukias į peleną pelenas traukias į niekad
ir iš niekad į niekad srovena ertmė po žeme

tamsumoj tamsumoj tamsumoj tamsumoj tamsumoj
mūsų oras retėja ir mūsų materija sklaidos
viskas parengta mirčiai kada prasiskleidžia skiemuo
ir juoduoja įspaustos į nesantį popierių raidės
štai šitoj tamsumoj štai šitoj aklumoj

Believe in winter. Drink the blessed cold.
Take pride in knowing that your home is lost.
Just like the ones who huddle in a boat,
Breathe darkness and the clarity of salt.

Sleep envelops Ithaca's hills and dales,
And injured children sleep without a murmur,
And only death will finally prevail,
And wet snow, and music, and nothing ever.

[DS]

In the Fire

WINTER DIALOGUE 1997 | THE JUNCTION 2008

in the fire in the fire in the fire in the fire in the fire
where space pulls over to the side and yields to time
cross out my soul make the not me in me expire
that the exalted nothing tasting peace may become
a spark a speck a line and a breach in the fire

in water in water in water in water in water
beneath the cupola filled with echo and ice
today you protect me and hand me out to others
may I not return home don't see me don't break my disguise
where eight bridges sway in the piercing cold in the water

underground underground underground underground underground
where the stone falls apart and the soundless stream stays together
where the winter matures and no colour in green can be found
the body retreats into ash and ash into never
and from never to never the void flows under the ground

in the dark in the dark in the dark in the dark in the dark
our matter becomes dispersed and our air grows slack
all things are ready for death when the syllable sparks
and pressed into fictional paper the letters grow black
in this darkness here in this blindness here in this dark

[DS]

69

Naujosios Anglijos Uoste

RINKTINE (SELECTED POEMS) 1999

Ne jūra, o tvankios miglos, betono luitai,
gelžgaliai, tarp kurių patamsėjęs karminas
retkarčiais trykšta į orą. Pūvančių dumblių
užgožtas, kyšo bangolaužis – prieglobstis kirui.
Stebėtojas smėlio ir sąsiaurio sandūroj laukia,
kol raudonis užges šiapus stiebų suirutės
ir bus jau laikas namo. Bet kame gi jo namas?
Čia ar kitam vandenyno krante? Kalnuos, kur lavinos
nuogai nusvidino šlaitą? Po užmiesčio kėniais,
kur dūluoja įgriuvę rūsiai? Nejaunėjančiam kūne,
kuris atsisako paklusti? Galbūt abejonėj,
kad gyvenai? Tikrume, kad išnyksi? Rūdžių apnuodytoj terpėj
ar žvilgsny, kuris net joje
pagauna simetriją, sandorą, saiką?

Emigrantė

SANKIRTA (THE JUNCTION) 2005

Tarp kitų, skubesnių naujienų – frazė ragely:
'Ar girdėjai? Senokai. Deja, ji labai kamavos.'
Nežinau, namie ar kitur. Dabar nedažnai
lankausi tuose vitrinų ir tunelių tyruos.
Neatspėju ir mėnesio. Rodos, pavasarį būna
kiek lengviau pasitraukti: juoduojančio sniego,
anglinų pumpurų ir valkų bjauratis apramina,
nes atgimti daros ne taip jau svarbu. Aleksandras,
Eduardas, Ksenija (ji dar gyva). Išsiblaškiusios kartos.
Menu tik pūką ant skruosto, grebluojančią tarseną, dideles pėdas.
Per ryškūs lūpų dažai. Ne iš karto suprantamos akys.
Stalčiuose kaspinas, kvitai ir čekiai, jau pusė gyvenimo šičia.

New England Harbour

THE JUNCTION 2008

Not the sea, but sultry mists, concrete slabs
and discarded rails, pierced by the sunset's sooty carmine
which, from time to time, streaks the sky. Curtained with
fetid algae, the breakwater protrudes – a refuge for seagulls.
Where the sand and strait converge, a figure waits for the crimson
to fade on the far side of the many-masted disorder
and to return home, when the moment comes. But, where is home?
Here, or on the ocean's far shore? In the mountains, where avalanches
have sheared off the slopes? Under back-road firs,
where one can glimpse old cellars' depths? In the ageing body,
which refuses to submit? Or perhaps in the uncertainty
that you have lived? The certainty you will disappear? In this place poisoned
       by rust –
or again, in the gaze that can still here divine
the symmetry, harmony and measure it manages to find?

[EH]

The Émigré

THE JUNCTION 2008

Among more urgent news – briefly, in the phone receiver:
'Didn't you know? A while ago. Alas, she suffered quite a bit.'
I don't know if it was at home. These days, I rarely visit
that deserted zone of shop windows and underpasses.
I don't know the month either. Perhaps it's easier
to pass away in spring: snow's blackening muck,
tree buds stained with coal, puddles – this calms one down,
until one loses interest in resurrection. Alexander,
Edward, Xenia (still alive). A scattered generation.
My memory calls up – a downy cheek, guttural accent, clumsy feet.
Lipstick, too bright. Eyes, not immediately concrete.
In a drawer, a ribbon, receipts and cheques: half a life spent here.

Treji pirmieji metai praslenka veltui –
taip sako kiekvienas. Nevisiškai tai, ko tikėjais:
šaltis retuos laiškuos iš gimtinės, kurioj nesikeičia
nei kalėjimų sienos, nei laikraščių skiltys. Už grotų pirmajam aukšte
reklamos, antenos ir purvas. Ties akiračiu smailas mormonų
šventyklos bokštas nei švirkštas (heroinas, ne opijus liaudžiai,
šiandien tvirtintų Karlas). Nematau, ar ji vagone,
ar jau sėdi už vairo: vis vien virš galvos grindinys,
betonas, gelžgaliai, būsimas kapas. Patamsyje girgžda liftai.
Sausas kontorų korys, kur tavo akcentas
nekliudo, tačiau neteikia vilčių. Nuo skausmo pagelbsti
ne žemynų kaita, o mirtis. Pradžioje ji padidina skausmą.

Iš tikrųjų, tiek laiko. Po smilkiniu renkasi raukšlės,
pro riešą, gal dar labiau pro pirštus prasišviečia kauliukai.
Kitame gyvenime buvom pažįstami. Ten sidabravo ožekšniai,
skroblynai riedėjo į slėnį. Ne, nieko tarp mudviejų. Ginčai,
apie skaitytas eiles, bičiulius. Vieną kartą net barnis prie durų,
kur pora benosių sfinksų iš juosvo cemento
tikriausiai stūkso ir šiandien. Paskui geresniojoj Bronxo daly
molbertas, iškreivintos šaknys, turinčios reikšti
nenykstantį ryšį su tėvynės gamta ir t. t. Nes gamta atsilygins:
kūnas nugali sielą, limfos greitkeliu skuba ląstelės,
bronchai džiūsta, ir medikas ištaria graikišką žodį,
paaukojantį mus Browno judesiui, šarmui ir rūgščiai.

Debesys, drėgnas granitas, pilkas vandens gomurys.
Šitos upės neteka niekur. Prie garažo prislinkęs meškėnas
snukeliu pabarbena duris, voverė kibirkščiuoja spygliuos.
Įžiūrėdamas pirmą žibintą, beveik negalvoji
apie naktį. Širdis atkakliai tarsi kūdikio kumštis
daužo tai, ko nemoka įvardyti. Lapai apipila šaką,
triūsia skruzdėlės, veidrody blizga dažų buteliukas,
neįrėmintos sensta trapecijos, plaštakos, žvaigždės,
brangios tik jai. Visa tai buvo senokai.
Kūno gėda ir vargas, kosulys, nenumaldomas išskyrų kvapas,
įsipykęs noras, kad tai greičiau pasibaigtų,
abejingi praeiviai. Atleisk man tylą ragely.

The first three years of exile are wasted –
everyone agrees. Not quite what you'd had in mind:
chilliness in rare letters from home, where neither prison walls,
nor newspaper columns change. Outside the basement window's grating –
ads, antennae, dirt. Near the horizon – the Mormon
Temple's needle spire, like a syringe (heroin, not opium, for the people
Marx would now declare). I can't see it – was she on the train,
or at the steering wheel: all the same, overhead – asphalt,
concrete, scrap metal, a future grave. Elevators complain in darkness.
The dry honeycombs of offices, where your accent
isn't a hindrance, nor does it inspire confidence. Changing continents
doesn't alleviate pain – only death does. To begin, it's worse.

The fact is, so much time has passed. Wrinkles knit by the temple.
Bones are prominent at the wrist – but more so through the fingers.
We knew each other in another life. Spindle trees shone like silver there,
hornbeam groves fell to the valley. There was nothing between us.
Just arguments about friends, poems read. A quarrel once by
a door where two grey-black cement sphinxes, perhaps,
still stand. Later, in the Bronx's better part –
her husband's easel: twisted roots, meant to signify
the enduring link to the motherland, nature, etc. For nature always gets even:
the body overcomes the soul, cells rush the lymph's highway,
the lungs dry, and a doctor utters the Greek word
that offers us up, in sacrifice, to the Brownian law of alkali and acid.

Clouds, damp granite – a grey larynx of water.
These rivers flow nowhere. A raccoon, skulking past the garage
knocks at the door with its snout. A squirrel sputters in the tree's needles.
When I focus on the first street lamp, I almost forget
the darkness. Like an infant's fist, the heart is knocking hard
at what it cannot name. A branch sheds its leaves.
Ants labour. A paint pot flames in the mirror.
Unframed trapezes, hands, stars – dear only to her –
are growing old. It was all long ago.
The shame, the body's degradation, the cough, the body fluid's stench,
the damned desire for the end to come quickly –
and indifferent passersby. Forgive my silence on this end of the line.

[EH]

Sankirta

SANKIRTA (THE JUNCTION) 2005

Nuo plento takas leidosi į drėgną
pievutę. Dubury matei, kaip gęsta
saulėlydis, užgavęs tviskią vielą.
Dryžuotą stulpą vainikavo herbas,
cementą brūžino šiurkšti svėrė.

Į šiaurės rytus traukėsi ankšta,
kantri šalis, jau sveikinanti naktį.
Alksnyno nuokraštyje stirna skabė
lapiją. Už akiračio bemaž
atspėjai ežerą, kurio pakrantėj
tamsoki vandens atspindėjo vaiką,
sutampantį su tavimi. Daina
vingiavo virš nendrynų, liepto, datos
užžėlusiame antkapyje. Laikas,
išsprūdęs atminčiai ar biografui,
turbūt visų svarbiausias, nes yra
drauge ir sunkmena, ir talismanas.

Į kairę tvyrojo laukinis miškas.
Jame švytėjo proskyna – plyšys,
atvėręs pelkę ar tiesiog purvynus,
kur spietės neįžiūrimos būtybės,
gauruotos, šypsančios, prasimanytos
bepročio grafiko. Labai toli
juodavo lankos ir įgriuvę tiltai.
Žvarbus kanalas siekė marių ribą,
nerasdamas nei miesto, nei laivyno.
Žinojai: kūdikiai tenai užgimsta
tam, kad pavartėse dalytųs švirkštais,
pagieža, sperma, nuorūkom, skatikais.

Už nugaros – balkšvi sodybos dūmai,
ir amsi šunys, sergėdami ūkį
nuo neprašyto svečio. Jau vėlu.
Tarp įdubų ir piliakalnių sukas
beveik nepravažiuojamos keliūtės,
ir netinkuotas mūras dengia ugnį.
Na ką gi, jei likimas lėmė, būk
šiame krašte prie pat gimtinės durų,

The Junction

From the highway, down to the meadow
led the path. In the ravine, you watched
the sunset brush up against wires, fade.
The State's mark crowned the signpost
and bittercress stems scratched cement.

A country, long-suffering and patient,
lay to the north-east welcoming night.
A doe nibbled brushwood and alder.
Beyond the horizon, you could almost
see a distant lake. In its clouded surface
was the indistinct reflection of a child
whose outline matched yours. Above,
a song hovered over the bridge and
rushes, on mossy tombstones' dates.
Time that escapes biographers and
memory is perhaps the most important:
both a heavy burden and a talisman.

To the left stretched the wild wood.
In it, a bright opening – a gap which
revealed a marsh, or simply mud or silt.
There, unseen, swarmed the grinning,
unkempt offspring of absurd designs
and schemes. In the distance ruined
bridges and glades showed black. Icy
canals took aim at the cold fringes
of the bay, but failed to hit the city
or the fleet. You know that children
there are born into side streets sharing
rage, cigarette butts, sperm, syringes.

Whitish chimney smoke behind you,
and growling dogs that keep guard
against unwelcome guests. It's late.
Impassable dirt roads wind round
past hollows and debris. Unplastered
brick walls conceal the fires. I guess
if fate has brought you here, you should
accept this territory at the threshold

kurčioj trilypėj sankirtoj, kur stūkso
stulpai, išlikę iš kitų laikų,
kadaise mirtini, ir atšiauriu
lanku dykynę kerta viadukas.

Palieski vėstančią vaikystės žolę.
Esi namie. Trilypė jūra ošia
nakties kriauklėj. Tau buvo dovanota
nyki era, sargybinis, kurio
nebėr, ir balso išsiilgęs oras.

of home. This triple-junction strewn
with rigid signposts – now outdated,
but one time deadly. The viaduct's
grim arch spans neglected grounds.

Touch the cold grass of childhood.
You are home. Night's shell enfolds
the three-fold sea. It's all a gift of grace:
these muddled times, the sentry no longer
on guard, the air that's longing for a voice.

[EH]

6 | SIMON ARMITAGE

Filmed by Pamela Robertson-Pearce at Sheffield University,
17 November 2014

This film marks the 25th anniversary of Bloodaxe's publication of Simon Armitage's first collection, *Zoom!*, the book which launched his meteoric rise to poetic stardom in 1989. He introduces and reads several of its poems, written at a time when he was still living at home in Huddersfield while working as a probation officer in Manchester. In the interview which follows, he recalls those times and the background to the writing of the book.

Unusually for a first collection, *Zoom!* was a Poetry Book Society Choice and was shortlisted for a Whitbread Poetry Award (forerunner of the Costa Awards). It established Armitage as one of the most distinctive new voices in British poetry. Reviewing the book in the *Sunday Times*, Peter Reading wrote: 'Armitage creates a muscular but elegant language of his own out of slangy, youthful, up-to-the-minute jargon and the vernacular of his native northern England. He combines this with an easily worn erudition, plenty of nous and the benefit of unblinkered experience... to produce poems of moving originality.'

I solicited the manuscript from him after being impressed by poems he was publishing in small magazines and pamphlets from small presses based in northern England around 1986-87, a support network whose importance he acknowledges in the interview. One key supporter of his work was Peter Sansom of the Poetry Business, who provided this endorsement for the back of the book: 'You couldn't mistake Simon Armitage for any other poet. He has found his voice early, and it really is his own voice – his language and rhythms drawn from the Pennine village where he lives: robust, no-nonsense and (above all) honest.'

He published a second book with Bloodaxe, *Xanadu* in 1992, before being poached by Faber. The rest, as they say, is history, but *Zoom!* has remained in print with Bloodaxe, selling over 12,000 copies. As well as producing this film for the book's 25th birthday, Bloodaxe has issued an e-book with audio edition of *Zoom!* incorporating recordings Simon made for Peter Sansom in Huddersfield in 1989. So the voice you hear there is that of the young probation officer, aged 26, who had just published his first book of poems. But as he says in our interview, he wouldn't want to change a word of what he wrote then. *Zoom!* will always be *Zoom!*

The Stuff

We'd heard all the warnings; knew its nicknames.
It arrived in our town by word of mouth
and crackled like wildfire through the grapevine
of gab and gossip. It came from the south

        so we shunned it, naturally;
        sent it to Coventry

and wouldn't have touched it with a barge pole
if it hadn't been at the club one night.
Well, peer group pressure and all that twaddle
so we fussed around it like flies round shite

        and watched,
        and waited

till one kid risked it, stepped up and licked it
and came from every pore in his body.
That clinched it. It snowballed; whirlpooled. Listen,
no one was more surprised than me to be

        cutting it, mixing it,
        snorting and sniffing it

or bulking it up with scouring powder
or chalk, or snuff, or sodium chloride
and selling it under the flyover.
At first we were laughing. It was all right

        to be drinking it, eating it,
        living and breathing it

but things got seedy; people went missing.
One punter surfaced in the ship-canal
having shed a pair of concrete slippers.
Others were bundled in the back of vans

        and were quizzed, thumped,
        finished off and dumped

or vanished completely like Weldon Kees:
their cars left idle under the rail bridge
with its cryptic hoarding which stumped the police:
'Oldham – Home of the tubular bandage.'

        Others were strangled.
        Not that it stopped us.

Someone bubbled us. C.I.D. sussed us
and found some on us. It was cut and dried.
They dusted, booked us, cuffed us and pushed us
down to the station and read us our rights.

        Possession and supplying:
        we had it, we'd had it.

In Court I ambled up and took the oath
and spoke the addict's side of the story.
I said grapevine, barge pole, whirlpool, chloride,
concrete, bandage, station, story. Honest.

Snow Joke

Heard the one about the guy from Heaton Mersey?
Wife at home, lover in Hyde, mistress
in Newton-le-Willows and two pretty girls
in the top grade at Werneth prep. Well,

he was late and he had a good car so he snubbed
the police warning-light and tried to finesse
the last six miles of moorland blizzard,
and the story goes he was stuck within minutes.

So he sat there thinking about life and things;
what the dog does when it catches its tail
and about the snake that ate itself to death.
And he watched the windscreen filling up

with snow, and it felt good, and the whisky
from his hip-flask was warm and smooth.
And of course, there isn't a punchline
but the ending goes something like this.

They found him slumped against the steering wheel
with VOLVO printed backwards in his frozen brow.
And they fought in the pub over hot toddies
as to who was to take the most credit.

Him who took the aerial to be a hawthorn twig?
Him who figured out the contour of his car?
Or him who said he heard the horn, moaning softly
like an alarm clock under an eiderdown?

On Miles Platting Station

the stitchwort has done well for itself, clinging
as it must to the most difficult corners
of near-derelict buildings. In the breeze
a broken cable mediates between the stanchions
and below the bridge a lorry has jack-knifed

attempting to articulate an impossible junction. This,
after all, is only a beginning. After the long
chicanery of the express train picking its way
across the fishplates we will rattle backwards
through the satellite towns. From Greenfield we will

fail to hold our breath the length of the tunnel
then chase the sixpence of the entrance and burst
the surface of light just over the border.
It will be the hour after rain. The streets will shine
and the trees bend, letting their soft load.

Until then, the platform holds us out against the townscape
high enough to see how Ancoats meshes with Beswick,
how Gorton gives onto Hattersley and Hyde, to where
Saddleworth declines the angle of the moor.
Somewhere beyond that the water in Shiny Brook

spills like a broken necklace into our village.
The police are there again; boxhauling the traffic,
adjusting the arc-lights. They have new evidence tonight
and they lift it from behind the windbreak, cradle it
along their human chain and lower it carefully down

into Manchester.

Ivory

No more mularkey,
no baloney. No more cuffuffle
or shenanigans;

all that caboodle
is niet dobra. It will end
this minute.

No more fuss
or palaver; no more mush
or blarney. No flowers,

by request; no offence meant,
and none taken. No more blab,
none of that ragtag

and bobtail business,
or ballyhoo
or balderdash

and no jackassery, or flannel,
or galumphing.
Listen:

from this point forward
it's ninety-nine
and forty-four hundredths

per cent pure.
And no remarks
from the peanut gallery.

Eighties, Nineties

Firstly, we worked in laughable conditions.
The photocopier
defied definition,
the windows were sealed with a decade of paintwork,
the thought of a cigarette triggered the sprinklers
and the security door
was open to question.
Any excuse got me out of the office.

I found the letter in the 'pending' folder,
a handwritten thing
signed T. Ruth O'Reilly
on a perfumed leaf of watermarked vellum.
It requested recognition, or maintenance even
from a putative father,
one William Creamstick
who was keeping shtum in the Scottish Borders.

At midnight I took the decision to risk it.
I darned the elbows
of my corduroy jacket,
threw a few things in an old army surplus
and thumbed it to Ringway for a stand-by ticket.
At dawn I was still
going round in circles
in a five-mile stack over Edinburgh airspace.

I accepted a lift to Princes Street Gardens
from an aftershave rep
who slipped me some samples.
It was Marie Celeste-ville in the shopping centre
so I borrowed a pinta from the library doorstep
and a packet of rusks
from the all-night chemist
then kipped for an hour in the cashpoint lobby.

Creamstick's house was just as I'd pictured:
pigs in the garden,
geese in the kitchen.
He was toasting his feet on the coal-fired Aga
as I rapped the window with my umbrella handle
and he beckoned me in,
thinking I'd come
to spay the bitches in his sheepdog's litter.

He listened, nodding, as though I were recounting
the agreeable facts
from another man's story.
Then producing a bread knife the size of a cutlass
he suggested, in short, that I vacate his premises
and keep my proboscis
out of his business
or he'd reacquaint me with this morning's breakfast.

In a private wood on the way to the trunk road
I stumbled on a fish farm
and beyond its embankment
was a fish that had jumped too far from the water.
Two more minutes of this world would have killed it.
I carried it, drowned it,
backstroked its gills
till it came to its senses; disappeared downwards.

Back at Head Office they were all going apeshit.
Hadn't I heard of
timesheets, or clearance,
or codes of conduct, or agency agreements?
As I typed out my notice and handed my keys in
I left them with this
old tandem to ride on:
if you only pay peanuts, you're working with monkeys.

It Ain't What You Do It's What It Does to You

I have not bummed across America
with only a dollar to spare, one pair
of busted Levi's and a Bowie knife.
I have lived with thieves in Manchester.

I have not padded through the Taj Mahal,
barefoot, listening to the space between
each footfall picking up and putting down
its print against the marble floor. But I

skimmed flat stones across Black Moss on a day
so still I could hear each set of ripples
as they crossed. I felt each stone's inertia
spend itself against the water; then sink.

I have not toyed with a parachute cord
while perched on the lip of a light aircraft;
but I held the wobbly head of a boy
at the day centre, and stroked his fat hands.

And 1 guess that the tightness in the throat
and the tiny cascading sensation
somewhere inside us are both part of that
sense of something else. That feeling, I mean.

Zoom!

It begins as a house, an end terrace
in this case
    but it will not stop there. Soon it is
an avenue
    which cambers arrogantly past the Mechanics' Institute,
turns left
    at the main road without even looking
and quickly it is
    a town with all four major clearing banks,
a daily paper
    and a football team pushing for promotion.

On it goes, oblivious of the Planning Acts,
the green belts,
    and before we know it it is out of our hands:
city, nation,
    hemisphere, universe, hammering out in all directions
until suddenly,
    mercifully, it is drawn aside through the eye
of a black hole
    and bulleted into a neighbouring galaxy, emerging
smaller and smoother
    than a billiard ball but weighing more than Saturn.

People stop me in the street, badger me
in the check-out queue
    and ask 'What is this, this that is so small
and so very smooth
    but whose mass is greater than the ringed planet?'
It's just words
    I assure them. But they will not have it.

7 | JAAN KAPLINSKI

Filmed by Neil Astley in Dalkey, Ireland, 25 March 2011

Jaan Kaplinski is one of Estonia's best-known writers and cultural figures, nominated for the Nobel Prize and given many other international awards and honours, including the European Prize for Literature in 2016. He was a member of the new post-Revolution Estonian parliament (Riigikogu) in 1992-95, and his essays on cultural transition and the challenges of globalisation are published across the Baltic region.

He was born in Tartu in 1941, shortly after the Soviet annexation of Estonia. His mother was Estonian, and his Polish father died in a labour camp in northern Russia when Jaan was still a child. 'My childhood,' he has said, 'passed in Tartu, a war-devastated university town. It was a time of repression, fear and poverty.'

After studying Romance Language and Linguistics at Tartu University, he worked as a researcher in linguistics, as a sociologist, ecologist and translator. He has lectured on the History of Western Civilisation at Tartu University and has been a student of Mahayana Buddhism and philosophies of the Far East. He has also translated poetry from French, English, Spanish, Chinese and Swedish (a book of poems by Tomas Tranströmer).

Kaplinski has much in common with Gary Snyder, who wrote that 'he is re-thinking Europe, revisioning history, in these poems of our times. Elegant, musing, relentless, inward, fresh. Poems of gentle politics and love that sometimes scare you.'

After publishing translations of three collections with Harvill in Britain, one of these from Breitenbush and one from Copper Canyon in the US, Kaplinski published *Evening Brings Everything Back* with Bloodaxe in 2004. I first met him at the launch of that book at Cúirt International Festival of Literature in Galway. Our second meeting was also in Ireland, when we launched his *Selected Poems* at Poetry Now in Dún Laoghaire in 2011, and Katie Donovan kindly let me film him reading his poetry and discussing his life and work at her house in Dalkey.

In the interview extracts which follow his reading on the film, he talks about the philosophical background of his poetry, his father's involvement with Frankism and Sufism, and his own explorations of Buddhism and the philosophy of language.

'Pesu ei saa kunagi pestud'

ÕHTU TOOB TAGASI KOIK 1985

Pesu ei saa kunagi pestud.
Ahi ei saa kunagi köetud.
Raamatud ei saa kunagi loetud.
Elu ei saa kunagi valmis.
Elu on nagu pall, mida tuleb kogu aeg
püüda ja lüüa, et ta maha ei kukuks.
Kui tara on ühest otsast korras,
laguneb ta juba teisest. Katus tilgub läbi,
köögiuks ei lähe kinni, vundamendis on praod,
laste püksipõlved katki...
Kõike ei jõua meeleski pidada. Ime on,
et selle kõige kõrval jõuab märgata
kevadet, mida on kõik nii täis,
mida jätkub igale poole – õhtupilvedesse,
vainurästa laulu ja igasse
kastepiiska igal rohuliblel niidul,
nii kaugele kui silm videvas seletab.

'Ida ja Lääne piir rändab ikka'

ÕHTU TOOB TAGASI KOIK 1985

Ida ja Lääne piir rändab ikka, vahel itta, vahel läände
ja vaevalt me päriselt teame, kus ta parajasti on,
kas Gaugamelas, Uuralis või hoopis meis endas,
nii et üks kõrv, üks silm, üks sõõre, üks käsi, üks jalg,
üks kops ja üks muna (naisel munasari)
jääb ühele, teine teisele poole. Ainult süda,
ainult süda on ikka ühel pool,
kui vaatame põhja, siis läänes,
kui vaatame lõunasse, siis idas,
ja suu ei tea, kumma poole eest
peab rääkima tema.

'The washing never gets done'

THE WANDERING BORDER 1987 / SELECTED POEMS 2011

The washing never gets done.
The furnace never gets heated.
Books never get read.
Life is never completed.
Life is like a ball which one must continually
catch and hit so that it won't fall.
When the fence is repaired at one end,
it collapses at the other. The roof leaks,
the kitchen door won't close, there are cracks in the foundation,
the torn knees of children's pants...
One can't keep everything in mind. The wonder is
that beside all this one can notice
the spring which is so full of everything
continuing in all directions – into evening clouds,
into the redwing's song and into every
drop of dew on every blade of grass in the meadow,
as far as the eye can see, into the dusk.

[JK/SH/RT]

'The East-West border is always wandering'

THE WANDERING BORDER 1987 / SELECTED POEMS 2011

The East-West border is always wandering,
sometimes eastward, sometimes west,
and we do not know exactly where it is just now:
in Gaugamela, in the Urals, or maybe in ourselves,
so that one ear, one eye, one nostril, one hand, one foot,
one lung and one testicle or one ovary
is on the one, another on the other side. Only the heart,
only the heart is always on one side:
if we are looking northward, in the West;
if we are looking southward, in the East;
and the mouth doesn't know on behalf of which or both
it has to speak.

[JK/SH/RT]

'Surm ei tule väljast'

Surm ei tule väljast. Surm on sees.
Sündinud-kasvanud koos meiega.
Käinud koos meiega lasteaias ja koolis.
Õppinud koos meiega lugema ja arvutama.
Käinud koos meiega kelgutamas ja kinos.
Otsinud koos meiega elu mõtet.
Püüdnud koos meiega aru saada Einsteinist ja Wienerist.
Saanud koos meiega esimesed seksuaalkontaktid.
Abiellunud, saanud lapsed, tülitsenud, leppinud.
Läinud lahku, võibolla ka ei ole, ikka meiega koos.
Käinud tööl, käinud arsti juures, käinud matkal,
puhkekodus ja sanatooriumis. Jäänud vanaks,
pannud lapsed paari, läinud pensionile,
hoidnud lapselapsi, põdenud, surnud
meiega koos. Ärme siis kardame. Meie surm
ei ela meist kauem.

'Death does not come from outside'

THROUGH THE FOREST 1991/1996 / SELECTED POEMS 2011

Death does not come from outside. Death is within.
Born-grows together with us.
Goes with us to kindergarten and school.
Learns with us to read and count.
Goes sledging with us, and to the pictures.
Seeks with us the meaning of life.
Tries to make sense with us of Einstein and Wiener.
Makes with us our first sexual contacts.
Marries, bears children, quarrels, makes up.
Separates, or perhaps not, with us.
Goes to work, goes to the doctor, goes camping,
to the convalescent home and the sanatorium. Grows old,
sees children married, retired,
looks after grandchildren, grows ill, dies
with us. Let us not fear, then. Our death
will not outlive us.

[HH]

'Once I got a postcard from the Fiji Islands'

THE WANDERING BORDER 1987 / SELECTED POEMS 2011

Once I got a postcard from the Fiji Islands
with a picture of sugar-cane harvest. Then I realised
that nothing at all is exotic in itself.
There is no difference between digging potatoes in our Mutiku garden
and sugar-cane harvesting in Viti Levu.
Everything that is is very ordinary
or, rather, neither ordinary nor strange.
Far-off lands and foreign peoples are a dream,
a dreaming with open eyes
somebody does not wake from.
It's the same with poetry – seen from afar
it's something special, mysterious, festive,
No, poetry is even less
special than a sugar-cane plantation or potato field.
Poetry is like sawdust coming from under the saw
or soft yellowish shavings from a plane.
Poetry is washing hands in the evening
or a clean handkerchief that my late aunt
never forgot to put in my pocket.

[JK/SH/RT]

'Silence of night'

THE WANDERING BORDER 1987 / SELECTED POEMS 2011

Silence of night. A cockroach
comes out from under the bathtub
in a fifteenth-storey flat; the switch
is out of order, and the lamp
often lights itself.
It climbs up the wall and stops
on the shelf just above the sink. Who knows why.
Perhaps the smell of odours oozing
from bottles, gallipots, and tubes with inscriptions
Wars After Shave Spartacus Sans Soucis Bocage
Arcancil Exotic Intim Desodor Pound's Cream
Cocoa Butter Pond's Dry Skin Cream Maquimat

Avon Chic Privileg Fath de Fath Aramis
Savon Ambre Ancien eau de Cologne...
Perhaps it has an inkling of something
great and mysterious, of a transcendental reality
behind these colourful labels or perhaps
the odours have simply obliterated other traces of smell
from its path leading into the socket hole and from there
into the kitchen behind the breadbox.

[JK/SH/RT]

'To eat a pie, and to have it'

THROUGH THE FOREST 1991/1996 / SELECTED POEMS 2011

To eat a pie and to have it – I
sometimes succeed – I exchange
a piece of lived life for poetry, and then on
for roubles and kopecks – I live off that same
life, eat my own tail and shins
and they grow again, always anew
and the eagle of poetry rises again into flight
and tries to rise with me away from this world
towards a higher world, from which, once,
I was expelled. I remember it
and in my dreams I see it over and over again,
but in reality I do not know how to go there,
although I go on reading stories and folklore studies,
believing that one day I shall discover the way.
Then I shall still need wings. Only wings.
Perhaps my own.

[HH]

Translators:

JK/SH/RT: Jaan Kaplinski with Sam Hammill/Riina Tamm
HH: Hildi Hawkins

8 | KO UN

Filmed with Brother Anthony of Taizé at Aldeburgh Poetry
Festival by Neil Astley, 3-4 November 2012

Born in 1933, Ko Un has long been a living legend in Korea, both
as a poet and as a person. Allen Ginsberg once wrote, 'Ko Un is a
magnificent poet, combination of Buddhist cognoscente, passionate
political libertarian, and naturalist historian.'

After immense suffering during the Korean War, he became a
Buddhist monk. His first poems were published in 1958, his first
collection in 1960. A few years later he returned to the world. After
years of dark nihilism, he became a leading spokesman in the
struggle for freedom and democracy during the 1970s and 1980s,
when he was often arrested and imprisoned.

He has published more than 150 volumes of poems, essays, and
fiction, including the monumental seven-volume epic *Mount Paekdu*
and the 30-volume *Maninbo* (Ten Thousand Lives) series. A selec-
tion from the first ten volumes of *Maninbo* relating to Ko Un's
village childhood was published in the US in 2006 under the title
Ten Thousand Lives. A selection from the second ten volumes was
published by Bloodaxe in 2015 as *Maninbo 2: Peace and War*, trans-
lated by Brother Anthony of Taizé and Lee Sang-Wha, translators
of his most recent poetry included in *First Person Sorrowful* (2012).
The film shows the launch reading for that book at Aldeburgh
Poetry Festival in 2012, followed by the finale of another Aldeburgh
event at which Ko Un delighted the audience with his rendering of
the traditional Korean folksong, 'Miryang Arirang' (밀양 아리랑).

Nothing shows more clearly his stature as a writer than the
variety of themes and emotions found in his most recent work,
acclaimed by Korean critics as bringing poetry to a new level of
cosmic reference. 'His abiding concern is nothing less than the
quintessentially human question of what it means to live in time,'
writes Andrew Motion in his foreword to *First Person Sorrowful*:
'On page after page in this book, in a wonderful cascade of different
forms and registers, we find him squaring up to the paradoxes this
entails. [...] Ko Un generally mixes the allegorical with the elem-
ental. Sure, he enjoys writing about ordinary things. But the recur-
ring motifs of his poems are generic clouds, rivers, flags, winds and
skies, and over the course of this book they create a panorama that
feels at once very particular and highly abstracted, and a style that
is both familiar and original – a kind of amplified Symbolism.'

죽은 시인들과의 시간

POETRY LEFT BEHIND 2002

우리는 우주의 한 지방에 있다.
어느 때는 무지막지한 황야였고
어느 때는 자궁인 곳.
지금 우리는
하나하나의 살아있는 시인만이 아니다.
이곳에서 우리는 살아있는 시인과
다른 무엇으로 된
낯선 오지이다

어떤 소리도 소멸의 경계를 넘지 않는다.
어느 때는 몸이 무겁고
어느 때는 몸이 마음보다 가볍다.
죽은 시인들의 영혼이
우리 각자의 몸 속에 들어와
지친 날개를 접고 깃들었다. 무겁다.
나는 나 이상이다.
너는 너 이상이다.
우리는 우주의 방언으로 노래하고
죽은 시인의 새로운 모국어로 노래한다.
시작은 혼자였으나
다음은 함께였다 짐이 가볍다.

거대한 파도기둥이 치솟으며 소용돌이치다가
다음날 아침 가라앉을 때.
그 동안 숨어버렸던 갈매기가
공포 끝에 나타나
더 이상 벌벌 떨지 않고
가장 세련된 원을 그리며 날아오를 때.
그는 죽었다.
누군가가 그를 시인이라고 수근거렸다.

하루가 느리게 진화되는 내장처럼 길었고
또 하루가 막 태어난 갈매기 새끼의 날개처럼 짧다.
죽은 시인의 남은 생애가
우리 각자의 난생설화의 생애 가운데 자리잡았기 때문이다.

Time with Dead Poets

FIRST PERSON SORROWFUL 2012

We are in one sector of the universe, sometimes a wilderness,
sometimes a womb.
Now each of us
is not just an individual living poet.
Here
we are also unfamiliar backcountries
made up of something different
from living poets.

No sound passes beyond the boundaries of extinction.
Our bodies sometimes feel heavy,
sometimes lighter than our hearts.
The souls of dead poets
enter and make their abode in each of our bodies,
folding their weary wings.
I am more than myself.
You are more than yourself.
We sing in the universe's dialect,
sing in the new mother-tongue of dead poets.
We begin alone,
then we are together all the time.

When huge waves rose suddenly
only to settle back the next morning,
when the gulls emerged from hiding
after the terror,
no longer a-tremble,
and went soaring high, drawing the most refined circles,
a person died.
A poet, people whispered.

At times, a day is as long as a slowly writhing intestine;
at times, a day is as short as a newborn gull's wings.
It's because the dead poet's remaining lifetime has settled
inside each of our lives born of the egg-laying myth.

고도 5천 미터 평원 위 상공이다.
바짝 마른 티벧 갈매기가 날고 있다.
아주아주 옛날
한 대륙이 달려와 부딪쳤을 때
그때까지 찬란한 바다였던 그 일대가
히말라야가 되어버렸다.
갈매기는 바다를 잃어버렸다.
마구 소리쳤다.
갈매기 2세 12세 혹은 1302세…
다음이 있다
다음이 있다
그 소리들은 마침내 노래가 되고 시가 되었다.

그리하여 우리는
하나하나의 살아있는 시인이다.
또한 하나하나의 살아있는 시인만이 아니라
이 세상과 이 세상 이후에도 하나가 아닌
셋이고 일곱이고 열 하나이지 않으면 안 된다.
우리가 오고
우리가 가는 시간의 관능이 우리이다.
지금 누구를 위한 추도는
누군가가
우리하나하나를 추도할 때와 함께이다.
우리가 이곳에서 만나는 일은
이곳 이외의 여러 곳에
수많은 이별과 죽음의 풍경을 남기는 일이다.

여기다!
우리들의 오지에 호수가 있다. 수상하다.
눈 감기 전과
눈 감은 뒤의 수면水面에
하양 수련 꽃 떠 있다
누구를 위한 만가를 써보지 않은 시인은 불행하다.
우리는 그런 불행을 지고
이따금 새로운 만가를 써야 한다.
그것은 연가의 다른 이름이다. 꽃이다.
아 슬픔이 필요하다.
그것은 연가의 다른 이름이다. 꽃이다.

In the void above high plateaux at 5000 metres
a dry, gaunt Tibetan gull is flying.
A very, very long time ago,
a continent came rushing near, collided.
Then what had been a sparkling sea
went mad and turned into the Himalayas.
The gulls lost their ocean.
They cried aloud.
They have continued their lives
through a second generation, a twelfth, even a 1302nd...
Each succeeded the next.
And the next.
Their cries at last became songs, became poems.

So each of us
is a living poet.
We are each not only a living poet;
we need to be three poets, seven poets, eleven, in this world and the world after.
We are the very sensuality
of the time in which we come and go.
When we hold a memorial for someone,
that is also the time when someone will hold a memorial for each of us.
Our meeting here
is our leaving many partings behind
in many other places, elsewhere.

Here we are!
In our backcountry there is a lake.
On the water's surface, before and after we close our eyes,
floats a white water lily.
Unfortunate is the poet who has never written an elegy for someone.
On that account we must sometimes write a new elegy.
That is another name for a love song. A flower.
Ah! we so need sorrow.
The lake remembers the middle of its ancient sea.

햇볕

FATHERLAND STARS 1984

어쩔 줄 모르겠구나
침을 삼키고
불행을 삼키자
9사상 반 평짜리 북창 감방에
고귀한 손님이 오신다
과장 순시가 아니라
저녁 무렵 한동안의 햇볕
접고 접은 딱지만하게 햇볕이 오신다
환장하겠다 첫사랑
거기에 손바닥 놓아본다
수줍은 발벗어 발가락을 쪼인다
그러다가 엎드려
비종교적으로 마른 얼굴 대고 있으면
햇볕 조각은 덧없이 미끄러진다
쇠창살 넘어 손님은 덧없이 떠난 뒤
방안은 몇 곱으로 춥다 어둡다
육군교도소 특감은 암실이다
햇볕 없이 히히 웃었다
하루는 송장 넣은 관이었고
하루는 전혀 바다였다
용하도다 거기서 사람들 몇이 살아난 것이다

살아 있다는 것은 돛단배 하나 없는 바다이기도 하구나

Sunlight

FIRST PERSON SORROWFUL 2012

I really don't know what to do.
Let me swallow my spit,
and my unhappiness, too.
An honoured visitor is coming
to my tiny cell with its north-facing window.
It's not the chief making his rounds,
but a gleam of sunlight for an instant late in the afternoon,
a gleam no bigger than a square of folded pasteboard.
I go crazy; it's first love.
I hold out the palm of my hand,
warm the toes of my shy, bared feet.
Then as I prostrate myself on the floor
and bask my gaunt, unreligious face
in that scrap of sunlight, all too fleeting it slips away.
When the visitor has receded beyond the iron bars,
the room becomes several times colder and darker.
This special cell in a military prison is a photographer's darkroom.
Without sunlight I sometimes laughed like an idiot.
One day it was a coffin.
One day it was altogether the sea.
Amazing! A few have survived here.

Being alive is itself being at sea without a single sail in sight.

그 속삭임

EMPTY SKY 2008

비가 오다
책상 앞에 앉다
책상이 가만히 말하다
나는 일찍이 꽃이었고 잎이었다 줄기였다
나는 사막 저쪽 오아시스까지 뻗어간
땅속의 긴 뿌리였다

책상 위의 쇠토막이 말하다
나는 달밤에 혼자 울부짖는 늑대의 목젖이었다

비가 그치다
밖으로 나간다
흠뻑 젖은 풀이 나에게 말하다
나는 일찍이 너희들의 희로애락이었다
너희들의 삶이었고 노래였다
너희들의 꿈속이었다

이제 내가 말하다
책상에게
쇠에게
흙에게
나는 일찍이 너였다 너였다 너였다
지금 나는 너이고 너이다

The Whisper

FIRST PERSON SORROWFUL 2012

Rain falls.
I sit at my desk.
The desk speaks softly:
Once I was a flower, was a leaf, was a stalk.
I was a long root beneath the ground
stretching as far as yon desert oasis

A scrap of iron on the desk speaks:
I was the uvula of a stillness howling alone on moonlit nights.

The rain stops.
I go outside.
Grass, thoroughly soaked, speaks to me:
Once I was your joy and sorrow.
I was your history and songs.

Now I speak
to desk
to iron
to earth:
Once I was you, was you, was you.
Now I am you, I am you.

일인칭은 슬프다
LATE SONGS 2002

슬프다 깨달음은 어느새 모습이 된다
지난 세기 초
혁명 뒤 소비에트 시인들은
'우리들'이라고만 말하기로 했다
'우리들'이라고만
시인 자신을 부르기로 했다
황홀했다
그 결정은
풋설 때문에
거리에 나가지 못한 채
방 안에 서성거릴 때도 유효했다
저 혼자
'우리들......'이라고 맹세했다
거울 저쪽에서
'나'는 어디론가 사라졌다
어느 화창한 날
뛰쳐나온 마야꼽스끼도
'우리들'이라고 외치고 다녔다

그는 거리의 시인이었다
어디에도 '나'는 허용되지 않았다
'나'는 죄악이었다
'우리들'
'우리들......'
오직그것만이 주문(呪文)의 권력이 되었다

차츰 하늘의 저기업이 눌러댔다
어른꽃들 누누이 짓밟혔다
혁명은
혁명을 먹었다
모든 아이들의 공에서 바람이 빠져갔다
'우리들'도
팽팽한 대기 속에서
바람이 빠졌다

누가 대담하게[
'나는 사랑한다'라고 섰으나
아직
'우리들은 사랑한다'라고 읽는 습관이 남아 있었다
겨울 눈이 다 녹지 않았다
몸은 늘 불안하다

First Person Sorrowful

FIRST PERSON SORROWFUL 2012

I am sad. Enlightenment soon becomes a contradiction.
After the revolution early last century
the Soviet poets
decided they would only say 'We'.
They decided they would only call themselves
'We'.
They were enchanted.
Their decision held
even when they could not go out into the streets,
even when they lingered indoors
due to heavy blizzards.
They took oaths saying 'We...'
by themselves.
'I' had disappeared somewhere
deep in the looking-glass.
Mayakovsky, too, one bright sunny day, dashed out
shouting and shouting 'We'.
He was a poet of the street.
'I' was not allowed anywhere.
'I' was wicked.
'We'
'We...'
That alone had incantatory power.

Little by little, a low-pressure front settled in.
Summer flowers kept being trampled.
Revolution
devoured revolution.
The air went out of every child's ball.
Likewise the taut round atmosphere
of 'We'
slowly went flat.

Someone boldly wrote
'I am in love',
but still, as long the custom,
it was read, 'We are in love'.
Winter snows had not all melted.
Spring is always uncertain.

지난 세기 말
소비에트가 죽었다
바르샤바조약 국가들이
하나하나 떨어져나갔다

그 이래
시인들에게 온통 '나'뿐이다
'나'로 시작해서
'나'로 하루가 저물었다
'나' 이외에는
아무 것도 없다
신도 '나'의 다른 이름이었다

오늘 환태평양
'우리'와 '나'의 유령들을 무한한 파도에 묻는다
누가 태어날 것인가
'우리'도 아닌
'나'도 아닌 누가 태어날 것인가
파도는 파도의 무덤이고 파도의 자궁이다

Late last century
the Soviet Union disappeared.
Countries dropped out of the Warsaw Pact
one after another.

Since then
poets have nothing but 'I'.
Starting with 'I'
they end the day with 'I'.
There is nothing
except 'I'.
God, too, is another name for 'I'.

Today I bury
the ghosts of 'We' and 'I' in the endless waves of the Pacific Rim.
Who will be born?
Who will be born,
neither 'We' nor 'I'?
Each wave is one wave's grave, another wave's womb.

작은 노래 24 편 중
POETRY LEFT BEHIND 2002

만약 10년 30년 또는 60년
이런 세월이 무상하지 않다면
이런 삶이 무상하지 않은 거라면
인간은 훨씬 더 야만이었으리라

오 숭고한 무상 만세

*

오늘이
하찮은 날일지라도
누가 태어나는 날이고
누가 떠나는 날이다
누가 기다리는 날이다

오늘도 해 지기 전 낙조 웅혼하여라

*

붉은 영산홍이 피어 있네
저만치 배롱나무 꽃필 생각 전혀 없네

이렇게 세상은 각각의 살림이네 나는 좋아 헤매네

from 24 Little Songs

FIRST PERSON SORROWFUL 2012

Ten years, thirty years, or fifty years,
if such time-spans were not transient,
if such life-spans were not transient,
humans would have become much more barbarous.

Oh, long live sublime transience!

*

Today
may be a trivial day,
the day someone is being born,
someone is leaving,
someone waiting.

Today too, the glow of the setting sun is glorious!

*

Scarlet rhododendrons are in blossom.
The crape myrtle trees beyond have no thought of blossoming.

So everything in the world has its own way of living. Glad of that,
I wander on.

All poems translated from the Korean by Brother Anthony of Taizé & Lee Sang-Wha

9 | THOMAS LUX
(1946-2017)

Filmed by Neil Astley at the Snape Maltings, Aldeburgh,
8 November 2014

Thomas Lux was born in Northampton, Massachusetts, in 1946, to working-class parents, and raised on a dairy farm. He studied at Emerson College, Boston, and later, briefly, at the University of Iowa. He taught for 27 years at Sarah Lawrence College, and was latterly Bourne Professor of Poetry and director of Poetry@Tech at the Georgia Institute of Technology in Atlanta. He died from lung cancer in February 2017, aged 70. We launched his Bloodaxe *Selected Poems* at Aldeburgh Poetry Festival in 2014, sadly the last time I saw him, when I filmed him in a music practice room at Snape Maltings. His totally engaged delivery of poems from the book and frank discussion of his life and work make for an unforgettable, deeply moving film.

After starting out as a neo-surrealist American poet in the 1970s, Lux 'drifted away from surrealism and the arbitrariness of all that. I got more interested in subjects, identifiable subjects other than my own angst or ennui'. The later Lux wrote more directly in response to more familiar but no less strange human experience, creating a body of work that is at once simple and complex, wildly imaginative and totally relevant. He used humour or satire 'to help combat the darkness... to make the reader laugh – and then steal that laugh, right out of the throat. Because I think life is like that, tragedy right alongside humour.'

Each of Lux's multi-faceted poems is self-contained, whether it is musing or ranting, lamenting or lambasting, first person personal or first person universal. 'Usually, the speaker of my poems is a little agitated,' Lux once said, 'a little smart-ass, a little angry, satirical, despairing. Or, sometimes he's goofy, somewhat elegiac, full of praise and gratitude.'

He published 12 collections of poetry. His 'switchover' collection was *Half Promised Land* in 1986, which marked a sea change in his work. *Split Horizon* in 1994 won him the Kingsley-Tufts Award, making it possible for him to devote much more time and energy to his poetry at a crucial stage in the evolution of his work. He published two books of poetry in Britain, *The Street of Clocks* from Arc in 2001, and Bloodaxe's *Selected Poems* in 2014, which shows the poet before and after his 'recovery' from Surrealism.

Wife Hits Moose

HALF PROMISED LAND 1986 | SELECTED POEMS 2014

Sometime around dusk moose lifts
his heavy, primordial jaw, dripping, from pondwater
and, without psychic struggle,
decides the day, for him, is done: time
to go somewhere else. Meanwhile, wife
drives one of those roads that cut straight north,
a highway dividing the forests

not yet fat enough for the paper companies.
This time of year full dark falls
about eight o'clock – pineforest and blacktop
blend. Moose reaches road, fails
to look both ways, steps
deliberately, ponderously.... Wife
hits moose, hard,

at a slight angle (brakes slammed, car
spinning) and moose rolls over hood, antlers –
as if diamond-tipped – scratch windshield, car
damaged: rib-of-moose imprint
on fender, hoof shatters headlight.
Annoyed moose lands on feet and walks away.
Wife is shaken, unhurt, amazed.

– Does moose believe in a Supreme Intelligence?
Speaker does not know.
– Does wife believe in a Supreme Intelligence?
Speaker assumes as much: spiritual intimacies
being between the spirit and the human.
– Does speaker believe in a Supreme Intelligence?
Yes. Thank You.

A Little Tooth

THE DROWNED RIVER 1990 | SELECTED POEMS 2014

Your baby grows a tooth, then two,
and four, and five, then she wants some meat
directly from the bone. It's all

over: she'll learn some words, she'll fall
in love with cretins, dolts, a sweet
talker on his way to jail. And you,

your wife, get old, flyblown, and rue
nothing. You did, you loved, your feet
are sore. It's dusk. Your daughter's tall.

The People of the Other Village

SPLIT HORIZON 1994 | SELECTED POEMS 2014

hate the people of this village
and would nail our hats
to our heads for refusing in their presence to remove them
or staple our hands to our foreheads
for refusing to salute them
if we did not hurt them first: mail them packages of rats,
mix their flour at night with broken glass.
We do this, they do that.
They peel the larynx from one of our brothers' throats.
We de-vein one of their sisters.
The quicksand pits they built were good.
Our amputation teams were better.
We trained some birds to steal their wheat.
They sent to us exploding ambassadors of peace.
They do this, we do that.
We canceled our sheep imports.
They no longer bought our blankets.
We mocked their greatest poet
and when that had no effect
we parodied the way they dance

which did cause pain, so they, in turn, said our God
was leprous, hairless.
We do this, they do that.
Ten thousand (10,000) years, ten thousand
(10,000) brutal, beautiful years.

An Horatian Notion

SPLIT HORIZON 1994 | SELECTED POEMS 2014

The thing gets made, gets built, and you're the slave
who rolls the log beneath the block, then another,
then pushes the block, then pulls a log
from the rear back to the front
again and then again it goes beneath the block,
and so on. It's how a thing gets made – not
because you're sensitive, or you get genetic-lucky,
or God says: Here's a nice family,
seven children, let's see: this one in charge
of the village dunghill, these two die of buboes, this one
Kierkegaard, this one a drooling

nincompoop, this one clerk, this one cooper.
You need to love the thing you do – birdhouse building,
painting tulips exclusively, whatever – and then
you do it
so consciously driven
by your unconscious
that the thing becomes a wedge
that splits a stone and between the halves
the wedge then grows, i.e., the thing
is solid but with a soul,
a life of its own. Inspiration, the donnée,

the gift, the bolt of fire
down the arm that makes the art?
Grow up! Give me, please, a break!
You make the thing because you love the thing
and you love the thing because someone else loved it
enough to make you love it.
And with that your heart like a tent peg pounded

toward the earth's core.
And with that your heart on a beam burns
through the ionosphere.
And with that you go to work.

'I Love You Sweatheart'

SPLIT HORIZON 1994 | SELECTED POEMS 2014

A man risked his life to write the words.
A man hung upside down (an idiot friend
holding his legs?) with spray paint
to write the words on a girder fifty feet above
a highway. And his beloved,
the next morning driving to work...?
His words are not (meant to be) so unique.
Does she recognise his handwriting?
Did he hint to her at her doorstep the night before
of 'something special, darling, tomorrow'?
And did he call her at work
expecting her to faint with delight
at his celebration of her, his passion, his risk?
She will *know* I love her now,
the *world* will know my love for her!
A man risked his life to write the words.
Love is like this at the bone, we hope, love
is like this, Sweatheart, all sore and dumb
and dangerous, ignited, blessed – always,
regardless, no exceptions,
always in blazing matters like these: blessed.

Refrigerator, 1957

NEW AND SELECTED POEMS 1997 | SELECTED POEMS 2014

More like a vault – you pull the handle out
and on the shelves: not a lot,
and what there is (a boiled potato

in a bag, a chicken carcass
under foil) looking dispirited,
drained, mugged. This is not
a place to go in hope or hunger.
But, just to the right of the middle
of the middle door shelf, on fire, a lit-from-within red,
heart red, sexual red, wet neon red,
shining red in their liquid, exotic,
aloof, slumming
in such company: a jar
of maraschino cherries. Three-quarters
full, fiery globes, like strippers
at a church social. Maraschino cherries, maraschino,
the only foreign word I knew. Not once
did I see these cherries employed: not
in a drink, nor on top
of a glob of ice cream,
or just pop one in your mouth. Not once.
The same jar there through an entire
childhood of dull dinners – bald meat,
pocked peas and, see above,
boiled potatoes. Maybe
they came over from the old country,
family heirlooms, or were status symbols
bought with a piece of the first paycheck
from a sweatshop,
which beat the pig farm in Bohemia,
handed down from my grandparents
to my parents
to be someday mine,
then my child's?
They were beautiful
and, if I never ate one,
it was because I knew it might be missed
or because I knew it would not be replaced
and because you do not eat
that which rips your heart with joy.

Cucumber Fields Crossed by High-Tension Wires

THE STREET OF CLOCKS 2001 | SELECTED POEMS 2014

The high-tension spires spike the sky
beneath which boys bend
to pick from prickly vines
the deep-sopped fruit, the rind's green
a green sunk
in green. They part the plants' leaves,
reach into the nest,
and pull out mother, father, fat Uncle Phil.
The smaller yellow-green children stay,
for now. The fruit goes
in baskets by the side of the row,
every thirty feet or so. By these bushels
the boys get paid, in cash,
at day's end, this summer
of the last days of the empire
that will become known as
the past, adoios, *then*,
the ragged-edged beautful blink.

Plague Victims Catapulted over Walls into Besieged City

THE STREET OF CLOCKS 2001 | SELECTED POEMS 2014

Early germ
warfare. The dead
hurled this way turn like wheels
in the sky. Look: there goes
Larry the Shoemaker, barefoot, over the wall,
and Mary Sausage Stuffer, see how she flies,
and the Hatter twins, both at once, soar
over the parapet, little Tommy's elbow bent
as if in a salute,
and his sister, Mathilde, she follows him,
arms outstretched, through the air,
just as she did on earth.

Tarantulas on the Lifebuoy

HALF PROMISED LAND 1986 | SELECTED POEMS 2014

For some semitropical reason
when the rains fall
relentlessly they fall

into swimming pools, these otherwise
bright and scary
arachnids. They can swim
a little, but not for long

and they can't climb the ladder out.
They usually drown – but
if you want their favor,
if you believe there is justice,
a reward for not loving

the death of ugly
and even dangerous (the eel, hog snake,
rats) creatures, if

you believe these things, then
you would leave a lifebuoy
or two in your swimming pool at night.

And in the morning
you would haul ashore
the huddled, hairy survivors

and escort them
back to the bush, and know,
be assured that at least these saved,
as individuals, would not turn up

again someday
in your hat, drawer,
or the tangled underworld

of your socks, and that even –
when your belief in justice
merges with your belief in dreams –
they may tell the others

in a sign language
four times as subtle
and complicated as man's

that you are good,
that you love them,
that you would save them again.

DVD 2

MONIZA ALVI – DEBORAH GARRISON

1 | MONIZA ALVI

Filmed at home in Wymondham, Norfolk,
by Neil Astley, 11 November 2013

Moniza Alvi was born in Lahore, Pakistan, in 1954, the daughter of an English mother and a Pakistani father. Her family left for Britain when she was just a few months old, and she grew up in Hertfordshire, only returning to Pakistan in the mid-90s, after publishing her first book of poems, *The Country at My Shoulder* (1993). In this book and in her second collection, *A Bowl of Warm Air* (1996), she drew on real and imagined homelands in poems which are 'vivid, witty and imbued with unexpected and delicious glimpses of the surreal – this poet's third country' (Maura Dooley).

Ruth Padel has called her 'a bold surrealist, whose poems open the world up in new, imaginatively absurd ways', and Moniza Alvi has said that her imagination has always been fed as much by 'fantasy and the strange-seeming' as by the strangeness of her background.

Originally published by OUP, her first two collections were reprinted in her first Bloodaxe title, *Carrying My Wife* (2000), together with a third collection of new work. In her later poems, her delicately drawn fantasies transform the familiar into strange evocations of the joys and tensions of relationships, of love, intimacy, frustration, jealousy and paranoia, exploring birth, death and parenthood as well as the fragility of life with a sure wit and lightness of touch. The title-sequence of *How the Stone Found Its Voice* (2005) is a series of poems inspired by creation myths. Begun in the wake of the tragedy of 9/11, they are imbued with the dark spirit of that time, with titles including 'How a Long Way Off Rolled Itself Up' and 'How the World Split in Two', the poem she reads first in the film.

Much of her 2008 collection *Europa* relates to ancient and modern traumas, including enforced exile, alienation, rape and "honour killing", with a re-imagining of the story of the rape of Europa by Jupiter as a bull as its centre-piece. The cover picture is a painting by American artist Tabitha Vevers, 'When We Talk About Rape' (1992), the inspiration for the poem 'Mermaid' which she reads in the film. She has since published *Homesick for the Earth* (2011), a bilingual edition of her versions of French poet Jules Supervielle, and *At the Time of Partition* (2013), a book-length poem set in 1947 when thousands of people were killed in civil unrest and millions displaced during the partition of India and Pakistan.

How the World Split in Two

HOW THE STONE FOUND ITS VOICE 2005

Was it widthways or lengthways,
a quarrel with the equator?
Did the rawness of the inside sparkle?

Only this is true:
there was an arm on one side
and a hand on the other,
a thought on one side
and a hush on the other.

And a luminous tear
carried on the back of a beetle
went backwards and forwards
from one side to the other.

I Would Like to be a Dot in a Painting by Miró

THE COUNTRY AT MY SHOULDER 1993 | SPLIT WORLD 2008

I would like to be a dot in a painting by Miró.

Barely distinguishable from other dots,
it's true, but quite uniquely placed.
And from my dark centre

I'd survey the beauty of the linescape
and wonder – would it be worthwhile
to roll myself towards the lemon stripe,

Centrally poised, and push my curves
against its edge, to get myself
a little extra attention?

But it's fine where I am.
I'll never make out what's going on
around me, and that's the joy of it.

The fact that I'm not a perfect circle
makes me more interesting in this world.
People will stare forever –

Even the most unemotional get excited.
So here I am, on the edge of animation,
a dream, a dance, a fantastic construction,

A child's adventure.
And nothing in this tawny sky
can get too close, or move too far away.

I Was Raised in a Glove Compartment

THE COUNTRY AT MY SHOULDER 1993 | SPLIT WORLD 2008

I was raised in a glove compartment.
The gloves held out limp fingers –

in the dark I touched them.
I bumped against the First Aid tin,

and rolled on notepads and maps.
I never saw my mother's face –

sometimes
her gloved hand would reach for me.

I existed in the quiet – I listened
for the sound of the engine.

The Sari

THE COUNTRY AT MY SHOULDER 1993 | SPLIT WORLD 2008

Inside my mother
I peered through a glass porthole.
The world beyond was hot and brown.

They were all looking in on me –
Father, Grandmother,
the cook's boy, the sweeper-girl,
the bullock with the sharp
shoulderblades,
the local politicians.

My English grandmother
took a telescope
and gazed across continents.

All the people unravelled a sari.
It stretched from Lahore to Hyderabad,
wavered across the Arabian Sea,
shot through with stars,
fluttering with sparrows and quails.
They threaded it with roads,
undulations of land.

Eventually
they wrapped and wrapped me in it
whispering *Your body is your country.*

Presents from My Aunts in Pakistan

THE COUNTRY AT MY SHOULDER 1993 | SPLIT WORLD 2008

They sent me a salwar kameez
               peacock-blue,
                       and another
      glistening like an orange split open,
embossed slippers, gold and black
               points curling.
      Candy-striped glass bangles
                 snapped, drew blood.
      Like at school, fashions changed
             in Pakistan –
the salwar bottoms were broad and stiff,
             then narrow.
My aunts chose an apple-green sari,
      silver-bordered
             for my teens.

I tried each satin-silken top –
      was alien in the sitting-room.
I could never be as lovely
             as those clothes
      I longed
for denim and corduroy.
      My costume clung to me
             and I was aflame,
I couldn't rise up out of its fire,
      half-English,
             unlike Aunt Jamila.

I wanted my parents' camel-skin lamp –
      switching it on in my bedroom,
to consider the cruelty
             and the transformation
from camel to shade,
      marvel at the colours
             like stained glass.

My mother cherished her jewellery –
      Indian gold, dangling, filigree.
             But it was stolen from our car.

The presents were radiant in my wardrobe.
    My aunts requested cardigans
        from Marks and Spencers.

My salwar kameez
    didn't impress the schoolfriend
who sat on my bed, asked to see
    my weekend clothes.
But often I admired the mirror-work,
    tried to glimpse myself
        in the miniature
glass circles, recall the story
    how the three of us
        sailed to England.
Prickly heat had me screaming on the way.
    I ended up in a cot
in my English grandmother's dining-room,
    found myself alone,
        playing with a tin boat.

I pictured my birthplace
    from fifties' photographs.
        When I was older
there was conflict, a fractured land
    throbbing through newsprint.
Sometimes I saw Lahore –
        my aunts in shaded rooms,
screened from male visitors,
    sorting presents,
        wrapping them in tissue.

Or there were beggars, sweeper-girls
    and I was there –
        of no fixed nationality,
staring through fretwork
        at the Shalimar Gardens.

Mermaid

(after Moniza Alvi)

EUROPA 2008

About human love,
                    she knew nothing.

I'll show you he promised.
But first you need legs.

And he held up
                 a knife

with the sharpest of tips
to the ripeness of her emerald tail.

She danced an involuntary dance
captive
           twitching with fear.

Swiftly
       he slit

down the muscular length
exposing the bone in its red canal.

She played dead on the rock

           dead by the blue lagoon
           dead to the ends of her divided tail.

He fell on her, sunk himself deep
into the apex.

Then he fled
           on his human legs.

Human love cried the sea,
the sea in her head.

2 | ANTONELLA ANEDDA

Filmed with Jamie McKendrick in Ledbury by Neil Astley,
6 July 2013

Antonella Anedda is one of Italy's leading poets. Her poetry has a searing, disruptive quality, an honesty that is hard won. Her words have the air of breaking the silence reluctantly, and they keep the silence with them. This stringent, ferrous element sets her at odds with the eloquence and lyricism characteristic of the Italian poetic tradition, and may owe something to an alternative nationality, a different landscape. Though born in Rome, she comes from a Sardinian family and has passed a great deal of her life between the capital and a small island, La Maddalena, off the coast of Sardinia. The languages she was brought up hearing were Logudorese, Catalan from Alghero, and Corsican French mixed with the dialect of La Maddalena – and of late she has found herself also writing a number of poems in Logudorese.

While her poems have a geographical sweep, there is also an insistence on domestic detail – balconies, crockery, sewing, cooking: elements often considered too humble to warrant poetic attention. But even here they are often set against a backdrop of war and insecurity, and a poem in these surroundings is as likely to be the site of a haunting.

Her first book, *Winter Residences*, already posited an elsewhere, that of St Petersburg, and an elective affinity with another culture. With time, and with the emergence of her next four books of poetry, this sense of apartness has increased, as has the force and particularity of her language – and has made her, along with Valerio Magrelli, one of the most valued and original poets of her generation.

Jamie McKendrick's first English translation of her work, *Archipelago* (Bloodaxe Books, 2014), a dual text selection from five collections published in Italy, won him the John Florio Translation Prize 2016. Filmed before their Ledbury Poetry Festival event in 2013, we see poet and translator interacting as they read and discuss details of the poems and translations, including 'Contro Scaurum' ('Against Scaurus'), a poem in Logudorese originally titled 'Name', and another written as a prose piece in the Italian which Jamie felt needed to be translated into free verse lines in English.

Settembre 2001. Arcipelago della Maddalena, isola di S. Stefano

IL CATALOGO DELLA GIOIA 2003

questa piccola isola forata sott'acqua dai sommergibili americani,
dove mio bisnonno piantò viti e agrumi
costruì stalle e portò dieci vacche dal Continente.
I loro zoccoli tremanti sulla barca, il vento sui dorsi
colpiti fino allora solo dalle piogge del nord.
Sono ancora lì, le corna miste a sabbia
gli scheletri profondi, stretti agli scogli senza più paura,
senza più distinzione tra i pascoli e il mare.

Contro Scaurum

DAL BALCONE DEL CORPO 2007

No ischio iscrivere de Roma.
Meda belluria, dechidu, mutas 'e linu.
Forzis gòi –sunt binti seculos– pessaint cuddos sardos
bennitos a dimandare zusstissia contra Scauro.

'Zente chene ide...terra ue peri su mele est 'ele'

Gòi nàrriat Cicero in faeddu suo. Ora, in mesu petras
bortat suo lumene, lestru, minutu. Ma sicutera
morint sos distimonzos, s' ape tribulat.
Reghet su mele: limba e'lidone, gardu et sale.

126

September 2001. Maddalena Archipelago. Island of S. Stefano

CATALOGUE OF JOY 2003

This small island riven underwater by U.S. submarines,
where my great-grandfather planted citrus fruits and vines,
built cowsheds and brought ten cows from the mainland.
Their trembling hoofs on the boat, the wind on their backs
only struck till then by rain from the north.
They're still there, horns mingled with the sand,
deep-rooted skeletons, close up to the rocks, no longer afraid,
no longer distinguishing pasture from sea.

translated from the Italian by Jamie McKendrick

Against Scaurus

FROM THE BODY'S BALCONY 2007

How can I write of Rome in one or seven days
– a glut of beauty, taste and linen tunics.
Maybe those Sards, 20 centuries ago, felt this
when they came to plead for justice against Scaurus.

'A truthless people…land where even the honey is gall'

Cicero said in his oration. But his name, now,
tiny and rapid, flits among the stones, and just as
then, witnesses die, the bee labours on.
Honey endures – a tongue of salt, arbutus, thistle.

translated from the Logudorese by Jamie McKendrick

In 54 BC, Scaurus, proconsul in Sardinia, was accused of extortion and of being the cause of the suicide of a woman he had raped. The Sards came to Rome to testify, but Scaurus had as his defence lawyer Cicero, who poured scorn on these unkempt figures, covered with animal skins, bewildered among the columns of the refined Tribunal. Although apparently guilty, Scaurus was absolved.

f

È la lettera della felicità terrena del soffio che fugge dalle labbra, è la fiducia dei fiori che si flettono quando scende il sole, ma è anche la lettera del fulmine, della fiamma che fende il buio.

'Fa freddo,' diciamo e la f si raddoppia nello stesso fiato della bocca sul fuoco.

* * *

> ...the years, the years.
> Down their carved names the raindrop ploughs.
>
> THOMAS HARDY

Non riesco a sentirti, sta passando un camion carico di ferro, ogni parola spenta dalle sbarre di ferro, ogni nome folgorato dal clangore del ferro, lucido e nero di pioggia senza passato o futuro. Il desiderio non è più l'affamato che guarda dalla finestra la casa illuminata.

f

Is the letter of felicity, of earthly joys, of the breath's flight from the lips, its fading; it's the faith of flowers that fold when the sun sets, but it's also the letter of the lightning flash, of the flame that, flickering, cleaves the dark.

'It's freezing' we say, and the f doubles in the same breath that feeds the fire.

translated from the Italian by Jamie McKendrick

*　　*　　*

> ...the years, the years.
> Down their carved names the raindrop ploughs.
>
> THOMAS HARDY

I can't hear you – a lorry laden with iron
is trundling past, and every word's drowned out
by the iron bars, every name erased
by the foundry thunder and clangour
of iron, shiny and black under a rain
without past, without future.
Desire's no longer the hungry creature
who peers through glass at the palace of light.

translated from the Italian by Jamie McKendrick

The poems in this selection are drawn from the following Italian collections by Antonella Anedda published by Mondadori: *Il catalogo della gioia* (Catalogue of Joy, 2003), *Dal balcone del corpo* (From the Body's Balcony, 2007), and *Salva con nome* (Save As, 2012). They also appear, with Jamie McKendrick's English translations, in the dual language edition *Archipelago* (Bloodaxe Books, 2014).

3 | JEAN 'BINTA' BREEZE

Filmed by Pamela Robertson-Pearce at the Y Theatre, Leicester,
8 March 2010

Jean 'Binta' Breeze is a popular Jamaican Dub poet and storyteller whose performances are so powerful she has been called a 'one-woman festival'. Her poems are Caribbean songs of innocence and experience, of love and conflict. They use personal stories and historical narratives to explore social injustice and the psychological dimensions of black women's experience. Striking evocations of childhood in the hills of Jamaica give way to explorations of the perils and delights of growth and change – through sex, emigration, motherhood and age.

Born in Hanover, Jamaica, she first visited London in 1985 to take part in the International Book Fair of Radical and Third World Books, and she has been writing, performing and teaching ever since. As well as several records and CDs, she has released seven poetry books, five of these with Bloodaxe: *On the Edge of an Island* (1997), *The Arrival of Brighteye* (2000), *The Fifth Figure* (2006), *Third World Girl: Selected Poems* (2011) and *The Verandah Poems* (2016).

Introduced by Colin McCabe, *Third World Girl* was published with a DVD featuring two Jean 'Binta' Breeze performances filmed by Pamela in 2010 at Leicester's Y Theatre, plus an onstage interview with Jane Dowson. The film included in *In Person: World Poets* is an excerpt from the first of these in which she reads and introduces four of the poems. The DVD which comes with *Third World Girl* includes 33 poems read in the course of the two performances.

Third World Girl doesn't cover *The Fifth Figure*, her book-length sequence mixing poetry and prose which chronicles the lives of five generations of Caribbean and Black British women of mixed ancestry. Part novel, part poem, part family memoir, its structure is based on the Jamaican quadrille, a hybrid version of the dance brought from Europe by the island's former colonial masters.

Her later collection *The Verandah Poems* is a book of coming home and coming to terms, of contemplation rather than contention – of mellow, musing, edgy poems drawn from the life and lives around her in Jamaica. It has a foreword by Kei Miller and features a selection of colour photographs by Tehron Royes of the coastal village setting of the poems.

simple tings

RIDDYM RAVINGS 1988 | THIRD WORLD GIRL 2011

de simple tings of life, mi dear
de simple tings of life

she rocked the rhythms in her chair
brushed a hand across her hair
miles of travel in her stare

de simple tings of life

ah hoe mi corn
an de backache gone
plant mi peas
arthritis ease

de simple tings of life

leaning back
she wiped an eye
read the rain signs
in the sky
evening's ashes
in a fireside

de simple tings of life

ordinary mawning

RIDDYM RAVINGS 1988 | THIRD WORLD GIRL 2011

it wasn't dat de day did start out bad
or dat no early mawning dream
did swing mi foot
aff de wrong side of de bed

it wasn't dat de cold floor
mek mi sneeze

an mi nose start run wid misery
wasn't a hangover headache
mawning
or a worry rising mawning

de sun did a shine same way
an a cool breeze
jus a brush een aff de sea
an de mawning news
was jus de same as ever
two shot dead
truck lick one
Israel still a bruk up
Palestine
an Botha still have de whole world han
twist back a dem

no
it wasn't de day dat start out bad
wasn't even pre m t
or post m t
was jus anadda ordinary get up
get de children ready fi school
mawning
anadda what to cook fah dinna dis evening
mawning
anadda wish me never did breed but Lawd
mi love dem mawning
jus anadda wanda if ah should a
tek up back wid dis man it would a
ease de situation mawning

no
it wasn't no duppy frighten mi
mek mi jump outa mi sleep
eena bad mood
nor no neighbour bring first quarrel
to mi door
wasn't de price rise pon bus fare
an milk an sugar

was jus anadda
same way mawning

anadda clean up de mess
after dem let mawning
a perfectly ordinary
mawning of a perfectly
ordinary day
trying to see a way
out

so it did hard fi understand
why de ordinary sight of
mi own frock
heng up pon line
wid some clothespin
should a stop mi from do nutten
but jus
bawl

spring cleaning

SPRING CLEANING 1992 | THIRD WORLD GIRL 2011

de Lord is my shepherd
I shall not want

an she scraping
de las crumbs
aff de plate
knowing ants will feed

maketh me to lie down
in green pastures
leadeth me beside de still
waters

an she han washing clothes
spotless
lifting dem outa de water
drying she han careful slow
pon she apron

restoreth my soul

she mixing
sugar
water
lime
she filling she favourite jug
de one wid de cool palm pattern

yea though I walk
troo de valley of de
shadow of death

she opening de fridge
de cowl stapping her breath
for a motion

I will fear no evil

she put een wah she want
tek out wah she want
shut de door

for thou art wid me
thy rod an thy staff
dey comfort me

an she looking wid a far eye
pon de picture a de children
side a de almanac
pon de wall

surely goodness an mercy
shall follow me

she pick up de broom,
an she sweeping

all de days of my life

an she sweeping

an I will dwell
in de house of de Lord

she sweeping out
sweeping
out

shake de broom
in de wind
dus fly
she beat it gains de fence
dus fly
she cup she han
unda de pipe
an she sprinkle water
roun she
stan up
hans akimbo

she watching
all de dark spirits
departing wid de dus

sunrise in er eyes

forever
an ever

Aid Travels with a Bomb

THIRD WORLD GIRL 2011

400 years
from the plantation whip
to the IMF grip

Aid travels with a bomb
Watch out
Aid travels with a bomb

Aid for countries in despair
aid for countries that have no share
they're dumping surplus food in the sea
yet they can't allow starvation to be

They buy your land to dump nuclear waste
you sell it so that food your children can taste

Aid travels with a bomb
Watch out
Aid travels with a bomb

They love your country
they want to invest
but your country don't get
when it come to the test

They rob and exploit you
of your own
then send it back
as a foreign loan
interest is on it
regulations too
they will also decide
your policy for you

Aid travels with a bomb
Watch out
Aid travels with a bomb

They come, they work
they smile so pleased
they leave and you discover
a new disease

Aid travels with a bomb
Watch out
Aid travels with a bomb

You don't know if they're on CIA fee
or even with the KGB
cause you think your country is oh so free
until you look at the economy

Aid travels with a bomb
Watch out!!

4 | ANA BLANDIANA

Filmed with Viorica Patea at the Romanian Cultural Institute,
London, by Neil Astley, 18 July 2014

Ana Blandiana is one of Romania's foremost poets, a leading dissi-
dent before the fall of Communism, and now her country's
strongest candidate for the Nobel Prize. A prominent opponent of
the Ceauşescu regime, Blandiana became known for her daring, out-
spoken poems as well as for her courageous defence of ethical values.
Over the years, her works have become the symbol of an ethical
consciousness that refuses to be silenced by a totalitarian government.

Blandiana redefines her poetics in every new book of poetry she
publishes. Her most recent collection, *My Native Land A4*, was
first published in Romania in 2010 and in Paul Scott Derrick and
Viorica Patea's English translation by Bloodaxe in 2014. In it she
recreates a land of words, water, trees, abandoned churches, fallen
angels and roller-skating gods. She projects visionary spaces within
the confines of a page – the A4 sheet of her title – which emerge
out of her imagination as anguished territories in which the lyrical
'I' is compelled to draw precise, clear boundaries out of a diffuse
magma of words.

The poems articulate a quest for love, beauty and truth and
affirm an urgent need for existential authenticity as a requisite for
the redemption of the self, chronicling the struggle between a
constantly deteriorating body that is learning how to die and the
spirit that strives to overcome its physical constraints. *My Native
Land A4* contains meditations on fundamental themes such as the
fragility and vulnerability of being, the inexorable toll of time, the
limitations of the human condition and the correspondence between
life and death within the cosmic rhythms of the universe.

When Ana Blandiana was in London in 2014 for Poetry Inter-
national at the Southbank Centre, Gabriela Mocan kindly offered
the use of a function room at the Romanian Cultural Institute for
us to film Ana Blandiana reading from *My Native Land A4* with
Viorica Patea. The excerpt from that reading shown in the film
ends with a virtuoso performance by poet and translator of the
poem which gives the book its title, 'Country of Unease' ('Patria
neliniştii') read simultaneously in both languages. Ana Blandiana
returned to London in 2015 to give a public reading from the book
in the same room at the Institute.

Rugăciune

PATRIA MIA A4 2010

Dumnezeu al libelulelor, al fluturilor de noapte,
Al ciocârliilor şi al bufniţelor,
Dumnezeu al râmelor, al scorpionilor
Şi al gândacilor de bucătărie,
Dumnezeu care i-ai învăţat pe fiecare altceva
Şi ştii dinainte tot ce i se va întâmpla fiecăruia,
Aş da orice să înţeleg ce-ai simţit
Când ai stabilit proporţiile
Otrăvurilor, culorilor, parfumurilor,
Când ai aşezat într-un cioc cântecul şi în altul croncănitul,
Şi-ntr-un suflet crima şi în altul extazul,
Aş da orice, mai ales, să ştiu dacă ai avut remuşcări
Că pe unii i-ai făcut victime şi pe alţii călăi,
Egal de vinovat faţă de toţi
Pentru că pe toţi i-ai pus în faţa faptului împlinit.
Dumnezeu al vinovăţiei de a fi hotărât singur
Raportul între bine şi rău,
Balanţa menţinută cu greu în echilibru
De trupul însângerat
Al fiului tău care nu-ţi seamănă.

Deasupra râului

PATRIA MIA A4 2010

În icoanele suspendate de secole
Deasupra râului
Moartea era îmbrăcată
La ultima modă
(Ultima modă atunci,
Când a fost construit podul
Şi pictată icoana).

Prayer

MY NATIVE LAND A4 2014

God of the dragonflies, of nocturnal moths,
Of larks and owls,
God of earthworms and scorpions,
Of kitchen cockroaches,
God that has taught each one something different
And who knows beforehand what will happen to them all,
I'd like to know what you felt
When you settled
On the sizes
Of their poisons, colours and perfumes,
When you placed a song in one beak
And a cackle in another,
Murder in one soul and ecstasy in another,
I'd give anything to know
If you felt remorse
For making some of them victims and
Others hangmen,
Equally guilty before them all
Because all of them were born with a *fait accompli.*
God of guilt, for having decided on your own
The ratio of evil and good,
The scales trembling always in a delicate balance
Above the wounded body
Of your son, who
Does not resemble you at all.

Above the River

MY NATIVE LAND A4 2014

In icons hung centuries ago
Above the river
Death is dressed
In the latest cut of clothes
(The latest cut of clothes
When the bridge was built
And the icon was painted).

Ea, cea eternă,
Se supunea unor reguli
Atât de trecătoare,
Avea deci umor,
Îi plăcea să se joace,
O distra propria ei imagine
Ilustrând efemerul
La zi.
Sau poate doar pictorul
Se amuzase
Făcându-şi
Deasupra râului
Mereu curgător
Autoportretul
În acest travesti viitor…

Un personaj transparent

PATRIA MIA A4 2010

Nu l-am înţeles niciodată,
Nu i-am cunoscut definiţia:
Un personaj transparent
Sau numai o boare
Pe care nici nu o simţi,
Deşi te atinge.

Doar după ani, după decenii
Începi să-i descoperi
Urmele
Întipărite în carne,
Adânci
Ca nişte urme de ghiare.
Tot ce ştiu despre el
Este că se grăbeşte
Spre locul
Unde încetează să fie.

Timeless Death
Submitted itself to such
Passing fancies.
This tells us that it had a sense of humour,
That it liked to have fun.
It amused itself by dressing up
In the changing fashions
Of the day.
Or maybe it was only the painter
Who amused himself
By painting
His own self-portrait
Above that river
That flows
Towards this future in disguise...

A Transparent Being

MY NATIVE LAND A4 2014

I've never understood him,
Never could define him:
A transparent being
Or only a breeze
That you don't even feel
Although it brushes your skin.

Only after years or decades
Have passed, you begin to find
His traces
Printed
Deeply on your flesh,
Like the marks of a claw.
The only thing I know about him
Is that he rushes to get
To the place
Where he ceases to exist.

Patria neliniştii

PATRIA MIA A4 2010

Aici este patria neliniştii,
Gata să se răzgândească
Din clipă în clipă
Şi, totuşi, nerenunţând să aştepte
Ceva nedefinit.
Aici este patria,
Între pereţii aceştia
La câţiva metri unul de altul,
Şi nici măcar în spaţiul întreg dintre ei,
Ci doar pe masa cu hârtii şi creioane
Gata să se ridice singure şi să scrie,
Schelete brusc animate ale unor condeie mai vechi
Nefolosite de mult, cu pasta uscată,
Lunecând pe hârtie frenetic
Fără să lase vreo urmă...
Aici este patria neliniştii:
Voi reuşi vreodată
Să descifrez urmele care nu se văd,
Dar eu ştiu că există şi aşteaptă
Să le trec pe curat
În patria mea A4?

Country of Unease

MY NATIVE LAND A4 2014

This is the country of unease,
Always about to change its mind
Any second now
Without, however, giving up hope of
Some indefinite possibility.
This is my native land,
Between these walls
The handful of metres between
And not even all of them –
Alone at the desk with paper and pencils
Ready to move on their own and begin to write,
Skeletons brought suddenly to life by ancient feathers
Unused for ages, the glue dried out –
They scribble in a frenzy on the paper
And leave no trace…
This is the country of unease:
Will I manage some day
To decipher these traces that no one can see
But that I know are there, and waiting
For me to write them out
In my native land: A4?

All poems translated from the Romanian
by Paul Scott Derrick & Viorica Patea

5 | DAN CHIASSON

Filmed at home in Sudbury, Massachusetts, USA,
by Pamela Robertson-Pearce, 19 September 2008

Dan Chiasson has been hailed in America as 'one of the most gifted young poets of his generation' (Frank Bidart) who 'has succeeded in writing the poetry many of his generation aim for: free-swinging, gorgeous in phrase, bold in imagination, athletic in movement' (Robert Pinsky).

His first UK publication was *Natural History & other poems*, published by Bloodaxe in 2016, bringing together poems from his first two US collections, *The Afterlife of Objects* (2002) and *Natural History* (2005), along with more recent work. This was followed by *Where's the Moon, There's the Moon* (2010) from Bloodaxe, and by *Bicentennial* (2014) from Knopf in the US. Both his Bloodaxe titles were Poetry Book Society Recommendations.

Where's the Moon, There's the Moon takes its title from an improvised children's game. It is a book about staged loss and staged recovery and how, in our games as in our poems, made-up losses depict real ones. At the book's centre is the title-poem, a long exploration of being a father in light of having lost one.

When we visited him in 2008, the collection was still in manuscript. In the film he reads three of its sequences of short poems, 'Swifts', 'Satellites' and 'Hide-and-Seek'. 'Satellites' draws on Coleridge's 'Frost at Midnight' and William Blake's 'The Sick Rose', as well as M.H. Abrams's study of Romanticism, *The Mirror and the Lamp*. The herbarium in 'Hide-and-Seek' is Emily Dickinson's, now available in facsimile from Harvard University Press.

Born in 1971 in Burlington, Vermont, he is an Associate Professor of English at Wellesley College in Massachusetts and poetry critic for *The New Yorker*. He has also published a critical study, *One Kind of Everything: Poem and Person in Contemporary America* (University of Chicago Press, 2007).

Swifts

WHERE'S THE MOON, THERE'S THE MOON 2010

1 *Fist*

It is impossible for me to remember
the cozy room I slept in as a child.
Somebody made my bed up to be paradise.
It was hard for me, a hard night, when I entered art.

The tendons in my wrist are visible.
What will I do now I have made this fist?
To loosen it feels weird, anticlimactic—
a misuse, a misunderstanding, of fists.

That's how it was with me that night.
And so, mysteriously, I lost my sweetness.
Weird, to feel intended for violence,
when what I wanted was an hour of rest.

2 *Thread*

I lack the rigor of a lightning bolt,
the weight of an anchor. I am
frayed where it would be highly useful—
and this I feel perpetually—to make a point.

I think if I can concentrate I might turn sharp.
Only, I don't know how to concentrate—
I know the look of someone concentrating,
indistinguishable from nearsightedness.

It is hard for the others to be near me,
my silly intensity shuffling
a zillion insignia of interiority.
Being near me never made anyone a needle.

(for Jason Dodge)

145

3 *Wind*

Find some other reason to sway, forest;
old people get bent over
from vitamin deficiencies; trees,
take them as your inspiration.

For I have neither time nor energy
any longer to write poems, to make feeling
out of what, without me, is silent;
I find your standing there disgusting.

And you, reader, I see you nod your head,
treelike, appraising these lines;
I find your standing there—
not disgusting, but not inspiring either.

4 *Tree*

All day I waited to be blown;
then someone cut me down.

I have, instead of thoughts,
uses; uses instead of feelings.

One day I'll feel the wind again.
A moment later I'll be gone.

5 *Cause*

Whitman wrote this, before he started writing poetry.
He was a journalist for years, you know;
a radical, a partisan for some ridiculous cause.

He wrote this to support—or was it to condemn?—a cause.
It doesn't matter if you aren't Whitman yet.
Now that he's been Whitman for so long, it would.

6 *Effect*

Everything scatters as the night wears on:
but you, don't scatter, will you?
I think we could make this night last forever.

With our joined heads, like mathematicians,
we could work all night, so that
where night once was, work would be; and night,

as long as work went on, would never end.
It is starting to sound a little tiring:
all this working, just to stave off morning.

7 *Needle's eye*

I wish I were as big as a basketball hoop.
It is actually painful to be this fine.
It is like squinting for no reason,
all night, choosing the pain of squinting
over going to sleep. And yet,
what does it matter how big
a target you are? Someone somewhere
will invent a game to make you hard to hit.

8 *Sound, 2 a.m.*

A minute ago I was a child coughing: having had
too much of everything today, except for air.

Now I am an animal, feeling, tonight, perplexed—
I fled the outside, the cold, the lack of food;

I meant to enter a house, which I connect with warmth,
which my body told me was the appropriate move.

Instead I entered a person's mind. Like the child,
I am trapped: I have no will, no life to call my own.

147

9 Swifts

Reality isn't one point in space.
It isn't one moment in time—
look at time, a spool of twine
one minute, idle in a sewing kit,
the next minute a shooting star.

Reality is an average of moods,
strike that, a flock of birds,
strike that, a single bird
tracked through dense forest:

you can lose it for hours or days,
but it isn't lost. You tired of the metaphor.

10 Caress

The tendons flattened and the knot untied.
You could do anything, then, with your hand;
you could forget the fact you had a hand.
This lasted, or so you were tempted to think,
for years; winter didn't matter,
yet spring arrived as a blessing to your body.
Sweetness, or what passed for it, returned;
and then, like an anchor yanked suddenly
from the sea, your muscles clenched.

Satellites

WHERE'S THE MOON, THERE'S THE MOON 2010

1 *Banquette*

The satellite that crisscrossed the sky
one day encountered gravity—
the moment it hit the water
it was in a different documentary.

So why would I give it a thought
what you do all night in your apartment
when you're mine on the street
and mine, now, in this suede banquette?

2 *Bullet*

What counts as a target and what does not
is not innate or inevitable.
One minute your eye falls limply
like a net. The next it becomes a bullet.

What counts as a bullet follows the same rule:
inert, a lump of something small,
chalky in the palm of your hand,
finds its fate (it has a fate) when it gets shot.

3 *Night scene*

Meanwhile, standing by: the stars;
a field where the moon shines;
clouds suddenly darken the field.
If nothingness were a rug, we'd buy it.

Houses go uncharted, week after week;
whole lifetimes happen on schedule,
a child arrives without incident,
grows up to be an astronaut I mean assassin.

4 *Orbit*

You have this big capacity, small speck:
barely there at all until
the sun detects your metal shell,
then only a pinprick;

and yet you can predict the moment,
having already lived it,
lived through it, laughed it off,
we thought our child would suffer forever.

5 *Next*

If you can orbit the planet, why can't you see
what makes the human heart happy?
Is it art or is it sex?
Or is it, as I suspect, just keeping going

from next thing to next thing
to next thing to next thing
to next to next to next to next
pulsating stupidly to outlast time?

6 *Coleridge*

'The inmates of my cottage, all at rest':
abstruse my ass, I want a sandwich.
The body is Conan the Barbarian.
Night walk and the sky is gigantic,

but not as lofty as its reputation,
just as I, Mr Friendless and Unloyal,
Conan the Nobody's Around,
now attempt to wash down lead with acid.

7 *Bluet*

Flowers have faces. They are happy or sad.
Their faces change, like ours;
unlike us, it doesn't mean
uh-oh a new mood out of nowhere dawned.

Technically it is immoral to kill a flower
but people do it all the time,
to smooth something over or to please a lover.
Nature just rolls right on, headless.

8 *Abstruser musings*

To be no one at all, merely the latest
to have had his brain
turned inside out by vanity,
so that it shine entirely on itself—

is this what M.H. Abrams called 'the lamp'?
I call it masturbation,
not as an insult but an accurate name:
it feels good doing it, and people like to watch.

9 *Blake*

A satellite sees into your heart.
It is blind to the rest of the planet.
Its giant eye stares all day
at the one bull's-eye on its one target.

It sees that your heart is sick. You're sick.
All that it sees is the fact
your heart, that once held endless joy,
now sick, soon will 'thy life destroy'.

Hide-and-Seek

WHERE'S THE MOON, THERE'S THE MOON 2010

Herbarium

Jasmine means passion and privet
means private. If they are bound together
in a book, hidden underground, a famous book,

off-limits in a library, which one wins:
privet, that kept the secret,
or jasmine, that made the privet shine?

Stadium

An empty stadium is an indrawn breath.
There hasn't been a team here in ages.
Futuristic is starting to look very old.

It's a vast cereal bowl; and in it,
bobbing like a raisin, there's my childhood.
I'm rooting for the nonexistent team.

Waterfall

Meanwhile like a treadmill a waterfall
pours its entire body
downstream, going nowhere, pours

and is filled by the nothing waters
upstream, as though gravity
needed something to gloat about.

Hide-and-Seek

Once, north of here, a child played
hide-and-seek. His part was to hide,
ergo he played his role and hid.

The seeker, embarrassed by his role,
thinking it beneath his dignity,
developed instead a personality disorder.

Herbarium (II)

Once, west of here, a child fastened
flowers to the pages of a book,
and wrote their names in Latin underneath.

This was the pinnacle of mimesis.
The flowers are so brittle now
nobody is allowed to open that book.

Olympic Stadium, Montreal

There is no name for the tendency
of things to start to fall apart
before they are complete, but

that isn't because the phenomenon
is rare: to the contrary,
little poem: this is the common condition.

Falls, Bristol, VT

The waterfall runs all day and night,
shedding big self on the rocks below,
refilling with more self, more self, more self,

while bathers visit in small groups, never
the same bathers, always the same river—
my local, inverted, redneck pre-Socratic.

Revolving Door

I spit and swallow with equal gusto.
Spitting is not a sign of disgust.
Swallowing is not a sign of hunger.

Casting out is not a sign of anger.
Allowing in is not affection.
I chug along, doing what I'm meant to do.

Hide-and-Seek (II)

Hide and seek, hide and seek: the magic trick
of keeping time in play by yo-yo
mini-episodes of loss and recovery.

One day that game goes dark, and you want
a new game whose object isn't loss.
The rule is: everyone stay close by, in sight.

Previews

It was the newest movie, and we arrived early.
Something bright and loud was playing,
not the movie, but not that different from the movie.

Infinitely elongated Beforehand, bright Not Yet:
our children grew impatient in your zone.
We left the movie before the movie began.

6 | POLLY CLARK

Filmed at home in Kilcreggan, Rosneath, Argyll and Bute,
Scotland, by Pamela Robertson-Pearce, 19 April 2010

The characters in Polly Clark's poems speak in many voices, both animal and human, bringing into focus the moments when we are most alive, and most alone. Her narrators search for answers to questions about the nature of human attachment and longing.

Her debut collection *Kiss* (2000) took the reader on a journey into the self. In *Take Me with You* (2005), the journey turns outwards and explores the ways in which we connect with others and the wider world. Her third collection *Farewell My Lovely* (2009) is about leaving one's life and returning a stranger. In poems which are moving and often darkly comic, she explores the ways in which we try to hang on to what we were, and how we accept that everything we were certain of has gone forever.

As she reads from all three collections in the film, connections between seemingly unrelated poems become clear. Changed lives is as much the central thread in poems relating to childbirth and marriage as it is in a detective's confession or a sequence in the voice of a young soldier sent to war in the Falklands, *I Thought It Was in Scotland*.

Born in Toronto in 1968, Polly Clark grew up in Lancashire, Cumbria and the Scottish Borders. She has worked variously as a zookeeper, a teacher of English in Hungary and in publishing at Oxford University Press. Her second collection, *Take Me With You*, was a Poetry Book Society Choice shortlisted for the T.S. Eliot Prize. *Afterlife: New & Selected Poems* is due from Bloodaxe in 2018. Her novel, *Larchfield*, inspired by Auden's formative years in Helensburgh, Scotland, was published by Quercus in their riverrun imprint in 2017. She now lives on the West Coast of Scotland and is Literature Programme Producer for Cove Park, Scotland's International Artist Residency Centre.

Elvis the Performing Octopus

TAKE ME WITH YOU 2005

hangs in the tank like a ruined balloon,
an eight-armed suit sucked empty,

ushering the briefest whisper
across the surface, keeping

his slurred drift steady with an effort
massive as the ocean resisting the moon.

When the last technician,
whistling his own colourless tune,

splashes through the disinfectant tray,
one might see, had anyone been left to look,

Elvis changing from spilt milk to tumbling blue,
pulsing with colour like a forest in sunlight.

Elvis does the full range, even the spinning top
that never quite worked out, as the striplight fizzes

and the flylamp cracks like a firework.
Elvis has the water applauding,

and the brooms, the draped cloths, the dripping tap,
might say that a story that ends in the wrong place

always ends like this –
fabulous in an empty room,

unravelled by the tender men in white,
laid out softly in the morning.

My Education at the Zoo

KISS 2000

There is a rule which I am born knowing,
from the moment I slip out, and my mouth

becomes that anguished, red, newborn hole,
its ridge of unborn teeth uselessly bared.

I know this rule and am flailing against it.
But in later years I come to an uneasy acceptance;

my unusual physical strength is a testament
to its weight. When I am 16

I can push a barrow overflowing
with rolling cow haunch and pony carcass

all the way up the hill to the wolves.
Only the strongest of the strong men can do it:

there is laughter, and something else, a recognition.
On New Year's Eve, when one year metamorphoses

into a dream of another, they kiss me
with uneasy, snarling kisses.

The Amazon parrot whirls at me,
a green screech as I approach his nest;

next door, the cockatoo is pacing up and down,
he clambers up me, as if I were a gnarled tropical tree,

lodges his head down my shirt between my breasts,
murmurs (you must incline your head to hear his words)

fuck you bitch, his yellow eyes blinking.
I'm afraid at the end I begin to fall apart,

and accidentally set three pairs of lovebirds free
and the cockatoo, who simply climbs the nearest tree

and hurls insults (but suddenly the words begin to come,
secretly, when I am alone at night).

The real men bask at lunchtime, like lions keeping
their violence to themselves while the sun is hot.

At night, at party after party, I find it hard
to keep from being discovered or blurting the truth.

I drink ten pints, laugh at all insults,
refuse to retreat, as finally amidst howls

of laughter at 3 a.m., one of them emerges
wearing two bras and a nightie, his face covered in paint,

and everyone cheering his victory in the game
that he is playing, that now I know the name of.

My Life with Horses

KISS 2000

Before I knew there were men,
I galloped a pony bareback;
it was a hard winter, but
how sure-footed we were, resolute
in frozen emptiness, stamping
the ice with our names.

Years later I lay like a foal in the grass,
wanting to touch your hair;
we clutched like shadows,
I twined the past through my fingers, kissing
great gulps of father, of mother,
galloping, with nothing to stop me.

Now in the evening I put on my dress
like a secret; will you see
how my elbow pokes like a hock,
the way I have carefully cut my mane,
the way my eyes roll from fear of you?
I'm trying to hide the animal I am;

and you give me a necklace,
bright as a bit, and you're
stamping your name
into the earth, and my arm
is around you, weak as a halter,
and nothing can stop me, no mother or father.

Hedgehog

TAKE ME WITH YOU 2005

Its leg was not broken. It was not homeless.
It clenched in my hands, a living flinch.
You cannot love so much and live,
it whispered, its spines clicking like teeth.
I hid it from itself in a cardboard box.

Overnight it nibbled a hole and slipped away.
I cried so much my mother thought I'd never stop.
She said, *you cannot love so* – and yet
I grew to average size and amused a lot of people
with my prickliness and brilliant escapes.

Dumbarton

TAKE ME WITH YOU 2005

In changing my life I got as far as Dumbarton.
It was midnight. She didn't believe I loved her,
so I rang her and said, *I'm getting in the car now*
and I found myself swallowing the road out of Glasgow,
the bridge screaming at me to leave then, leave.

I rang her. I hated my voice. *I'm so tired
darling, tired*, I said. The click told me
that the future is as uncertain as the past.
The road was empty, my whole body ached.
I had nine points on my licence and so

had to crawl my way to my brand new life.
She didn't believe I loved her. I rang her.
I've left everything for you, I said. Or,
You're everything to me. Or perhaps
I said nothing at all, being smashed

upside-down in the central reservation.
The lights of Dumbarton were mostly out
as I turned back. The stars were gibberish,
the road flat on its back. I rang her. I hated my voice.
I'm so tired, darling, tired. Forgive me.

Buffalo Mozzarella

TAKE ME WITH YOU 2005

When I say that I tasted him
I mean that I knew the stale
baby-press of his mouth,
his cold breath, and the way
he scratched the cushion of his thumb
on his stubbled cheek. See –

how he leans in the litter bin,
his arm digging deep,
to feel among the cut of beer cans
the abominable plastic, the rub of old fat,
as if there should be flesh there,
something gentle to welcome him.

And then he finds it – the sundried tomato
and buffalo mozzarella sandwich
I had just one bite out of because I saw
the one thing that scared me most,
and I dropped my sandwich with its one
shell-shaped ticklishly damp bite out.

I didn't think that a mouth
more silent than mine
would nuzzle where my lips had been
and bite out a shape to caress mine,

160

nibbling, delicate, not rushing at all –
and that someone else's hunger

and sorrow and spit would devour mine.
When I say that I tasted him
I mean that the night shook me awake
and I saw the back of his head clearly
as he bent down into darkness and shame
to find out the truth about me.

Farewell My Lovely

FAREWELL MY LOVELY 2009

> A really good detective never gets married.
>
> RAYMOND CHANDLER

I'd gotten used to that roomy grin,
the face like a bag of facts,
the flank round as a pony's,
and the way she had of blending in
so badly. But after all,
I didn't really know her,
neither she nor I being the intimate type.

I take a slug of something
that I've been craving, make a note
of everything that's gone with her.
But my notes become a list
of immovables: this slouching house,
the sea with a face I'd like to smack,
the loosening sky, fit to drop –

as I'm dusting the mirror
I glimpse her, smart as a rat
in the company of rocks –
but the day's slammed shut
and it's time to file the file.
This is a face to be turned over
for answers from now on.

She's left nothing behind her
to show what was between us.
Always meticulous,
        I find she's slipped
like a last dram into my dreams,
hunched at the scene, wiping fingerprints,
knowing that it's over, that it's time to go.

Landing

FROM *I Thought It Was in Scotland: A Falklands Memoir*
FAREWELL MY LOVELY 2009

Just to make things more frustrating
they show us porno films all night.

Rapiers are breaking up in the hold.
No news in case it puts us off.

In April, it's the height of winter.
When we land the sea is bright blue.

I thought it was in Scotland.
I thought it would be like *Platoon*.

The planes roar in & and drop & turn.
The beach blows up before my eyes

and the thought crosses my mind –
I was going to take Stacey to meet

my parents, but I never did.
And I never slept with her either.

I said goodbye from a phone box.
Couldn't wait for the pips to cut me off.

Beheaded

FAREWELL MY LOVELY 2009

I hear perfectly: the thud
onto linen, the strange gasp
like the cry of a premature baby,
just once and then silence.

And I see perfectly:
how my lashes scratch the light,
a hair glittering in shadow,
the winded hollow

where my lips rest.
I still have all my words.
I move my mouth,
like someone begging for water.

Fingers grab my hair
and I soar high above my sad
old body, slumped and tiny.
Tears of pity for it fill my eyes.

They are tending it,
the blank women in blue.
They are washing it,
as if they loved it.

Look, the people are cheering me,
look, they are glad to see me,
now that I've been removed
without a single word of protest.

Last Will and Testament

FAREWELL MY LOVELY 2009

To Hamish the dog: my blankets, my best rattle, the blocks he chewed.
To my mother: my mattress where my head has made a dip,
                     all the photographs.
To my father: his spectacles, which he let me take from his nose and break,
                     also my lacy shoes and all my frozen spinach.
To Auntie Jan: the pink cardigan she made me, also my butterfly.
To my mother in addition: my washable nappies (for re-sale), Gina Ford,
                     my weaning spoons.
To my father in addition: my words (my *da-da*, my *ba-ba*), my mother,
                     my best red trousers.

7 | STEWART CONN

Filmed at home in Edinburgh by Pamela Robertson-Pearce,
5 June 2010

'Stewart Conn's soft-spoken, gravely graceful verse has been among the most distinguished produced in Britain in the last thirty years… Having found a sonorous, lyric voice early in his career, he seemed, even as a young poet, mature beyond his years. Now the voice has deepened and darkened with age and we are invited to share with the poet his perplexity and joy at the passing of time. No Scottish poet is as firmly rooted, none so eloquently elegiac.' This was Donny O'Rourke writing 20 years ago.

For David McCordick, 'Stewart Conn is one of Scotland's most skilled and wide-ranging poets. A sympathetic, if quite unsentimental, treatment of the natural world, or the rural one at least, does run throughout his poetry, but so do the themes of love, family relationships, the nature and power of art, and that time-honoured subject of poetry – the fragility and transitoriness of life itself.' (*Scottish Literature in the Twentieth Century*)

Bloodaxe has published seven books of Stewart Conn's poetry over the past 30 years, including three retrospective selections: *In the Kibble Palace* (1987), *Stolen Light* (1999) and *The Touch of Time* (2014). The poems he reads in the film range across the years also.

With what Professor Carla Sassi sees as 'his thoughtful attention to small details, his redeeming gaze, his formal control of impeccably constructed verses, and his deep and warm humanity' he movingly explores everyday events and revelations, and how – like our lives and those of our loved ones – they are transformed by time.

Stewart Conn was born in Glasgow in 1936 and grew up in Ayrshire, the setting for much of his early poetry. Since 1977 he has lived in Edinburgh, where until 1992 he was based as BBC Scotland's head of radio drama. He was Edinburgh's first Makar or Poet Laureate in 2002-05. As well as publishing a memoir, *Distances* (2001), and several anthologies, he has written many plays for stage and radio, including *I Didn't Always Live Here*, *Play Donkey*, and *The Burning*, about witch trials in 16th-century Scotland.

Todd

STOATS IN THE SUNLIGHT 1968 | THE TOUCH OF TIME 2014

My father's white uncle became
   arthritic and testamental in
   lyrical stages. He held cardinal sin
was misuse of horses, then any game

won on the sabbath. A Clydesdale
   to him was not bells and sugar or declension
   from paddock, but primal extension
of rock and soil. Thundered nail

turned to sacred bolt. And each night
   in the stable he would slaver and slave
   at cracked hooves, or else save
bowls of porridge for just the right

beast. I remember I lied
   to him once, about oats: then I felt
   the brand of his loving tongue, the belt
of his own horsey breath. But he died,

when the mechanised tractor came to pass.
   Now I think of him neighing to some saint
   in a simple heaven or, beyond complaint,
leaning across a fence and munching grass.

Ferret

STOATS IN THE SUNLIGHT 1968 | THE TOUCH OF TIME 2014

More vicious than stoat or weasel
because caged, kept hungry, the ferrets
were let out only for the kill:
an alternative to sulphur and nets.

Once one, badly mauled, hid
behind a treacle-barrel in the shed.
Throwing me back, Matthew slid
the door shut. From outside

the window, I watched. He stood
holding an axe, with no gloves.
Then it sprang; and his sleeves
were drenched in blood

where the teeth had sunk. I hear
its high-pitched squeal,
the clamp of its neat steel
jaws. And I remember

how the axe flashed, severing
the ferret's head,
and how its body kept battering
the barrels, long after it was dead.

Driving Through Sutherland

STOATS IN THE SUNLIGHT 1968 | THE TOUCH OF TIME 2014

Here too the crofts were burned
to the ground, families stripped
and driven like cattle to the shore.
You can still hear the cursing,
the women shrieking.

                    The Duke
and his lady sipped port, had
wax in their ears. Thatch
blazed. Thistles were torn up
by the root.

            There are men
in Parliament today could
be doing more.

            With these thoughts
in mind we drive from Overscaig
to Lairg, through a night as blue
as steel.

Leaving Loch Shin behind
we find facing us an even colder
firth, and a new moon rising
delicately over a stubble field.

Tremors

AN EAR TO THE GROUND 1972 | THE TOUCH OF TIME 2014

We took turns at laying
an ear on the rail –
so that we could tell
by the vibrations

when a train was coming.
Then we'd flatten ourselves
to the banks, scorched
vetch and hedge-parsley,

while the iron flanks
rushed past, sending sparks
flying. It is more and more
a question of living

with an ear to the ground:
the tremors, when they come,
are that much greater –
for ourselves and others.

Nor is it any longer
a game, but a matter
of survival: each explosion
part of a procession

there can be no stopping.
Though the end is known,
there is nothing for it
but to keep listening ...

168

Under the Ice

UNDER THE ICE 1978 | THE TOUCH OF TIME 2014

Like Coleridge, I waltz
on ice. And watch my shadow
on the water below. Knowing that
if the ice were not there
I'd drown. Half willing it.

In my cord jacket
and neat cravat, I keep
returning to the one spot.
How long, to cut
a perfect circle out?

Something in me
rejects the notion.
The arc is never complete.
My figures-of-eight
almost, not quite, meet.

Was Raeburn's skating parson
a man of God, poised
impeccably on the brink;
or his bland stare
no more than a decorous front?

If I could keep my cool
like that. Gazing straight ahead,
not at my feet. Giving
no sign of knowing
how deep the water, how thin the ice.

Behind that, the other
question: whether the real you
pirouettes in space,
or beckons from under the ice
for me to come through.

Visiting Hour

UNDER THE ICE 1978 | THE TOUCH OF TIME 2014

In the pond of our new garden
were five orange stains, under
inches of ice. Weeks since anyone
had been there. Already by far
the most severe winter for years.
You broke the ice with a hammer.
I watched the goldfish appear,
blunt-nosed and delicately clear.

Since then so much has taken place
to distance us from what we were.
That it should have come to this.
Unable to hide the horror
in my eyes, I stand helpless
by your bedside and can do no more
than wish it were simply a matter
of smashing the ice and giving you air.

Carpe Diem

THE BREAKFAST ROOM 2010 | THE TOUCH OF TIME 2014

From my study window
        I see you
below in the garden, a hand
        here pruning
or leaning across to snip
        a wayward shoot,

a daub of powder-blue in a
        profusion of green;
then next moment, you are
        no longer there –
only to reappear, this time
        perfectly framed

in dappling sunlight, with
    an armful of ivy
you've trimmed, topped by
    hyacinth blooms,
fragrant survivors of last
    night's frost.

And my heart misses a beat
    at love for you,
knowing a time will come
    when you are
no longer there, nor I here
    to watch you

on a day of such simplicity.
    Meantime let us
make sure we clasp each
    shared moment
in cupped hands, like water
    we dare not spill.

The Breakfast Room

THE BREAKFAST ROOM 2010 | THE TOUCH OF TIME 2014

> Bonnard frequently placed the most important objects
> on the periphery of a picture.
>
> PIERRE SCHNEIDER

1

That poster has been on my wall for years.
The other night a woman appeared in it,
a nondescript figure, more a housekeeper
than the wife whom the bohemian in him
painted in her bathtub, over and over down
the decades. Holding a cup, the other arm
slack, she merges with the curtains' muted
tones. A balustrade, shady garden beyond.

Waif-like, half her body outwith the frame,
she seems almost spectral, as if dissolving
or part of a transformation scene. I'd gladly
join her: brioches and baguettes to share,

171

tea in the pot, a chair easily drawn up. But
unlikely, given her forlorn stare. Not once
has there been a prelude to an invitation,
or the least indication she has noticed me.

2

Whether the artist's wife or his châtelaine
why in heaven's name would I invite you in?
You scarcely endear yourself by dismissing me
as some drab. That, or a moody phantom.
While I make no claim to beauty, a little
sensitivity wouldn't come amiss. It can be
hard enough dispelling the notions of those
who ogle my husband's nude studies of me.

As to not noticing you, quite the reverse.
I'm far too aware of your presence, my room
lit at all hours while you pursue your obsession;
loud music putting an end, albeit temporarily,
to my tranquility. But between marginality
and impermanence lies a fine distinction.
Whichever of us you believe to be the fiction,
I'll look out long after you've stopped looking in.

3

You find my Marthe unobtrusive? For a spell
she was so self-effacing, whenever I wanted
to paint her she would hide behind the curtain.
In one portrait not dissimilar to this she virtually
disappears. Here, simultaneously concealed
and revealed, she blends in perfectly. Small
compensation for what she has undergone,
illness held in abeyance by immersion in water:

hence my depictions of her as Venus emerging,
the light casting a spell on her skin as it was
when I first met her. A vision of young love
preserved, my palette imbues her with the blue-
violet of memory. No need to choose between
smelling the scent and plucking the flower –
painting her has been like bottling a rare spirit.
Now, if you'll excuse me, I have her bath to run.

8 | PETER DIDSBURY

Filmed at home in Hull by Neil Astley, 8 November 2010

Peter Didsbury's first collection *The Butchers of Hull* was launched alongside Douglas Dunn's iconic Hull poets anthology *A Rumoured City* in 1982. *The Classical Farm* (1987) won him a Cholmondeley Award and was a Poetry Book Society Recommendation, as was *That Old-Time Religion* (1994). His retrospective, *Scenes from a Long Sleep: New & Collected Poems,* was published by Bloodaxe in 2003, including a fourth collection, *A Natural History*. All his books have been well reviewed, yet he has remained a poet's poet.

Despite working away from the literary limelight as an archaeologist, this 'secular mystic with the lugubrious tongue' (*Independent on Sunday*) has attracted a dedicated readership. The *TLS* called him the best new poet published by Bloodaxe and 'one of the most eccentric and unpredictable, of English poetic holymen'. The Poetry Archive's characterisation of his work was particularly apt: 'Peter Didsbury has described himself as "someone who's constitutionally fascinated by myth and the weight of the past" and indeed his poems seem to conjure a particular, possibly bygone England peopled with men working the land, butchers, fishermen, kings and classical scholars. While the poems take in urban settings as well as rural, the intimacy of the poet's relationship to his environment is perhaps something more commonly associated with nature poetry. It's this that gives the poems their unusual texture, as Peter Porter suggests when he notes, in a review of Didsbury's first collection, the poems' "seedy urban pastoral".'

His Hull compatriot Sean O'Brien wrote that 'Didsbury's is the kind of work which makes you realise what you've been putting up with in the meantime. The product of a large and peculiar imagination, it shows a sense of adventure hardly to be paralleled in contemporary poetry... In Didsbury's work there is glimpsed an alternative history where Catholic Europe and the East are strangely mixed, where matters of faith and damnation are still alive...its power to delight, terrify and enlighten comes from a way of seeing for which most contemporary categories are meaningless.' (*London Magazine*)

Born in 1946 in Fleetwood, Lancashire, he moved to Hull at the age of six, read English and Hebrew at Oxford, and taught English in Hull for eight years before turning to the past for employment as well as for inspiration, becoming an archaeologist.

In Britain

THE BUTCHERS OF HULL 1982 | SCENES FROM A LONG SLEEP 2003

The music, on fat bellied instruments.
The fingers, swarming down ladders
into the bubbling cauldrons of sound.
The mouths, greasy, encouraging the prying fingers
with songs of fecund stomachs.
The hands, transferring to the singing mouths
whatever is lifted through the scum.
The choicest morsels, the collops of dog and the
gobbets of pig. The orchestras and bands,
the minstrelsy arranged in tiers,
dripping on each other. The larded steps.
The treacherous floors in the wooden galleries.
The garlands of offal, plopping on heads
from a height of some feet.
The offal sliding off down the front of the face,
or over the neck and ears. The offal reposing like hats.
The curly grey-white tubes, dangling jauntily
above the left eye of the bagpipe player.
The guests, similarly festooned.
The guests at their conversation,
abundance of dogs and pigs in these islands.
The guests at their serious business, lying in pools.
The stories, farting and belching across the puddled boards.
The gross imaginations, bulging with viscera.
The heads full of stories, the stories thwacked like bladders.
The stories steaming in time to the music.
The stories, chewed like lumps of gristle.
The stories describing extravagant herds.
The stories, reasons for killing each other.

The Drainage

THE BUTCHERS OF HULL 1982 | SCENES FROM A LONG SLEEP 2003

When he got out of bed the world had changed.
It was very cold. His breath whitened the room.
Chill December clanked at the panes.

There was freezing fog.
He stepped outside.
Not into his street but a flat wet landscape.
Sluices. Ditches. Drains. Frozen mud and leafcake. Dykes.
He found he knew the names of them all.
Barber's Cut. Cold Track. Lament. Meridian Stream.
He found himself walking.
It was broad cold day but the sky was black.
Instead of the sun it was Orion there.
Seeming to pulse his meaning down.
He was naked. He had to clothe himself.
The heifers stood like statues in the fields.
They didn't moan when he sliced the hides from them.
He looked at the penknife in his hand.
The needle, the thread, the clammy strips.
Now his face mooned out through a white hole.
The cape dripped. He knew he had
the bounds of a large parish to go.
His feet refused to falter.
Birds sat still in the trees.
Fast with cold glue. Passing their clumps
he watched them rise in their species.
The individuals. Sparrow. Starling. Wren.
He brought them down with his finger.
Knife needle and thread again.
It happened with the streams.
Pike barbel roach minnow gudgeon.
Perch dace eel. Grayling lamprey bream.
His feet cracked puddles and were cut on mud, They bled.
There was movement. He pointed. He stitched.
His coat hung reeking on him.
He made cut after cut in the cold.
Coldness and the colours of blood.
Red blue and green. He glistened.
He stitched through white fat.
Weight of pelts and heads. Nodding at the hem.
Feathers. Scales. Beaks and strips of skin.
He had the bounds of a large parish to go.
Oh Christ, he moaned. Sweet Christ.

A Priest in the Sabbath Dawn Addresses His Somnolent Mistress

THE CLASSICAL FARM 1987 | SCENES FROM A LONG SLEEP 2003

Wake up, my heart, get out of bed
and put your scarlet shirt back on and leave,
for Sunday is coming down the chimney
with its feet in little socks,
and I need a space in which to write my sermon.
Although the hour's already late
it can still be done, if only you'll depart!
Down the pipe and out across the lawn
would take you to the station yard
in which you left your bicycle last week
and give me time to clothe in flesh the text
I have in mind for the instruction of my flock.
Please hurry, dear. The earliest note of the matin bell
has left its tower like an urgent dove
and is beating its way to woods outside the town.
The sun is up, the parish breakfasted,
the ghosts are all returned into the flint
yet still you lie here, shaming me with sleep.
Wake up, I say, for Sabbath legs
are landing in the grate. Go naked if you must
but grant me these few minutes with my pen
to write of how I cut myself while shaving.
Be useful, at least, and fetch my very razor,
for the faithful have set their feet upon the road
and are hurrying here with claims on the kind of story
which I cannot fittingly make from your sudden grin.

A Winter's Fancy

THE CLASSICAL FARM 1987 | SCENES FROM A LONG SLEEP 2003

> To write a *Tristram Shandy* or a *Sentimental Journey* there is no way
> but to be Sterne; and Sternes are not turned out in bakers' batches.

A winter's fancy.
I look out of my window
and perceive I am Laurence Sterne.
I am sitting in Shandy Hall.
It is raining.
I am inventing a Bag,
which will accommodate everything.
I'd weave it out of air if I could
but the rain slants down like a page of Greek
and the afternoon is a dish of mud,
far removed from gentle opinion.
I am heavy with God.
The weather used
to cloak itself in sentiment
but today it imitates the tongues of men
and wags in curtains at me, along a yard.
I am also John, an elderly bibliophile.
Once, long after I died, I returned to Coxwold
on a literary pilgrimage.
A red-faced lout leaned over my gate
and instructed me curtly to Sodding Sod Off.
He was full of choler.
I sometimes feel I can understand
what's been eluding me ever since Christmas.
I'm exhausting my karma of country parson
in a dozen lives of wit and kidneys,
caritas, the pox, and marbled endpapers.
Looking out from here, this afternoon,
I can just discern the porch of my church
where Nick and Numps are sheltering from
Thucydides, Books Six and Seven.
By the look of that cloud looming up like a skull
there will soon be nothing left to do
but to take to my bed.
The cattle squelch past beneath a sodden sky,
below my windows and before the eyes

of Peter Didsbury, in his 35th year.
I consider other inventions of mine,
which rise before me in the darkening pane.
Light me that candle, oh my clever hand,
for it is late, and I am admirably tired.

A Malediction

THAT OLD-TIME RELIGION 1994 | SCENES FROM A LONG SLEEP 2003

Spawn of a profligate hog.
May the hand of your self-abuse
be afflicted by a palsy.
May an Order in Council
deprive you of a testicle.
May your teeth be rubbed with turds
by a faceless thing from Grimsby.
May your past begin to remind you
of an ancient butter paper
found lying behind a fridge.
May the evil odour of an elderly male camel
fed since birth on buckets of egg mayonnaise
enter your garden and shrivel up all your plants.
May all reflective surfaces
henceforth teach you to shudder.
And may you thus be deprived
of the pleasures of walking by water.
And may you grow even fatter.
And may you, moreover, develop athlete's foot.
May your friends cease to excuse you,
your wife augment the thicket of horns on your brow,
and even your enemies weary of malediction.
May your girth already gross
embark on a final exponential increase.
And at the last may your body, in bursting,
make your name live for ever,
an unparalleled warning to children.

A Bee

THAT OLD-TIME RELIGION 1994 | SCENES FROM A LONG SLEEP 2003

Become at last a bee
I took myself naked to town,
with plastic sacks of yellow turmeric
taped to my wizened thighs.

I'd been buying it for weeks,
along with foods I no longer had a need for,
in small amounts from every corner grocer,
so as not to arouse their suspicion.

It was hard, running and buzzing,
doing the bee-dance. I ached
at the roots of my wings, and hardly yet discerned
that I flew towards reparation,
that in my beehood my healing had been commenced.

Words they use in this hive. To me it seems still
that clumps of tall blue flowers,
which smiled as they encroached,
had been born of my apian will,
in which to my shame I struggled for a moment,
and stained the air with clouds of my dearly bought gold.

9 | KATIE DONOVAN

Filmed at home in Dalkey, Co. Dublin, Ireland,
by Pamela Robertson-Pearce, 5 June 2009

Katie Donovan writes about the hungers which haunt our flesh
and our fantasies, the conjunction of myth and the physical world
of body and earth. Her visceral poems render new sensations, land-
scapes and perceptions, taking a fresh look at family and history,
with daring imagery interwoven with language by turns playful
and elegiac. The need for role models, how to cope with loss, the
way we interact with the natural world, the play of power between
people, and how women cope with love and its aftermath are among
the many topics she addresses in her poetry.

Her retrospective *Rootling* (2010) draws on three previous
books, *Watermelon Man* (1993), *Entering the Mare* (1997) and *Day
of the Dead* (2002), together with a new collection, *Rootling*. Here
her lively sensibility explores motherhood, following the birth of her
two children: from the blues to the pleasures of breastfeeding, she
charts the shock of birth and the delights of watching her babies
develop. Enmeshed in the familial and domestic, the death of her
father prompts her to shuttle back to scenes of her own rural
childhood, as well as mourning the passing of a remarkable man.

Pamela filmed her reading poems from her first four books in
2009. She has since published a later collection, *Off Duty* (2016),
which charts the years of her late husband's throat cancer. That
book was shortlisted for the *Irish Times*–Poetry Now Award.

Born in 1962, she spent her childhood on a farm in Co. Wexford,
and has lived in Dalkey for much of her life. She has worked as a
journalist with *The Irish Times*, and taught creative writing at the
Institute of Art, Design and Technology in Dún Laoghaire and
latterly at NUI Maynooth. In 2017 she was named as the recipi-
ent of the 21st Lawrence O'Shaughnessy Award for Poetry.

Butter

WATERMELON MAN 1993 | ROOTLING 2010

In the first glow
of my laying out
I am all smooth
and golden –
a rich taste
waiting to melt
on the right tongue.

Then the knives come.
Dipping and scavenging,
they seek an easier passage
for dry bread,
they nibble at my edges
and stab at my heart,
leaving me pockmarked;
smudged with crumbs.

My plundered parts
are gloated over, licked,
spread out thin
with careful scrapes,
or smeared in thick welts
by greedy takers.

My solid sunshine
creams down their throats
for the gentle swallow –
the ooze between the teeth.

Broken into oily bubbles
by the churning
of their innards,
I endure the slow journey
of reconstitution,
biding my time
as I fatten again
to choke their veins
and stop their blood.

Yearn On

ENTERING THE MARE 1997 | ROOTLING 2010

I want you to feel
the unbearable lack of me.
I want your skin
to yearn for the soft lure of mine;
I want those hints of red
on your canvas
to deepen in passion for me:
carmine, burgundy.
I want you to keep
stubbing your toe
on the memory of me;
I want your head to be dizzy
and your stomach in a spin;
I want you to hear my voice
in your ear, to touch your face
imagining it is my hand.
I want your body to shiver and quiver
at the mere idea of mine.
I want you to feel as though
life after me is dull, and pointless,
and very, very aggravating;
that with me you were lifted
on a current you waited all your life to find,
and had despaired of finding,
as though you were wading
through a soggy swill of inanity and ugliness
every minute we are apart.
I want you to drive yourself crazy
with the fantasy of me,
and how we will meet again, against all odds,
and there will be tears and flowers,
and the vast relief of not I,
but us.
I am haunting your dreams,
conducting these fevers
from a distance,
a distance that leaves me weeping,
and storming,
and bereft.

Stitching

(for my grandmother, Marjorie Troop)

ENTERING THE MARE 1997 | ROOTLING 2010

I send my needle
through ravelled wool,
catching the loose ends
into a cross-hatched darn.
This is how your freckled hands
smoothed the worn spot
over the wooden mushroom.
Pigeon-breasted in your mustard dress,
you bent your head,
snicking in the needle tip,
your fingers light and careful,
as you impressed upon me
the importance
of learning how to sew.
Your favourite backdrop:
a soprano soaring from the gramophone,
the sun sweeping in from the garden,
flouncing yellow swathes over your shoulder.
I have the quilt you made –
my limbs are lapped
in its glowing sunflower heads –
your last opus,
left for your daughter to finish,
and me to admire.

Tomorrow the quilt will be packed away,
part of the unpicking
of the home I stitched together.
I will wander the empty rooms
like you,
when your darning days were done,
and you woke up
in a strange place,
surrounded by strangers,

pulled apart,
the gap too wide
for mending.

Day of the Dead, New Orleans

(for Lar Cassidy)

DAY OF THE DEAD 2002 | ROOTLING 2010

You would have loved one last night
of the syncopated 'Funky Butt',
with Big Al rolling
his great, luscious voice
out of the massive black mountain
of his chest,
the boys lifting their silver trumpets,
the flush in their cheeks
going right up to their thinning hair,
while the tomcat on the piano
sends his hands a-jitter
for the 'Charleston Rag',
and the sweet molasses drummer
drops his long lashes
and shimmies his cymbal.

All the vaults in the graveyard
are rollicking their brollies
with the beat and swish,
twirl and flourish;
in the voodoo haunt on Bourbon Street,
the obeah woman's hair stands up
with the tongues of serpents,
the clay ladies open their legs
and little heads peek out;
even Christ on his crucifix
has all the time in the world
for dixie.

My tears roll
when I think of the freezing day
we tried to warm
with our drums and poetry,
when we laid you down,
and carried your jazzy hat away.

Rootling

ROOTLING 2010

Little wrestler,
you snort, snuffle
and lunge;
latching on
like a cat
snatching and worrying
her prey.
Once attached,
you drag on me
like a cigarette,
puffing between sucks,
nose pressed close,
somehow catching
your wheezy breath.
Between rounds,
in your white wrap
you arch your back
for a rub,
like I'm your coach,
readying you
for newfound strength
in the ring.
Your fists flail,
fingers hooking
my nursing bra,
your feet curl and kick,
toes a feast
of tiny action.
There is nothing romantic
in this vital ritual,
yet I crane over you,
a loose sack,
liquid with the loss
of your form,
with the tears of labour
and lolling hormones
making me gush
along with my womb,
still churning out afterbirth.

So when
you dandle my nipple
with a gummy smile,
I tell myself
your grin's for me,
even if you've got
that look
of a seasoned souse
on his most
delicious tipple.

Buying a Body

ROOTLING 2010

I would go to the mall
in my white rental car
and shop for a new heart for you,
father; choose lungs,
as strong and light
as parachutes.
I would purchase
the finest pair of wrists,
the fastest feet,
and legs as fleet
as a stag's.
I would go
to the sleep dispenser
and find you dreams
blue and serene
as your favourite summer sky.
I'd buy you time.
But I'm home
from the land of malls,
and I've turned in
the rental car.
It's just you and me
in the cold Sunday afternoon,
you gasping as the lamb
you thought your hands could hold

slips free; the mother bleating,
me not moving as quick
as you'd like
to shut the gate.

You urge me up the yard
the lamb's black legs
in my fist, and I wonder
why it takes so long for you
to follow.
I learn later
you're hardly able to walk it now,
but today you aimed
to pull the wool
over my eyes.

10 | TISHANI DOSHI

Filmed in Ledbury by Neil Astley, 8 July 2012

The central theme of Tishani Doshi's poetry is the body, but its scope extends beyond the corporeal to challenge the more metaphysical borders of space and time. Her poems are powerful meditations born on the joineries of life and death, union and separation, memory and dream, where lovers speak to each other across the centuries, and daughters wander into their mothers' childhoods. As much about loss as they are about reclamation, Doshi's poems guide us through an 'underworld of longing and deliverance', making the exhilarating claim that through the act of vanishing, we may be shaped into existence again.

An award-winning writer and dancer of Welsh-Gujarati descent, she was born in Madras, India (now Chennai) in 1975, studied in the US and then worked in London in advertising before returning to India in 2001 to work with the choreographer Chandralekha, with whom she performed on many international stages. She has published six books of poetry and fiction as well as essays, interviews and travel writing in newspapers and magazines.

She won an Eric Gregory Award for her poetry in 2001. In 2006, she won the All-India Poetry Competition, and her debut collection, *Countries of the Body* (Aark Arts), won the Forward Prize for Best First Collection. Her first novel, *The Pleasure Seekers* (Bloomsbury, 2010), was longlisted for the Orange Prize and shortlisted for the Hindu Fiction Award, and has been translated into several languages. Her second poetry collection, *Everything Begins Elsewhere*, was published by Bloodaxe Books in 2012, and launched at Ledbury Poetry Festival and at London's Southbank Centre. Her third, *Girls Are Coming Out of the Woods*, is due from Bloodaxe in 2018.

She currently lives on a beach between two fishing villages in Tamil Nadu with her husband and three dogs, and sometimes moonlights as a dancer.

The Art of Losing

EVERYTHING BEGINS ELSEWHERE 2012

It begins with the death
of the childhood pet –
the dog who refuses to eat
for days, the bird or fish
found sideways, dead.
And you think the hole
in the universe,
caused by the emission
of your grief, is so deep
it will never be rectified.
But it's only the start
of an endless litany
of betrayals:
the cruelty of school,
your first bastard boyfriend,
the neighbour's son
going slowly mad.
You catch hold of losing,
and suddenly, it's everywhere –
the beggars in the street,
the ravage of a distant war
in your sleep.
And when grandfather
hobbles up to the commode
to relieve himself like a girl
without bothering to shut
the door, you begin to realise
what it means to exist
in a world without.
People around you grow old
and die, and it's explained
as a kind of going away –
to God, or rot, or to return
as an ant. And once again,
you're expected to be calm
about the fact that you'll never see
the dead again,
never hear them enter a room
or leave it,

never have them touch
the soft parting of your hair.
Let it be, your parents advise:
it's nothing.
Wait till your favourite aunt
keels over in a shopping mall,
or the only boy you loved
drives off a cliff and survives,
but will never walk again.
That'll *really* do you in,
make you want to slit your wrists
(in a metaphorical way, of course,
because you're strong and know
that life is about surviving these things).
And almost all of it might
be bearable if it would just end
at this. But one day your parents
will sneak into the garden
to stand under the stars,
and fade, like the lawn,
into a mossy kind of grey.
And you must let them.
Not just that.
You must let them pass
into that wilderness
and understand that soon,
you'll be called aside
to put away your paper wings,
to fall into that same oblivion
with nothing.
As if it were nothing.

Walking Around

(after Neruda)

EVERYTHING BEGINS ELSEWHERE 2012

It happens that I am tired of being a woman.
It happens that I cannot walk past country clubs
or consulates without considering the hags,
skinny as guitar strings, foraging in the rubbish.

All along the streets there are forlorn mansions
where girls have grown up and vanished.
I am vanishing too. I want nothing to do with gates
or balconies or flat-screen TVs.

It happens that I am tired of my veins and my hips,
and my navel and my sorrows.
It happens that I am tired of being a woman.

Just the same it would be joyous
To flash my legs at the drivers playing chess,
to lead the old man at house 38
onto the tarred road to lie down
under the laburnum dripping gold.

I do not want to keep growing in this skin,
to swell to the size of a mausoleum.
I do not want to be matriarch or mother.
Understand, I am only in love
with only these undrunk breasts.

And when Monday arrives with the usual
battalion of pear-shaped wives who do battle
in grocery store aisles,
I'll be stalking the fields of concrete and ash,

the days pushing me from street
to street, leading me elsewhere –
to houses without ceiling fans
where daughters disappear and the walls weep.

I will weep too for high-heeled beauty queens,
for sewing machines and chickens in cages.
I will walk with my harness
and exiled feet through cravings
and renunciations, through heaps
of midnight wreckages
where magistrates of crows gather
to sing the same broken song
of unforgiving loss.

The Memory of Wales

EVERYTHING BEGINS ELSEWHERE 2012

This is how it arrives, the memory
of Wales, on a day of scanty light.
I'm walking towards the playground.
I will never know newness like this,
or fear. I'm walking, and I'm eight.
I see a girl on the swing – my mother,

or at least, a version of my mother:
fair-haired, small. In the memory
of Wales it is often cold. I'm eight
and the cows are stalking light
like monsters in the playground.
I will never know newness like this.

I will never know a world like this.
This is my childhood and my mother's.
Everything begins in the playground:
beauty, decay, love, lilies. Memory
starts here on the stairs, in skylight.
Cows chew eternally. I'm eight

in this memory, I'm always eight.
There's a painting that speaks to this
malady of recurrence – an indigo twilight
of melting clocks, which shows Mother
Time as a kind of persistence, memory
and dream, coupling on the ground.

Everything we love returns to the ground.
Mother, father, childhood. When I'm eight
I know nothing of betrayal, but the memory
persists. Only once, is it different from this.
The playground is empty, and my mother,
no longer a girl, is walking a ridge of light.

Now she's at the wooden gate. Light
from Welsh stars tumbles to the ground.
Bronze cliffs in the distance sing. My mother
has met a man. She's going away. I'm eight,

but I've always known she'll leave all this.
Forsaking, after all, is a kind of memory.

My mother is eight and in Wales again.
She's in the playground of memory,
swinging towards light, towards this.

The Adulterous Citizen

EVERYTHING BEGINS ELSEWHERE 2012

> I am an adulterous resident; when I am in one city, I am dreaming
> of the other. I am an exile; citizen of the country of longing.
>
> SUKETU MEHTA, *Maximum City*

When it comes to it,
there's only the long, paved road
that leads to a house
with a burning light.
A house you can never own,
but allows you
to sleep in its bed
without demanding sex,
eat from its cupboards
without paying,
lie in the granite cool of its tub
without drowning.
And only when the first shards
of day slice through
the blinds
of the basement windows,
nudging you
with something of a whisper,
something like, *Maybe it's time to go* –
do you finally drag
your suitcases
up the carpeted stairs,
out the front door,
on to the summer pavements.

It is nothing
like losing a lover,
or leaving behind
the lanes of childhood.
Nothing like scaling
the winged walls of memory
to discover your friends
have packed up their boxes
and vanished.
More like stumbling
into a scene from the future,
where the ghost
of a husband
beckons with pictures
of a family
you no longer recognise,
and other people's children
race across the grass,
lulling you into belief
that you can always return like this –
without key in hand,
to lie in the folds of one city,
while listening to the jagged,
carnal breaths of another.

Homecoming

COUNTRIES OF THE BODY 2006

I forgot how Madras loves noise
loves neighbours and pregnant women
and Gods and babies

and Brahmins who rise
like fire hymns to sear the air
with habitual earthquakes.

How funeral processions clatter
down streets with drums and rose-petals,
dancing death into deafness.

How vendors and cats make noises
of love on bedroom walls and alleyways
of night, operatic and dark.

How cars in reverse sing 'Jingle Bells'
and scooters have larynxes of lorries.
How even colour can never be quiet.

How fisherwomen in screaming red
with skirts and incandescent third eyes
and bangles like rasping planets

And Tamil women on their morning walks
in saris and jasmine and trainers
can shred the day and all its skinny silences.

I forgot how a man dying under the body
of a tattered boat can ask for promises;
how they can be as soundless as the sea

on a wounded day, altering the ground
of the earth as simply as the sun filtering through
the monsoon rain dividing everything.

11 | RUTH FAINLIGHT

Filmed at home in London by Neil Astley, 8 November 2011

Ruth Fainlight's poems 'give us truly new visions of usual and mysterious events' (A.S. Byatt). Each is a balancing act between thought and feeling, revealing otherness within the everyday, often measuring subtle shifts in relationships between women and men. Images of the moon, however interpreted – whether as stern and stony presence or protective maternal symbol – recur throughout her work. Peter Porter described one of her collections as having 'the steadiness and clarity of the moon itself'.

Her *New & Collected Poems*, published by Bloodaxe in 2010, covers work written over 50 years, drawing on over a dozen books as well as a whole new collection and a selection of her translations of Sophia Mello de Breyner and Victor Manuel Mendiola. Four of those collections were originally published by Bloodaxe: *Climates* (1983), *Sugar-Paper Blue* (1997), which was shortlisted for the Whitbread Poetry Award, *Burning Wire* (2002), and *Moon Wheels* (2006). Other collections were published by Macmillan, Hutchinson and Sinclair-Stevenson.

Born in New York City in 1931, she has lived in England, mostly in London, since the age of 15. She also lived in Spain for four years in her 20s, and spent long periods in France and Morocco. Her first collection, *Cages*, was published in 1966.

She was married to the writer Alan Sillitoe for over 50 years. He died in 2010, and his bust can be seen behind her in the film. When I began trying to film Ruth reading her poems, I had to stop rightaway because of constant interference picked up by the radio mic which we couldn't account for at first, her radio and phone being switched off before we started. Then she remembered that Alan had been a keen CB radio ham and discovered that the old set in his study was still transmitting his signal. After that somewhat unsettling prelude, Ruth read a selection of poems written over 50 years, with no background buzz, but with, we hoped, Alan's blessing. The chained angel described in the last poem she reads stands on the landing outside her Notting Hill flat.

Passenger

FIFTEEN TO INFINITY (1983) | NEW & COLLECTED POEMS (2010)

Not watching trains pass and dreaming of when
I would become that traveller, glimpsed
inside the carriage flashing past a watching
dreaming child, but being the passenger

staring out at tall apartment blocks
whose stark forms cut against the setting sun
and bars of livid cloud, balconies crowded
with ladders, boxes, washing, dead pot-plants,

into lighted, steamy windows where women
are cooking and men just home from work, shoes
kicked off and sleeves rolled up, are smoking, stretched
exhausted in their sagging, half-bought chairs,

under viaducts where children busy
with private games and errands wheel and call
like birds at dusk: all that urban glamour
of anonymity which makes me suffer

such nostalgia for a life rejected
and denied, makes me want to leave the train,
walk down the street back to my neighbourhood
of launderettes, newsagents, grocery shops,

become again that watching dreaming girl
and this time live it out – one moment only
was enough before a yawning tunnel-
mouth obscured us both, left her behind.

Handbag

FIFTEEN TO INFINITY (1983) | NEW & COLLECTED POEMS (2010)

My mother's old leather handbag,
crowded with letters she carried
all through the war. The smell
of my mother's handbag: mints
and lipstick and Coty powder.
The look of those letters, softened
and worn at the edges, opened,
read, and refolded so often.
Letters from my father. Odour
of leather and powder, which ever
since then has meant womanliness,
and love, and anguish, and war.

The Crescent

THE KNOT 1990 | NEW & COLLECTED POEMS 2010

My stick of lipsalve is worn away
into the same curved crescent
that was the first thing I noticed
about my mother's lipstick.
It marked the pressure of her existence
upon the world of matter.

Imagine the grim fixity
of my stare, watching her smear
the vivid grease across her lips
from a tube shiny as a bullet.
The way she smoothed it
with the tip of a little finger
(the tinge it left, even after
washing her hands, explained
the name 'pinky') and her pointed tongue
licking out like a kitten's,
fascinated, irritated.

It was part of the mystery
of brassières and compacts and handbags
that meant being grown-up. I thought
my own heels would have to grow
a sort of spur to squeeze right down
the narrow hollow inside high-heels.

Now I am calmer and no longer
paint my lips except with this,
pale as a koshered carcass
drained of blood in salty water
or a memorial candle,
wax congealed down one side,
as though it stood in the wind
that blows from the past, flame
reflected like a crescent
moon against a cloud,
in the pool of molten light.

I carry the sign of the moon
and my mother, a talisman
in a small plastic tube
in my handbag, a holy relic
melted by believers'
kisses; and every time
I smooth my lips with the unguent
I feel them pout and widen
in the eternal smile
of her survival through me,
feel her mouth on mine.

Elegant Sybil

TWELVE SIBYLS 1991 | NEW & COLLECTED POEMS 2010

Having become an expert at false tones
as the voices slide lower or higher than intended
out of control, having heard so many lies
seen so many faces altering crazily
trying to hide their real motives,

having pondered the fate of those who came to consult her
and how little difference any words make,
her gaze is now withdrawn and watchful as a diplomat's.
Her lips, though still full, meet firmly in a straight hard line.

But her feathered cloak and tall head-dress of glorious plumage
are so elegant, no one can resist her.
The Emperor comes to hear her pronounce almost daily.
All the rich men's wives copy her style.

Alone at last, she strips off her regalia
lets the fine cloak drop to the floor
pushes strong fingers through the stubble of cropped hair
and climbs into the deep stone bath of water so cold
that even at the height of summer she shudders, and in winter
the effort of will the action demands
has become her greatest indulgence.

Opera in Holland Park

BURNING WIRE 2002 | NEW & COLLECTED POEMS 2010

Raucous peacocks like abandoned babies
counterpoint the final chorus of *Tosca*, Act I.

Every table in the café is occupied
by drinkers halted in the posture of listeners:
abstracted gaze, alertly lifted head.

The fumy blaze of flowerbeds, smouldering braziers
in the summer dusk. Vortices of midges
vibrate above the hedges like heat mirages.

To stare at the waterfall in the Japanese garden
for more than a few moments alters the scale:
a thousand-metre plunge down an Andean precipice.

In the interval, the audience eat ice cream, stroll
past the orangery. Violinists tighten their strings.

I have never been so close to a peacock before.
It struts, stops, opens its beak, emits a creaking,
tentative call and makes me jump with fright.

The small blue head swivels, crowned by feather-antennae
searching a signal. Precise articulation of
spurred legs like precious mottled enamel, clawed feet.

Massed trees darken into carbon-paper silhouettes
against the glassy tension of a paling sky
perfecting its spectrum of yellow, mauve and red.

Scarpia's room in the palace. Magnificence.
I can hear Tosca singing. The anguish starts again.

Chained Angel

SUGAR-PAPER BLUE 1997 | NEW & COLLECTED POEMS 2010

Since I stood it outside my front door,
this almost life-sized wooden figure,
I've questioned visitors on their opinion
of my angel's gender – whether it more resembles
a Duccio virgin or Uccello warrior.
The angel's attribute: a branch of palm,
its dress: a simple robe, and hair curled
to the shoulder, are not specific to either.

At first you think it's there to guard the door.
Then you notice a length of chain attached
between statue and floor – how else to defend
my captive, so ambiguous and helpless,
whose plumy wings are shackled, pinioned,
who cannot protect me nor itself from harm?
It has another purpose. I fear my angel
soon will utter what I do not want to hear.

12 | ROY FISHER

(1930-2017)

Filmed at home in Earl Sterndale, Derbyshire,
by Pamela Robertson-Pearce, 14 October 2008

Playing the language, pleasuring the imagination and teasing the senses, Fisher's witty, inventive and anarchic poetry has given lasting delight to his many dedicated readers for over half a century. He published over 30 poetry books, including four with Bloodaxe, most notably his retrospective, *The Long and the Short of It*, which Ian McMillan chose on *Desert Island Discs*, praising Fisher as 'Britain's greatest living poet'. This covers the entire range of Fisher's work, from its fraught beginnings in the 1950s through major texts of the 1960s and 1970s such as *City*, *The Ship's Orchestra* and 'Wonders of Obligation', to *A Furnace*, his 1980s masterpiece, and then the later work set in the scarred and beautiful North Midlands landscape where he lived for over 30 years, including the Costa-shortlisted *Standard Midland* (2010), added to the 2012 expanded edition of *The Long and the Short of It*. His final collection, *Slakki: New & Neglected Poems*, edited by Peter Robinson, was launched at a celebratory event in October 2016 in Birmingham Cathedral, which Roy was unable to attend, due to ill health. He died in March 2017, aged 86.

Reviewing Roy Fisher's poetry in *The Guardian*, Sean O'Brien wrote: 'Fisher stands outside, or alongside, whatever else is happening, an English late modernist whose experiments tend to come off. He is a poet of the city – his native Birmingham, which he describes as "what I think with". He is a redeemer of the ordinary, often a great artist of the visible... His range is large: he suits both extreme brevity and book-length exploration; his seeming improvisations have a way of turning into architecture. The best place to start is *The Long and the Short of It*. It might look and sound like nothing on earth at first, but then it becomes indispensable.'

Born in 1930 in Handsworth, Birmingham, he retired as Senior Lecturer in American Studies from Keele University in 1982. He was also a jazz musician, playing any style from Dixieland to bebop. He lived in the Derbyshire Peak District in his later years, where Pamela filmed him at home in 2008. The audio of him playing jazz piano is from Tom Pickard's film portrait, *Birmingham's What I Think With* (Pallion Productions, 1991).

The Thing About Joe Sullivan

THE THING ABOUT JOE SULLIVAN 1978 | THE LONG AND THE SHORT OF IT 2005/2012

The pianist Joe Sullivan,
jamming sound against idea

hard as it can go
florid and dangerous

slams at the beat, or hovers,
drumming, along its spikes;

in his time almost the only
one of them to ignore

the chance of easing down,
walking it leisurely,

he'll strut, with gambling shapes,
underpinning by James P.,

amble, and stride over
gulfs of his own leaving, perilously

toppling octaves down to where
the chords grow fat again

and ride hard-edged, most lucidly
voiced, and in good inversions even when

the piano seems at risk of being
hammered the next second into scrap.

For all that, he won't swing
like all the others;

disregards mere continuity,
the snakecharming business,

the 'masturbator's rhythm'
under the long variations:

Sullivan can gut a sequence
in one chorus –

– approach, development, climax, discard –
and sound magnanimous.

The mannerism of intensity
often with him seems true,

too much to be said, the mood
pressing in right at the start, then

running among stock forms
that could play themselves

and moving there with such
quickness of intellect

that shapes flaw and fuse,
altering without much sign,

concentration
so wrapped up in thoroughness

it can sound bluff, bustling,
just big-handed stuff –

belied by what drives him in
to make rigid, display,

shout and abscond, rather
than just let it come, let it go –

And that thing is his mood
a feeling violent and ordinary

that runs in among standard forms so
wrapped up in clarity

that fingers following his
through figures that sound obvious

find corners everywhere,

marks of invention, wakefulness;

the rapid and perverse
tracks that ordinary feelings

make when they get driven
hard enough against time.

The Entertainment of War

CITY 1961 | THE LONG AND THE SHORT OF IT 2005/2012

I saw the garden where my aunt had died
And her two children and a woman from next door;
It was like a burst pod filled with clay.

A mile away in the night I had heard the bombs
Sing and then burst themselves between cramped houses
With bright soft flashes and sounds like banging doors;

The last of them crushed the four bodies into the ground,
Scattered the shelter, and blasted my uncle's corpse
Over the housetop and into the street beyond.

Now the garden lay stripped and stale; the iron shelter
Spread out its separate petals around a smooth clay saucer,
Small, and so tidy it seemed nobody had ever been there.

When I saw it, the house was blown clean by blast and care:
Relations had already torn out the new fireplaces;
My cousin's pencils lasted me several years.

And in his office notepad that was given me
I found solemn drawings in crayon of blondes without dresses.
In his lifetime I had not known him well.

Those were the things I noticed at ten years of age:
Those, and the four hearses outside our house,
The chocolate cakes, and my classmates' half-shocked envy.

But my grandfather went home from the mortuary
And for five years tried to share the noises in his skull,
Then he walked out and lay under a furze-bush to die.

When my father came back from identifying the daughter
He asked us to remind him of her mouth.
We tried. He said 'I think it was the one'.

These were marginal people I had met only rarely
And the end of the whole household meant that no grief was seen;
Never have people seemed so absent from their own deaths.

This bloody episode of four whom I could understand better dead
Gave me something I needed to keep a long story moving;
I had no pain of it; can find no scar even now.

But had my belief in the fiction not been thus buoyed up
I might, in the sigh and strike of the next night's bombs
Have realised a little what they meant, and for the first time been afraid.

The Nation

POEMS 1979–1987 1988 | THE LONG AND THE SHORT OF IT 2005/2012

The national day
had dawned. Everywhere
the national tree was opening its blossoms
to the sun's first rays, and from all quarters
young and old in national costume
were making their way to the original National
Building, where the national standard already
fluttered against the sky. Some breakfasted
on the national dish as they walked, frequently
pausing to greet acquaintances with a heartfelt
exchange of the national gesture. Many
were leading the national animal; others carried it
in their arms. The national bird
flew overhead; and on every side
could be heard the keen strains
of the national anthem, played on
the national instrument.

Where enough were gathered together,
national feeling ran high, and concerted cries of
'Death to the national foe!' were raised.
The national weapon was brandished. Though
festivities were constrained by the size of
the national debt, the national sport was
vigorously played all day
and the national drink drunk.
And from midday till late in the evening
there arose continually from the rear
of the national prison the sounds of the national
method of execution, dealing out rapid
justice to those who had given way
– on this day of all days –
to the national vice.

from Texts for a Film

BIRMINGHAM RIVER 1994 | THE LONG AND THE SHORT OF IT 2005/2012

1 *Talking to Cameras*

Birmingham's what I think with.

It's not made for that sort of job,
but it's what they gave me.

As a means of thinking, it's a Brummagem
screwdriver. What that is,
is a medium-weight claw hammer
or something of the sort, employed
to drive a tapered woodscrew home
as if it were a nail.
                                    It's done
for lack of a nail, a screwdriver, a drill,
a bradawl, or the will to go looking.

The results come out mixed. It blunts
the screw-point, strains the shank,
bashes the head-slot flat. But

forced straight into the splitting wood,
it won't wind loose, and it can't
be twisted back out, even
if there's enough slot left for the bit.

It's instant, and it's obstinate,
and it's nobody else's future.
The screw dies in the attempt.
But you can be sure, if it's Birmingham,
that everything'll be altered
by the time you'd have wanted it again.
This isn't Yorkshire, or Paris.

[...]

2 *Birmingham River*

Where's Birmingham river? Sunk.
Which river was it? Two. More or less.

History: we're on our tribal ground. When they
moved in from the Trent, the first English

entered the holdings and the bodies of the people
who called the waters that kept them alive

Tame, *the Dark River*; these English spread their works
southward then westward, then all ways

for thirty-odd miles, up to the damp tips of the thirty-odd
weak headwaters of the Tame. By all of the Tame

they settled, and sat, named themselves after it:
Tomsaetan. And back down at Tamworth, where the river

almost began to amount to something,
the Mercian kings kept their state. Dark

because there's hardly a still expanse of it
wide enough to catch the sky, the Dark River

mothered the Black Country and all but
vanished underneath it, seeping out from the low hills

by Dudley, by Upper Gornal, by Sedgley, by
Wolverhampton, by Bloxwich, dropping morosely

without a shelf or a race or a dip,
no more than a few feet every mile, fattened

a little from mean streams that join at
Tipton, Bilston, Willenhall, Darlaston,

Oldbury, Wednesbury. From Bescot
she oozes a border round Handsworth

where I was born, snakes through the flat
meadows that turned into Perry Barr,

passes through Witton, heading for the city
but never getting there. A couple of miles out

she catches the timeless, suspended
scent of Nechells and Saltley – coal gas,

sewage, smoke – turns and makes off
for Tamworth, caught on the right shoulder

by the wash that's run under Birmingham,
a slow, petty river with no memory of an ancient

name; a river called Rea, meaning river,
and misspelt at that. Before they merge

they're both steered straight, in channels
that force them clear of the gasworks. And the Tame

gets marched out of town in the policed calm
that hangs under the long legs of the M6.

These living rivers
turgidly watered the fields, gave

drink; drove low-powered mills, shoved
the Soho Works into motion, collected waste

and foul waters. Gave way to steam,
collected sewage, factory poisons. Gave way

to clean Welsh water, kept on collecting
typhoid. Sank out of sight

under streets, highways, the back walls of workshops;
collected metals, chemicals, aquicides. Ceased

to draw lines that weren't cancelled or unwanted; became
drains, with no part in anybody's plan.

For Realism

THE MEMORIAL FOUNTAIN 1966 | THE LONG AND THE SHORT OF IT 2005/2012

For 'realism':
the sight of Lucas's
lamp factory on a summer night;
a shift coming off about nine,
pale light, dispersing,
runnels of people chased,
by pavements drying off
quickly after them,
away among the wrinkled brown houses
where there are cracks for them to go;
sometimes, at the corner of Farm and Wheeler Streets,
standing in that stained, half-deserted place

– pale light for staring up
four floors high
through the blind window walls
of a hall of engines,
shady humps left alone,
no lights on in there
except the sky –

there presses in
– and not as conscience –
what concentrates down in the warm hollow:

plenty of life there still,
the foodshops open late, and people
going about constantly, but not far;

there's a man in a blue suit
facing into a corner,
straddling to keep his shoes dry;
women step, talking, over the stream,
and when the men going by call out, he answers.

Above, dignity. A new precinct
comes over the scraped hill,
flats on the ridge get the last light.

Down Wheeler Street, the lamps
already gone, the windows have
lake stretches of silver
gashed out of tea green shadows,
the after-images of brickwork.

A conscience
builds, late, on the ridge. A realism
tries to record, before they're gone,
what silver filth these drains have run.

It Is Writing

THE THING ABOUT JOE SULLIVAN 1978 | THE LONG AND THE SHORT OF IT 2005/2012

Because it could do it well
the poem wants to glorify suffering.
I mistrust it.

I mistrust the poem in its hour of success,
a thing capable of being
tempted by ethics into the wonderful.

13 | CAROLYN FORCHÉ

Filmed in London by Neil Astley, 20 July 2014

Carolyn Forché is one of America's most outspoken poets – renowned as an advocate for 'poetry of witness' in her own work and in books such as the seminal *Against Forgetting: Twentieth-Century Poetry of Witness* (1993) – as well as an indefatigable human rights activist. Her later collections are visionary works drawing on work written over many years: *The Angel of History* (1994), *Blue Hour* (2003), and *In the Lateness of the World*, due out in 2018, only her fifth collection since her debut in 1976.

Her meditative poetry has a majestic sweep, with themes ranging from life on earth and human existence to history, war, genocide and the Holocaust. Jane Miller called *Blue Hour* 'a masterwork for the 21st century'. According to Joyce Carol Oates (*New York Times Book Review*), Forché's ability to wed the "political" with the "personal" places her in the company of such poets as Pablo Neruda, Philip Levine and Denise Levertov.

The film begins with her reading of 'The Colonel' from *The Country Between Us* (1981), which bears witness to what she saw in El Salvador in the late 1970s, when she travelled around a country erupting into civil war. Documenting killings and other brutal human rights abuses as a journalist and while working with Archbishop Oscar Romero's church group, she found herself drawn back into poetry as the only possible way to come to terms with what she was experiencing first-hand.

She follows this with several extracts from the title-poem of *The Angel of History*, which bears witness to the moral disasters of our times: war, genocide, the Holocaust, the atomic bomb. The book is a meditation on memory – how memory survives the unimaginable. The poems are fragmented, discordant, reflecting the effects of such experience, but forming a haunting mosaic of grief, evoking the necessary accommodations we make to survive what is unsurvivable. It is divided into five sections dealing with the atrocities of war in France, Japan and Germany as well as Forché's own experiences in Beirut and El Salvador. The title figure, the Angel of History – a figure imagined by Walter Benjamin – can record the miseries of humanity yet is unable either to prevent these miseries from happening or from suffering from the pain associated with them.

The Country Between Us is to be reissued by Bloodaxe in 2018 to coincide with the publication of *In the Lateness of the World*.

The Colonel

THE COUNTRY BETWEEN US 1981

WHAT YOU HAVE HEARD is true. I was in his house. His wife carried a tray of coffee and sugar. His daughter filed her nails, his son went out for the night. There were daily papers, pet dogs, a pistol on the cushion beside him. The moon swung bare on its black cord over the house. On the television was a cop show. It was in English. Broken bottles were embedded in the walls around the house to scoop the kneecaps from a man's legs or cut his hands to lace. On the windows there were gratings like those in liquor stores. We had dinner, rack of lamb, good wine, a gold bell was on the table for calling the maid. The maid brought green mangoes, salt, a type of bread. I was asked how I enjoyed the country. There was a brief commercial in Spanish. His wife took everything away. There was some talk then of how difficult it had become to govern. The parrot said hello on the terrace. The colonel told it to shut up, and pushed himself from the table. My friend said to me with his eyes: say nothing. The colonel returned with a sack used to bring groceries home. He spilled many human ears on the table. They were like dried peach halves. There is no other way to say this. He took one of them in his hands, shook it in our faces, dropped it into a water glass. It came alive there. I am tired of fooling around he said. As for the rights of anyone, tell your people they can go fuck themselves. He swept the ears to the floor with his arm and held the last of his wine in the air. Something for your poetry, no? he said. Some of the ears on the floor caught this scrap of his voice. Some of the ears on the floor were pressed to the ground.

May 1978

There are times when the child seems delicate, as if he had not yet crossed
  into the world.
When French was the secret music of the street, the café, the train, my own
    receded and became intimacy and sleep.
In the world it was the language of propaganda, the agreed-upon lie, and it
    bound me to itself, demanding of my life an explanation.
When my son was born I became mortal.

[...]

In the night-vaulted corridors of the Hôtel-Dieu, a sleepless woman pushes
  her stretcher
      along the corridors of the past. *Bonjour, madame. Je m'appelle Ellie.*

There were trains, and beneath them, laddered fields.

Autumns the fields were deliberately burned by a fire so harmless children ran
    through it making up a sort of game.
Women beat the flames with brooms and blankets, so the fires were said to be
  under control.

As for the children, they were forbidden to ask about the years before they
  were born.
Yet they burned the fields, yet everything was said to be *under control*
    with the single phrase *death traffic.*

This is Izieu during the war, Izieu and the neighboring village of Bregnier-
  Cordon.
This is a farmhouse in Izieu.
Itself a quiet place of stone houses over the Rhône, where between Aprils,
    forty-four children were
        hidden successfully for a year in view of the mountains.
Until the fields were black and snow fell all night over the little plaque which
    does not mention
        that they were Jewish children hidden April to April in Izieu near
  Bregnier-Cordon.

Comment me vint l'écriture? Comme un duvet d'oiseau sur ma vitre, en hiver.
In every window a blank photograph of their internment.

Within the house, the silence of God. Forty-four bedrolls, forty-four metal cups.
And *the silence of God is God.*

In Pithiviers and Beaune-la-Rolande, in Les Milles, Les Tourelles, Moussac
   and Aubagne,
       the silence of God is God.

The children were taken to Poland.
The children were taken to Auschwitz in Poland
      singing *Vous n'aurez pas L'Alsace et la Lorraine.*
In a farmhouse still standing in Izieu, *le silence de Dieu est Dieu.*

[…]

We lived in Ste Monique ward over the main corridor, Ellie and myself, in
      the Hotel-Dieu on the Place du Parvis Notre-Dame.
Below us jonquils opened.
Ellie was afflicted with scales again, tiny Ellie, at the edge of her bed, peeling
      her skin from her arm as if it were an opera glove,
and weeping *cachée, cachée, cachée* all during the war.

Barn to barn in the haylight, field to cellar. Winter took one of her sons, and
      her own attempt to silence him, the other.

Le Dieu? Le Dieu est un feu. A psychopath. Le Dieu est feu.

It isn't normal for a mother to outlive her children.
It isn't normal that my sons should be dead.

Paris! Oh, how I loathe this city because of its past.

Then you wish to leave Paris?

Mais oui. I wish to leave life, my dear.
My parents? Deported. My aunts and uncles? Deported. My friends? All of them
   deportees.
I don't know what became of a single one. How they came to the end.
My papers said I was Polish. When the money ran out, we ran. When the Nazis
   came, we ran. Cachée, cachée, cachée!

The tubercular man offers his cigarette and the snow falls, patiently, across the spring flowers.

My life, triste. Do you understand? This place. No good! France. No good! Germany. No good! Ni l'Union soviétique. Fascists! It is no good.

Then why not leave Paris?

I am Jewish. Do you understand? Alone in a small room on the third floor, always alone.
To remain sane, I sing librettos to myself, and German lullabies, can you imagine?

> *Mein Flügel ist zum Schwung bereit*
> *ich kehrte gern zurück,*
> *denn bleib ich auch lebendige Zeit*
> *ich hätte wenig Glück*

My husband was a soldier against the Nazis.   Resistance. Agir.   He wasn't killed in the war.
He even returned to me. It was after the war he died. He died of cholera.
And the world is worse now than it was then.

Worse?
Mais oui!

––––––––––––

We must wear our slippers and not smoke. We must not go further than the sign No Admittance.

No — a little residue of nothing.   And admittance, what does it mean? That they are not going to blame themselves for anything.
But the deportees, no, there is nothing between the word and those who are not, who do not reviennent.
And if language is an arbitrary system, one must not go further than the sign No Admittance
in the Hôtel-Dieu on the Place du Parvis Notre-Dame.

[…]

216

Surely all art is the result of one's having been in danger, of having gone
   through an experience all the way to the end.

As the last helicopter lifted away from the deck of the Manitowac and the
   ship turned

Bonsoir, madame. Je m'appelle Ellie.

A colander of starlight, the sky in that part of the world.

A wedding dress hanging in a toolshed outside Warsaw.

Bonsoir. Est-ce que je vous dérange?

On the contrary, I'm happy to practise speaking.

*Then you aren't French. How fortunate for me. I couldn't have shared this room
with a French woman.*

While the white phosphorus bombs plumed into the air like ostrich feathers
   of light and I cursed you for
            remaining there without me, for tricking me into this departure.

Parlez-vous francais? Est-ce que vous le parlez bien?

So beautiful, ma'am, from here, the sailor said, if you don't stop to think.

And it went on like that all night, questions in French, and it went on, radiant
   white feathers along the coast of Lebanon, until Ellie slept.

How can one confuse that much destruction with one woman's painful life?

Est-ce que je vous dérange? she asked. *Et pourquoi des questions?*

Because in French there is no auxiliary verb corresponding to our English *did*

As in

Did you wait for him to come back? and Did he return from the war alive?

Or

Did you decide in Beirut to go on without him?

As if someone not alive were watching:
Bonsoir. Est-ce que je vous dérange?

Night terrors. A city with all its windows blank.
A memory through which one hasn't lived.

You see, I told Madame about my life.
I told her everything.
And what did she say?

14 | TUA FORSSTRÖM

Filmed at home in Helsinki, Finland,
by Pamela Robertson-Pearce, 22 August 2009

Tua Forsström is a visionary Finland-Swedish poet who has become Finland's most celebrated contemporary poet. Her breakthrough came when she was still only 30 with her sixth collection, *Snow Leopard* (1987), which brought her international recognition, with its English translation by David McDuff winning a Poetry Book Society Translation Award. That book later became the first part of a trilogy, *I studied once at a wonderful faculty* (2003), also *The Parks* (1992) and *After Spending a Night Among Horses* (1997), coupled with a new cycle of poems, *Minerals* (2003). All the poems she reads in our film are from the trilogy, first published in a complete English edition by Bloodaxe in 2006, most of it translated by David McDuff, apart from *After Spending a Night Among Horses* (tr. Stina Katchadourian).

She has since published one further collection, *One Evening in October I Rowed Out on the Lake* (2012), published in a bilingual edition with David McDuff's English translation by Bloodaxe in 2015.

Her poetry draws its sonorous and plangent music from the landscapes of Finland, seeking harmony between the troubled human heart and the threatened natural world. As Sweden's August Prize jury commented, this is poetry 'both melancholy and impassioned', expressing a 'struggle against meaninglessness, disintegration, destruction – against death in life'.

For Claes Andersson, 'Tua Forsström's poems give a sense of having crystallised under a great pressure…a survey of the landscape of grief, exercises in renunciation and in the affirmation of loss of love, sexuality and communion with others… She belongs to a tradition that includes Rilke, Hölderlin, Paul Celan and the great Swedish poet Gunnar Ekelöf.'

When the Finnish Literature Information Centre invited British publishers of Finnish and Finland-Swedish writers to Helsinki in 2009, we were fortunate in being able to visit Tua at the same time, and to film her reading a selection of poems from her trilogy.

IV

For there is no place that does not
see you. You must change your life.

RAINER MARIA RILKE

1

Kom hem från de mörka vattnen
Kom hem därutifrån blåsten
Som en förstaklassist med den röda
väskan på ryggen, kom
hem. Förblandande det som
var, förblandande dig.
Dagarna liknar varandra.
Rader av burkar med slem och blod.
Det gäller att inte minnas
Det gäller att inte minnas den morgonen
nere vid det blanka vattnet, verklig
som en inbillning!
En gång fanns det oskuld och lust
En gång fanns det en besinningslös renhet
Man är ett ögonblick
Man är ett golv av sand i marknadstältet
Man transporterar små barn och skridskor
av och an längs hala vintervägar i sin längtan
till det svala ljuset, kom hem

3

För att förinta dem vi älskar
styr vi ut dem till narrar vid den
Nattliga teatern. Och de gör uppror!
Vi står där som gycklare själva!
Maskerade till dröm var de än mer
sig själva. Ömfotade kattdjur. Starka,
oförvanskade. De skall bedra oss.

from **Snow Leopard**

(translated by David McDuff)

IV

> For there is no place that does not
> see you. You must change your life.
>
> RAINER MARIA RILKE

1

Come home from those dark waters
Come home from out of the storm
Like a first-former with your red
schoolbag on your back, come
home. Confusing what
was, confusing you.
The days look like one another.
Rows of jars filled with blood and mucus.
It's a question of not remembering
It's a question of not remembering that morning
down by the shiny water, real
as an imagining!
Once there was innocence and pleasure
Once there was a reckless purity
One is a moment
One is a floor of sand in the market tent
One ferries small children and ice-skates
to and fro along slippery winter roads in one's yearning
for the cool light, come home

3

In order to destroy those we love
we dress them up as fools in the
Nocturnal Theatre. And they rise in revolt!
We stand there like clowns ourselves!
Masked into dream they were even more
themselves. Tender-footed felines. Strong,
uncorrupted. They are going to deceive us.

Det som vi kallar tid bedrar oss.
Själv är jag till exempel en sådan människa
som fortsätter att vandra av och an
den korta välbekanta sträckan mellan höghus
med de alltför svåra noterna i väskan och
en saklig, växande förtvivlan över
att vara jag. Det är oktober med metallisk
luft, metallisk himmel och de fördrivna
älskade som går med oss i röken
av vår andedräkt. Vi ser på dem,
vi måste aldrig förlora dem mer.

* * *

Det var sommarens hetaste dag.
Vi gick nere vid vattnet, och du
har blivit mitt syskon talade om
någon som insjuknat, fotbollsmatcher,
Thelonious Monk och anläggningen
du hade besökt i drömmen, välbekant
och olika för varje människa
Du sade att ingenting går över
Du sade att allt är övergående

med undantag för några lysande
och solkiga bilder som är sorg, som
är den sorg som genomströmmar
vänskapen som vatten,

några överexponerade sekvenser som
vi trycker skamset mot vårt hjärta.

What we call time deceives us.
I myself for example am the sort of person
who continues to wander up and down
the short familiar stretch between high-rise blocks
with the far too difficult music in my bag and
an objective, growing despair at
being myself. It is October with metallic
air, metallic sky and the banished
loved ones who walk with us in the smoke
of our breath. We look at them,
we must never lose them again.

* * *

It was the hottest day of the summer.
We walked down by the water, and you
who have become my brother talked about
someone who had fallen ill, football matches,
Thelonious Monk and the factory
you had visited in your dream, familiar
and different for each person
You said that nothing is ever finished
You said that everything is transitory

except for a few glowing
and soiled pictures that are sorrow, that
are the sorrow that flows through
friendship like water,

a few over-exposed sequences that
we press ashamedly to our hearts.

från **Parkerna**
1992

* * *

Snön yr över
Tenala kyrkogård

Vi tänder ljus för att
de döda skall vara mindre

ensamma, vi tror att de är
underställda samma lagar

som vi. Ljusen blinkar oroligt:
de döda längtar kanske efter

sällskap, vi vet ingenting om
deras verksamhet, snön yr

De döda tiger som bomull.
En skock tunna barn som

ohörbart tar ett steg närmare
Ser de på oss uppmärksamt ett

ögonblick: är det för att de
glömt, eller minns? Snön

yr över Tenala kyrkogård

Som när man flyger in
över en stad om natten på

låg höjd: ljusen blir
motorvägar, fordonens

strålkastare, man kommer
någonstans ifrån

from The Parks

(translated by David McDuff)

* * *

The snow whirls over
Tenala churchyard

We light candles so that
the dead will be less

lonely, we believe they are
subject to the same laws

as ourselves. The lights twinkle restlessly:
perhaps the dead are longing for

company, we know nothing of
their doings, the snow whirls

The dead are silent as cotton.
A flock of thin children who

inaudibly take one step nearer
They look at us closely for a

moment: is it because they've
forgotten, or remember? The snow

whirls over Tenala churchyard

As when you fly in
over a city at night at

low altitude: the lights become
motorways, the headlamps of

the traffic, you arrive
from somewhere

Snart kör man bil längs en
väg, ett av de blinkande

ljusen i yrsnön

* * *

Vi utgör en sådan ömklig
syn att cirkusdirektören
gråter. Dessutom fryser vi. Ach!
Han önskar oss åt helvete, han önskar
denna leriga marknadsplats i Ekenäs åt
helvete, med slutna ögon reser han från
denna gyttjepöl till kontinenten, en
annan ort: där ballerinans spetsar icke
är solkiga, där trapetskonstnären icke
stinker sprit, där lejonet ej stirrar
modlöst. Där det icke slår upp sprickor
i pudret. Där det icke slår upp sprickor
överallt! Cirkusdirektören känner ingen
sådan stad, men det är smärtsamt att
åldras och minnas utan smärta. Någonstans
glänser hästarnas hårrem, glittrar
paljetter, brusar publiken fjärran
från dessa tölpar. Där är det aldrig
oktober med snöblandat regn, där är
konsten minne och skimrande mynt.

* * *

Vi utrustar hästarna med det
som vi saknar: trofasthet och
mod. Vi älskar dem för deras
trofasthet och mod. Det är november,
det blåser milt mot ansiktet, små kalla

Soon you are driving along a
road, one of the twinkling

lights in the whirling snow

* * *

We make such a pitiful
sight that the circus-master
is in tears. What is more, we're cold. Ach!
He wishes us to hell, he wishes
this muddy market-place in Ekenäs to
hell, with eyes closed he leaves
this slush-puddle for the continent, a
different place: where the ballerina's lace isn't
dirty, where the trapeze artist doesn't
smell of spirits, where the lion doesn't stare
despondently. Where cracks don't open
in the powder. Where cracks don't open
everywhere! The circus-master doesn't know
any such city, but it is painful to
grow old and remember without pain. Somewhere
the horses' coats are shining, spangles
glitter, the audience roars far away
from these bumpkins. There it is never
October with snow-mingled rain, there art
is memory and shimmering coins.

* * *

We equip the horses with what
we lack: loyalty and
courage. We love them for their
loyalty and courage. It's November,
the wind blows gently in our faces, cold little

vattenskurar störtar från trädens
kronor   Hästarna skräms av sin
inbillning. Hästarna skräms av
vad som helst och sätter iväg.
Naturen slösar inte; naturen följer
strikt ekonomiska lagar. Träden
står kvar i dimman, orörliga
Något har långsamt förändrats, jag
vet: det som jag minns kommer
inte tillbaka.

* * *

Den fågeln rör sig aldrig
om dagen, du måste ha misstagit
dig, du måste ha förväxlat dess
vingslag med blåsten i asparnas
lövverk. Man fäster sig lätt vid allt: litet
krimskrams och fattiga skor, en häst.
Den Mörka Kamraten följer oss
Känslan av nederlag följer oss
Men klara dagar ser jag stranden genom
ett mönster klippt i silkespapper!
Klara dagar ser jag ingenting alls!
Jag vet inte längre hur du fördriver
tiden, man skall ju hålla på med något.
Man skall tro att det betyder något.
Stjärnbeströdda hus, mulen himmel
Det är som om någon sjöng en
mörk, entonig sång.

showers splash from the tree-
tops   The horses are frightened by their
imagination. The horses are frightened by
anything at all and set off.
Nature is not wasteful; nature follows
strict economic laws. The trees
stay put in the mist, motionless.
Something has slowly changed, I
know: what I remember doesn't
come back.

* * *

That bird never moves
in the daytime, you must have been
mistaken, you must have confused the beat
of its wings with the wind in the aspen's
foliage. It's easy to get attached to anything: a few
knick-knacks and poor shoes, a horse.
The Dark Companion follows us
The sense of defeat follows us
But on clear days I see the shore through
a pattern cut in tissue paper!
On clear days I don't see anything!
I don't know any more how you kill
time, after all, one must do something.
One must think that it means something.
Star-strewn houses, cloudy sky
It's as though someone were singing a
dark, monotonous song.

Staden glittrade

Staden glittrade på avstånd, och
jag stannade. Det var så vackert med
anläggningar och terrasserade trädgårdar,
liksom vattengenomlyst, och jag såg allt
mycket tydligt. Jag tänkte på de stora städerna
med katedraler, och hembygdsmuseerna på
landsorten i Sverige, och älggräset som doftade
så starkt, och jag mindes hur fäst jag hade varit
vid den lilla katten med de fläckiga tassarna som
sprang bort och hur jag hade saknat den.
Jag såg mig om och någon grät, jag kunde
inte beakta det. Staden var av genomskinligt glas.
Jag stod där. Jag såg min dominerande kärlek.
Av pärlor skimrande. De svarta svanarna. Kalcedon.
Jag försökte locka på den lilla katten. Allt glittrade.
Jag tvekade, jag visste allt, jag skulle
inte komma tillbaka.

Hästarna

Efter att ha tillbringat en natt
bland hästar minns jag hur friskt

det doftade av ammoniak och
smältsnö, den gröna månen

över den gröna skaren, en råtta
gnisslade i foderkammaren, hur jag frös

i min overall och yllemössa mot
morgonen och hur lugnt hästarna sov.

230

from After Spending a Night Among Horses

(translated by Stina Katchadourian)

The city was sparkling

The city was sparkling at a distance, and
I stopped. Everything looked so beautiful,
the street plans and the terraced gardens,
as if water-transparent, and I saw it all
very clearly. I thought about the great cities
with cathedrals, and the small local museums in
the countryside in Sweden, and the meadowsweet with its
strong fragrance, and I remembered how attached I had been
to the little kitten with the spotted paws who
ran away and how I had missed it.
I turned around and someone was crying, I couldn't
pay attention to it. The city was made of transparent glass.
I stood there. I saw my pre-eminent love.
Shimmering of pearls. The black swans. Chalcedony.
I tried calling the small kitten. Everything was sparkling.
I hesitated, I knew everything, I would
not come back.

The horses

After spending a night
among horses I remember the fresh

smell of ammonia and
melting snow, the green moon

over the green snow's crust, a rat
creaking in the hay room, how I shivered

in my overalls and wool cap toward
morning and how calmly the horses slept.

15 | TESS GALLAGHER

Filmed at her Irish home at Ballindoon by Lough Arrow, Co. Sligo, by Neil Astley, 29 April 2012

Born in 1943 in Port Angeles, Washington, the daughter of a logger and longshoreman, Tess Gallagher is a leading American poet as well as an essayist, fiction writer and playwright. She has published many books, including four poetry titles in Britain with Bloodaxe: *My Black Horse: New & Selected Poems* (1995), *Portable Kisses* (1996), *Dear Ghosts*, (2007), and most recently, *Midnight Lantern: New & Selected Poems* (2012), which draws on several collections, including *Moon Crossing Bridge* (1992), the poems of remembrance, mourning and recovery she wrote after the death of her husband, the writer Raymond Carver. Other poems relate to illness and remission, love and friendship, her tough childhood, the changing Pacific Northwest, and life in the West of Ireland, where she spends part of each year.

William Heyen wrote that 'Tess Gallagher's is perhaps the most deeply moving and spiritual and intensely intelligent poetry being written in America today', while Stanley Kunitz called her 'outstanding among her contemporaries in the naturalness of her inflection, the fine excess of her spirit, and the energy of her dramatic imagination'.

She co-authored two screenplays with Raymond Carver, and later contributed to the making of the Robert Altman film *Short Cuts*, based on Carver's work. She has also written introductions to books such as *A New Path to the Waterfall* and *All of Us* by Raymond Carver and *Carver Country*. She collaborated with the Irish storyteller Josie Gray to set his stories into print in *Barnacle Soup* (Blackstaff, 2007).

For Yvonne

(Yvonne McDonagh-Gaffney)

MY BLACK HORSE 1995 | MIDNIGHT LANTERN 2011/2012

Swept to her shoulders and out of the house –
the boys' sweaters, Granny's cardigan – that way
she had as a girl of borrowing
until we forgot to own. Now we coax her back
like a favorite garment that bears her scent,
laughter unravelling, like water breeze
pensive as a bride. How can she be
so everywhere and gone? Just like her to
store up warmth for us, stretching memory
like a sleeve until we are reshaped
by her absence. Coming upon *her* boat
marooned there on shore at Lough Arrow
is such wistfulness toward life
we know enough to turn it over,
climb in, let her hold us across the water.

Black Silk

WILLINGLY 1984 | MIDNIGHT LANTERN 2011/2012

She was cleaning – there is always
that to do – when she found,
at the top of the closet, his old
silk vest. She called me
to look at it, unrolling it carefully
like something live
might fall out. Then we spread it
on the kitchen table and smoothed
the wrinkles down, making our hands
heavy until its shape against Formica
came back and the little tips
that would have pointed to his pockets
lay flat. The buttons were all there.
I held my arms out and she
looped the wide armholes over

them. 'That's one thing I never
wanted to be,' she said, 'a man.'
I went into the bathroom to see
how I looked in the sheen and
sadness. Wind chimes
off-key in the alcove. Then her
crying so I stood back in the sink-light
where the porcelain had been staring. Time
to go to her, I thought, with that
other mind, and stood still.

The Hug

WILLINGLY 1984 | MIDNIGHT LANTERN 2011/2012

A woman is reading a poem on the street
and another woman stops to listen. We stop too,
with our arms around each other. The poem
is being read and listened to out here
in the open. Behind us
no one is entering or leaving the houses.

Suddenly a hug comes over me and I'm
giving it to you, like a variable star shooting light
off to make itself comfortable, then
subsiding. I finish but keep on holding
you. A man walks up to us and we know he hasn't
come out of nowhere, but if he could, he
would have. He looks homeless because of how
he needs. 'Can I have one of those?' he asks you,
and I feel you nod. I'm surprised,
surprised you don't tell him how
it is – that I'm yours, only
yours, etc., exclusive as a nose to
its face. Love – that's what we're talking about, love
that nabs you with 'for me
only' and holds on.

So I walk over to him and put my
arms around him and try to
hug him like I mean it. He's got an overcoat on

234

so thick I can't feel
him past it. I'm starting the hug
and thinking, 'How big a hug is this supposed to be?
How long shall I hold this hug?' Already
we could be eternal, his arms falling over my
shoulders, my hands not
meeting behind his back, he is so big!

I put my head into his chest and snuggle
in. I lean into him. I lean my blood and my wishes
into him. He stands for it. This is his
and he's starting to give it back so well I know he's
getting it. This hug. So truly, so tenderly
we stop having arms and I don't know if
my lover has walked away or what, or
if the woman is still reading the poem, or the houses –
what about them? – the houses.

Clearly, a little permission is a dangerous thing.
But when you hug someone you want it
to be a masterpiece of connection, the way the button
on his coat will leave the imprint of
a planet in my cheek
when I walk away. When I try to find some place
to go back to.

Yes

MOON CROSSING BRIDGE 1992 | MIDNIGHT LANTERN 2011/2012

Now we are like that flat cone of sand
in the garden of the Silver Pavilion in Kyōto
designed to appear only in moonlight.

Do you want me to mourn?
Do you want me to wear black?

Or like moonlight on whitest sand
to use your dark, to gleam, to shimmer?

I gleam.   I mourn.

Wake

MOON CROSSING BRIDGE 1992 | MIDNIGHT LANTERN 2011/2012

Three nights you lay in our house.
Three nights in the chill of the body.
Did I want to prove how surely
I'd been left behind? In the room's great dark
I climbed up beside you onto our high bed, bed
we'd loved in and slept in, married
and unmarried.

There was a halo of cold around you
as if the body's messages carry farther
in death, my own warmth taking on the silver-white
of a voice sent unbroken across snow just to hear
itself in its clarity of calling. We were dead
a little while together then, serene
and afloat on the strange broad canopy
of the abandoned world.

Choices

(for Drago Štambuk)

DEAR GHOSTS, 2006 | MIDNIGHT LANTERN 2011/2012

I go to the mountain side
of the house to cut saplings,
and clear a view to snow
on the mountain. But when I look up,
saw in hand, I see a nest clutched in
the uppermost branches.
I don't cut that one.
I don't cut the others either.
Suddenly, in every tree,
an unseen nest
where a mountain
would be.

I Stop Writing the Poem

MOON CROSSING BRIDGE 1992 | MIDNIGHT LANTERN 2011/2012

to fold the clothes. No matter who lives
or who dies, I'm still a woman.
I'll always have plenty to do.
I bring the arms of his shirt
together. Nothing can stop
our tenderness. I'll get back
to the poem. I'll get back to being
a woman. But for now
there's a shirt, a giant shirt
in my hands, and somewhere a small girl
standing next to her mother
watching to see how it's done.

16 | DEBORAH GARRISON

Filmed in New York by Pamela Robertson-Pearce,
11 September 2008

Deborah Garrison has published two collections, *A Working Girl Can't Win* (Faber, 1999) and *The Second Child* (Bloodaxe Books, 2008). In our film, shot in New York seven years on from 9/11, she reads from *The Second Child*, a book of poems about family in a world both more exciting and more frightening than ever before. It explores many facets of motherhood – ambivalence, trepidation and joy – coming to terms with the seismic shift in her outlook and in the world around her. She confronts her post-9/11 fears as she commutes daily into New York City, continuing to seek passion in her marriage and wrestling with her feelings about faith and the mysterious gift of happiness.

A Working Girl Can't Win chronicled the progress and predicaments of a young career woman. Her second book shows her moving into another stage of adulthood, starting a family and saying goodbye to a more carefree self. Sometimes sensual, sometimes succinct, always candid, *The Second Child* is a meditation on the extraordinariness resident in the everyday – nursing babies, missing the past, knowing when to lead a child and knowing when to let go. With a voice sound and wise, Deborah Garrison examines a life fully lived.

John Updike wrote that 'with their short lines, sneaky rhymes, and casual leaps of metaphor, Garrison's poems have a Dickinsonian intensity'. For Robert Pinsky, her 'directness, modesty and unshowy wit' won readers with her first book: 'It takes agility and imagination to write well about the ordinary... Those qualities also mark her new collection, *The Second Child*. This time the material includes parenthood and the attacks of September 11, 2001, with their aftermath... Garrison keeps her blessed and quotidian balance, in a remarkable way.'

Born in 1965 in Ann Arbor, Michigan, she worked on the editorial staff of *The New Yorker* for 15 years before becoming poetry editor at Alfred A. Knopf and senior editor at Pantheon Books.

Goodbye New York

(song from the wrong side of the Hudson)

THE SECOND CHILD 2007/2008

You were the big fat city we called hometown
You were the lyrics I sang but never wrote down

You were the lively graves by the highway in Queens
the bodega where I bought black beans

stacks of the *Times* we never read
nights we never went to bed

the radio jazz, the doughnut cart
the dogs off their leashes in Tompkins Square Park

You were the tiny brass mailbox key
the joy of 'us' and the sorrow of 'me'

You were the balcony bar in Grand Central Station
the blunt commuters and their destination

the post-wedding blintzes at 4 A.M.
and the pregnant waitress we never saw again

You were the pickles, you were the jar
You were the prizefight we watched in a bar

the sloppy kiss in the basement at Nell's
the occasional truth that the fortune cookie tells

Sinatra still swinging at Radio City
You were ugly and gorgeous but never pretty

always the question, never the answer
the difficult poet, the aging dancer

the call I made from a corner phone
to a friend in need, who wasn't at home

the fireworks we watched from a tenement roof
the brash allegations and the lack of any proof

my skyline, my byline, my buzzer and door
now you're the dream we lived before

I Saw You Walking

THE SECOND CHILD 2007/2008

I saw you walking in Newark Penn Station
in your shoes of white ash. At the corner
of my nervous glance your dazed passage
first forced me away, tracing the crescent
berth you'd give a drunk, a lurcher, nuzzling
all comers with ill will and his stench, but
not this one, not today: one shirt arm's sheared
clean from the shoulder, the whole bare limb
wet with muscle and shining dimly pink,
the other full-sheathed in cotton, Brooks Bros
type, the cuff yet buttoned at the wrist, a
parody of careful dress, preparedness –
so you had not rolled up your sleeves yet this
morning when your suit jacket (here are
the pants, dark gray, with subtle stripe, as worn
by men like you on ordinary days)
and briefcase (you've none, reverse commuter
come from the pit with nothing to carry
but your life) were torn from you, as your life
was not. Your face itself seemed to be walking,
leading your body north, though the age
of the face, blank and ashen, passing forth
and away from me, was unclear, the sandy
crown of hair powdered white like your feet, but
underneath not yet gray – forty-seven?
forty-eight? the age of someone's father –
and I trembled for your luck, for your broad
dusted back, half shirted, walking away;
I should have dropped to my knees to thank God
you were alive, O my God, in whom I don't believe.

September Poem

THE SECOND CHILD 2007/2008

Now can I say?
On that blackest day,

When I learned of
The uncountable, the hell-bent obscenity,

I felt, with shame, a seed in me,
Powerful and inarticulate:

I wanted to be pregnant.
Women in the street flowing toward

Home, dazed with grief, and my daze
Admixed with jealous awe, I wondered

If they were,
Or wished for it, too,

To be full, to be forming
To be giving our blood's food

To the yet to be.
To feel the warp of morning's

Hormonal chucking, the stutter kiss
Of first movement. At first,

The idea of sex a further horror:
To take pleasure in a collision

Of bodies was vile, self-centered, too lush.
But the pushy, ennobling pulse

Of the ordinary won't halt
For good taste. Or knows nothing of tragedy.

Thus. Today I have a boy
A week old. Blessed surplus:

A third child.
Have you heard mothers,

Matter-of-fact, call the third
The insurance policy?

That wasn't why.
And not because when so many people

Die we want, crudely pining,
To replace them with more people.

But for the wild, heaven-grazing
Pleasure and pain of the arrival.

The small head crushed and melony
After a journey

Out. Sheer cliff
Of the first day, flat in bed, gut-empty,

Ringed by memories and sharp cries.
Sharp bliss in proximity to the roundness,

The globe already set aspin, particular,
Of a whole new life.

Which might in any case
End in towering sorrow.

Into the Lincoln Tunnel

THE SECOND CHILD 2007/2008

The bus rolled into the Lincoln Tunnel,
and I was whispering a prayer
that it not be today, not today, please
no shenanigans, no blasts, no terrors,
just please the rocking, slightly nauseating
gray ride, stop and start, chug-a
in the dim fellowship of smaller cars,

bumper lights flickering hello and warning.
Yes, please smile upon these good
people who want to enter the city and work.
Because work is good, actually, and life is good,
despite everything, and I don't mean to sound
spoiled, but please don't think I don't know
how grateful I should be
for what I do have –

I wonder whom I'm praying to.
Maybe Honest Abe himself,
craggy and splendid in his tall chair,
better than God to a kid;
Lincoln whose birthday I shared,
in whom I took secret pride: born, thus I was,
to be truthful, and love freedom.

Now with a silent collective sigh
steaming out into the broken winter sun,
up the ramp to greet buildings, blue brick
and brown stone and steel, candy-corn pylons
and curving guardrails massively bolted and men
in hard hats leaning on resting machines
with paper cups of coffee –

a cup of coffee, a modest thing to ask
Abe for,
dark, bitter, fresh
as an ordinary morning.

On New Terms

THE SECOND CHILD 2007/2008

I'd like to begin again. Not touch my
own face, not tremble in the dark before
an intruder who never arrives. Not
apologise. Not scurry, not pace. Not
refuse to keep notes of what meant the most.
Not skirt my father's ghost. Not abandon
piano, or a book before the end.

Not count, count, count and wait, poised – the control,
the agony controlled – for the loss of
the one, having borne, I can't be, won't breathe
without: the foregone conclusion, the pain
not yet met, the preemptive mourning
without which
                  nothing left of me but smoke.

Pink and White

THE SECOND CHILD 2007/2008

Peonies are the only flower I care for
and when I saw them from the window
yesterday, tumbled and heavy along
a fence, fully exploded, nodding
at the ground, hanging their heads but not
yet spoiled, I remembered
a summer (maybe seven years
ago, or was it ten?) I wasn't sure
our love would come again,
and here I am, almost

kissing the grass like that,
bursting and rich, cracked
all over like broken cake –
makes you cry but still sweet.

Add One

THE SECOND CHILD 2007/2008

She's five.
Wants to know
What infinity is.

I try: you take the biggest
Number, you think the last
Number there is, and you add

One more.
See?
You can always add one.
So then the number's
Bigger still.
Infinity means –
The numbers go on
Forever.

She thinks. Index finger raised.
Swiveling innocently Elvis-style
Hips in her big-girl jeans
And shaking her pigtails
In a trance of musing. Then
Cocks her head, terrier-set:

'Is it like, God is still
Alive, making numbers?'

Now, who told her – it wasn't me! –
That God and infinity
Are spoken in one breath?
That what's infinite
Must be divine?

The Necklace
THE SECOND CHILD 2007/2008

He lay idling along me,
one leg crossed at the other knee, jauntily,

tiny man at his dinner, when
with brio sucked me in and wah-wahed

his jaw in quasi parody of his quest –
drinking but playing at drinking,

rhyming his eye with mine
and his was full of laughter as his starfish hand

upstretched, twirling to conduct the air,
to turn a song from nothing, waved

high and snagged of a sudden
the slender chain, platinum whisper

at my neck (dangled from which,
a diamond his father gave when *she* was born):

He couldn't care!
Just tugging there – by accident,

or in a freshman stumble toward
intent? – was for him a joyous

purpose, a study of texture,
of that solid link that might resist

his pull,
or not.

It took me a long minute
to unpeel that clutching paw,

and by the way it felt all wrong,
against nature.

See, if left to my own I'd let him
grasp without a thought

what was mine
and break it.

DVD 3

JANE GRIFFITHS – LEANNE O'SULLIVAN

1 | JANE GRIFFITHS

Filmed by Pamela Robertson-Pearce in Ledbury, 11 July 2009

Jane Griffiths writes mysteriously resonant poems about home, exile and shifting frontiers in classically precise language. Where her earlier collections are shot through with a migrant's sense of estrangement, the poems in her later books explore what it might mean to settle in a place. A number of her poems relate to the tension between displacement and acceptance of a new life, caught between love of a place and the fear of losing it.

Her poetry celebrates the landscapes she lives in by observing and recording them, yet with a strong awareness that these places exist in and of themselves, regardless of her observation. Hers are poems that delight in being in the world, despite the threat of loss.

Born in Exeter in 1970, she grew up in Holland and Devon, and now teaches English Literature at Wadham College, Oxford. She won an Eric Gregory Award for her poetry in 1996. Her Forward-shortlisted *Another Country* (2008) included large selections from two previous Bloodaxe collections, *A Grip on Thin Air* (2000) and *Icarus on Earth* (2005), as well as a new collection, *Eclogue Over Merlin Street*. Her most recent collections are *Terrestrial Variations* (2012), and *Silent in Finisterre* (2017), a Poetry Book Society Recommendation. Pamela filmed her reading a selection of poems from *Another Country* and from the manuscript of *Territorial Variations* before her reading at Ledbury Poetry Festival in 2009.

Emigrants

A GRIP ON THIN AIR(2000) | ANOTHER COUNTRY (2008)

Will know where they are by the absence
of trees, of people – the absence
even of anything to do. All
luggage is in transit; nothing at all
to do but watch from the empty house

through the empty window. The sky
is underlit, and under the sky
a lake; pewter, reflecting. A road.
Yellow buses turn at the end of the road,
if it is an end. Reeds block the view.

This bus is wheel-deep in them; it swims
along the lake's edge and a swan swims
towards it. They pass. And here, at last,
are two people, waiting for the last
bus out, or just standing, as people must

stand here often, leaning on the wind,
deep in reeds, and speechless in the wind
as if *lake* and *sky* were foreign words
to them as well: standing without words
but without need of them, being at home.

Migration

A GRIP ON THIN AIR (2000) | ANOTHER COUNTRY (2008)

First, there was the waking,
each day, to a lightness
they couldn't place. The air
stretched tight as a sheet;
the sun on their whitewashed

walls was flexible, or at any rate
warm and rounded to the touch.
It clung about them; they moved
shadowless, footsteps dropping like
stones to the light-resounding bay.

Daily their home gathered weed,
names, string. Sea-changed,
their eyes lost transparency;
they saw the house as it was:
a wholly new thing.

When the dreams came:
tarred and feathered bundles
of prehistory, their webbed feet
clay. They came overnight,
silently, as homing birds

to their owners, whose waking
each day was to a clogged grey
dawn, whose night-time shadows
had wings, scything steeply
above their narrow beds.

Bilingual

A GRIP ON THIN AIR (2000) | ANOTHER COUNTRY (2008)

New weight of language on the tongue;
the tongue tied: intractable, dumb.
The mouth takes shape in a new medium.
Its own breath is less than malleable.
                    Speech becomes sculpture:
a six-month-slow baroque contortion
to form one sentence:

ik stond met m'n mond vol tanden

Sounds freshly unearthed; the mouth
furred, lichen-locked; the tongue's tip curled.
Translation's a technicality: muscular
mastery of the letter R; long division
of the plaintive seagull syllables *ee, ui, ij:*

een enkele reis, alstublieft

The first words are rotund: pristine,
hard-pressed pebbles on the tongue.
Until the moment of revelation
when they burst like grapes against
the palate, and the tongue, unleashed,
unfurls like a cat and cries: *I am loose*
(los). Undone. Just look. I am translated.

Russian Dolls

ICARUS ON EARTH (2005) | ANOTHER COUNTRY (2008)

So they arrived, and found the shape of things
was a pear tree, a run of red brick
garden walls like the anatomy of a lost
civilisation, and a black and white cat
balled against pink peonies.

So they bought paint and papers and made
the house an interior. They took things in.
Sun spotted the ripening pears.
The evenings stretched like an elegy.
And they looked down on the skeletal north-

north-westerly semaphore of aerials, grew
self-contained. In autumn, as the fruit fell,
they could feel it: a new core shouldering
into place like a gold pear hardening
under the motley pear's skin.

Auricular

ECLOGUE OVER MERLIN STREET (2008) | ANOTHER COUNTRY (2008)

The first night home we leave the windows open.
The dark shifts softly as a curtain in its frame
while bats come out, swiftean

and irregular as the thin edge of a prayer
sounding the pitch of the gable, the timbre
of the slatted fence, and quicker

than compass needles in the crossfire of responses.

We imagine the inaudible exchange, remember
our train stretching the length of the coast

to the length of an afternoon, stopping and
starting down the line south from the mountains,
the soundtrack like a running question

and the leaden echo of all the intervening towns.

The bats flick darkly past invisible and familiar barns,
make current the spaces between the solids.

Another Country

ECLOGUE OVER MERLIN STREET (2008) | ANOTHER COUNTRY (2008)

Returning, the words were singular as stones
dropped in a still sheet of water, the clear
sense of them sinking under the surface
confusion, the prolific umming and erring.

The roads refused to add up. The school
was a coppice, the field where they'd flown
kites, a mere. There was a wild profusion
of magpies, and everyone was building

something – the prow of a church high
above the river that was the skyline.
Still, there were the vistas, the parks
with small white bridges crossing into an idea

of distance. They were just passing through.
The language returned like an underground
stream to its source: the repeats, the three
recurrent monosyllables to describe the view.

Border Crossing

TERRESTRIAL VARIATIONS (2012)

You'll never again say *this is where I stand* and mean it.
Your fists in your pockets each mould a stone, test the slight
differentiation of weight.

If you see a tree there's always another tree behind it,
if you turn a leaf you note the thin division of the centrefold,
the mismatched lifelines,

and you won't speak without a slip of the tongue – *forked*
would have been the word for it, before, or *split*.

The truth is, you have seen both sides of the horizon,
remember what the light was like, opposite:
the fish in the garden pond lipping the limpid
ceiling of their world, the suffocating seal of air,

and the apple tree in the foreground standing for all
a tree can stand for – barbed, black, shimmering.

So now when you see the wind ravel up the wind chimes
you think of fish rising, feel your tongue palm the unpalatable
similitudes, *like* and *like* and *like*.

There's the dark mass of the pool under its quick-shivered surface.
There's the neat phrase, *to get to the bottom of it*: like your fists
in your pockets, like the men who fished for the moon with a net.

And there's the third thing, that doesn't fit.

2 | PHILIP GROSS

Filmed at home in Penarth, Wales, by Pamela Robertson-Pearce,
13 July 2009

Philip Gross has published 19 books of poetry, ten of these from
Bloodaxe, most notably *The Water Table*, winner of the T.S. Eliot
Prize. Each of his collections is unified by a particular focus sustained throughout the poems and always related in some way to
the nature of embodiment and existence: space and absence in *The
Egg of Zero* (2006); the nature of water in *The Water Table* (2009);
the role of language and speech in identity and the self in *Deep
Field* (2011) and *Later* (2013); love and ageing in *Love Songs of
Carbon* (2015); space, sound and silence in *A Bright Acoustic* (2017).

The central concern of his earlier collection *The Wasting Game*
(1998) was much more personal, as Helen Dunmore observed at
the time: 'At the core of this new collection are the harrowing and
beautiful poems in which a father witnesses his daughter's near-
fatal struggle with anorexia. There is terror at watching a child
shrink to bone, longing to bring her back to the sunlit world,
anger, remorse, and above all an agonised love which resonates
throughout the poems. These are elegies for the living, piercing in
their clarity and depth of feeling.' In Pamela's film he introduces
and reads the whole sequence. Another poem from the same book,
'Imago', is included at the end, acting as a kind of postscript.

The Wasting Game is one of seven earlier collections included
in his retrospective volume *Changes of Address: Poems 1980-1998*
(1999).

Born in 1952 in Cornwall, Philip Gross lived in Bristol and
Bath for many years, and now lives in Penarth in South Wales.
He has also published several books of poetry for children and
nine novels for young people, and is Professor of Creative Writing
at Glamorgan University.

The Wasting Game

THE WASTING GAME (1998) | CHANGES OF ADDRESS (2001)

1

'I'm fat, look, *fat...*'

Yes and the moon's made of cheese,
that chunk she won't touch in the fridge

dried, creviced, sweating in its cold
like someone with a killing fever.

Half a scrape-of-marmite sandwich,
last night's pushed-aside

potatoes greying like a tramp's teeth,
crusts, crumbs are a danger to her,

so much orbiting space junk
that's weightless for only so long.

Burn it up on re-entry, burn it,
burn it. So she trains

with weights, she jogs, she runs
as if the sky were falling.

2

Curled like a lip, a crust dries in the bin,
the supermodel's come-on-don't-touch sneer
for the camera – desire
caught, teased, time and again

till all the wants run dry
and there's only this rictus,
a cat raking claws
down the arm of the chair,

eyes closed, lips apart
like the girl's head she drew
arching back to a lover's long
bone fingers tangled in her hair.

3

The eating thing:

the slouching beast
that's come to stay,

to spatter the slops
and foul the manger,

to snap at the hand
that tries to feed it, so

we leave it and we lie
in darkness, trying not to know,

not to hear it gnawing
in the next room, gnawing

itself to the bone.

4

Dry priestess at the shrine
of nothing. Maid-saint
fierce against the flesh
(burn it, burn it) denouncing
the witch in herself, see,
she's mounting the stake,
no, *becoming* it *and*
the tinder and the heartless
blaze you might mistake
for holiness. My homegrown
Manichee, almost 'perfected'
as the Cathars had it
fasting unto death. 'I want
a perfect figure.' Saying no
to the pull of the world.
Straight out, she said it
(burning but not yet
consumed) she said 'Weight
is bad. Bad.' On the blanket.
In the desert of her bed.

5

To be perfect...? 'Nothing's
perfect in this life,' I say.

Mealy middle-aged wisdom,

eat your words. See how
precisely she'll come to agree.

6

Close now, this nothing-

hungry thing that fills
her, that empties her... Once

in aquarium twilight a grey-
silver bass brought a face

big as mine up to the glass,
chewing water, with the weight

of deep ocean behind it. The cold.
Its tuppenny eye had a gleam

like contempt. For me? Or worse:
maybe its own reflection in the glass

was all it saw?

7

It's the Dark Ages now. I believe
in possession, in demons that speak
in crone voices out of fifteen-year-old lips,

her lips that have taken a tuck in
at the corner, a small crease like age
or disapproval when she (seldom) smiles.

I believe fairy tales like hot news,
how the Snow Queen's pinched
enraptured child might desire

nothing but to spell ETERNITY
from jags of ice, how Rumpelstiltskin
with the rage of any secret thing

that's named for what it is
might stamp so hard the splintering
could go on for ever,

how the scientists at Los Alamos
watched the fireball grow
and thought: it might not stop,

it might consume us all.

8

She's been paying her dues to gravity
in dud coin once a week

checking in on the doctor's scales
which wobble to a judgment: *holding steady*

though she's less and less able to hoist
what mass she still has, and she sways,

the rush of faintness in her ears like sea
hissing in over mud and in and in

as she steadies herself and walks towards it
with stones in her pockets, adding one a week.

9

Inside her, the slowing,
the faltering
voltage.
But still

there's this brilliant
flicker on the surface,
arc lights
on a dragged canal,

moving pictures
that don't quite
finesse the eye;
there are moments

you almost see through
(freeze *there*)
when the screen
shows nothing but a grey

room and gradually
shapes, near-transparent,
near-familiar,
like the threadbare home video

mailed with impossible demands.
You see the hostages,
a family,
staring out at you.

10

Ketones: a sour chemical smell on her skin
like a darkroom with blackouts on windows,
with shallow trays of fluid silky-still
as a swimming pool after lights-out,
their monochromes hardening. Developed,
they will close the family album.

11

I could hate

those frail maids fading beautifully
in books, wax lilies, pale-succulent

stalks that might snap
at a touch. The bird-dropping of blood

in a lace-bordered handkerchief
like the monstrance on the nuptual sheet.

A consummation most devoutly wished
by death. The maiden turns,

in woodcuts from another age
of plagues, to his knuckleboned touch,

half smiling; the consumptive turns
on her lace-bordered pillow

weakly and away
from any warmth of flesh

as if stung; the anorexic turns
her face towards these stories, stories

which, because I love the girl,
I hate.

12

She left home months ago.
Somehow we never noticed.
She was going solo

as a conjuror:
the egg we found rotting
in the body-folds of the sofa;

caked wads
of tissues in the bin with weetabix
compacted in them like the Mob's

car-crusher sandwiches;
potatoes spirited away
with one pass of the baggy-wristed

sweater she draped
on her bones. (What applause
when she whips it off one day

and she's gone!) Co-ordination
slipping now, caught out –
fraud, fraud! –

she plays the cheapest trick of all.
A toothmug of tap water,
sixty paracetamol.

She tries hissing herself offstage.

13
Drip. Drip.

Those stripped
twigs of her fingers.
Ivy torsions in the wrist.

Two spikes bandaged
to drip in her veins.

Sap sunk
at fifteen, she's been old
for too long, always cold
in her matt blacks, always
in some sort of mourning.

Mulched like leafmould,
mushroom-breathed, shit-smelling,
she's a question: Can
you love this?
Can you sit

and watch the hours dissolving
in the drip
of Parvolax and glucose
clear as rinsings from bare twig tips
when the downpour's gone?

They're trying to wash the river
in her blood. They're on the phone
to the Poisons Unit:
the readings aren't clear.
Nothing's perfect

but it's all there is.
This. Now. The drip
of plain words. Yes.
Love.
This.

Imago

THE WASTING GAME (1998) | CHANGES OF ADDRESS (2001)

She spent winter and spring
in her chrysalis, a strait world
shrunk and puckered like a mis-stitched scar.

Inside it held a breaking down of things
like a drop of original swamp sea.
Which is one way not to speak

of unopening windows resigned to the view
of the CAUTION PATIENTS CROSSING
speedbumped drive; the coded sign

NO CASUALTY DEPARTMENT here
among so many casualties;
the swabbed smells and the sounds off

like that sobbing on legs
down the corridor, and the dribbling
overspill from the padlocked pool

where a green beach ball scuds slow
eccentric orbits
to the pipe and back and round...

*

Hawk moth caterpillars
dropped from the limes in our street,
pointless manna she'd save

like the good girl she was,
on damp earth in a jam-jar.
They shrank to sealed flasks

for the usual great experiment.
We found a blood-brown drip
in the husk where one vanished;

another that, shrink-
wrapped too tight in itself,
couldn't ever split free.

So seeing her now
rise from the station subway
with bags marked for home,

to the lip of the crowd, and hesitate,
not a child now, and not any image
I could make to hold her,

I can't call her name,
I can't find words for her,
I wouldn't dare.

3 | CHOMAN HARDI

Filmed by Pamela Robertson-Pearce in Newcastle,
12 November 2015

In her second English collection, *Considering the Women* (2015), Choman Hardi explores the equivocal relationship between immigrants and their homeland – the constant push and pull – as well as the breakdown of an intermarriage, and the plight of women in an aggressive patriarchal society and as survivors of political violence.

Five of the poems she reads in the film are from the book's central sequence, *Anfal*, which draws on her post-doctoral research on women survivors of genocide in Kurdistan. The stories of eleven survivors (nine women, an elderly man and a boy child) are framed by the radically shifting voice of the researcher: naïve and matter-of-fact at the start; grieved, abstracted and confused by the end.

Knowledge has a noxious effect in this book, destroying the poet's earlier optimistic sense of self and replacing it with a darker identity where she is ready for 'all the good people in the world to disappoint her'. The collection ends with a new beginning found in new love and in taking time off from the journey of traumatic discovery to enjoy the small, ordinary things of life, as in 'A Day for Love', a translation of one of her own poems originally written in Kurdish, which she reads at the end.

Choman Hardi was born in Iraqi Kurdistan just before her family fled to Iran. She returned home at the age of five, but when she was 14 the Kurds were attacked with chemical weapons, and her family were forced back into exile. Her poems chart lives of displacement and terror, repression and the subjugation of women, family love, flight and survival. Granted asylum in the UK in 1993, she was educated at the universities of Oxford, London and Kent, and awarded a scholarship from the Leverhulme Trust to carry out her post-doctoral research about women survivors of genocide in Kurdistan-Iraq, publishing her study *Gendered Experiences of Genocide: Anfal Survivors in Kurdistan-Iraq* with Ashgate in 2011. Her collections of poetry in Kurdish and English include her first English collection, *Life for Us*, published by Bloodaxe Books in 2004, and *Considering the Women*, which was shortlisted for the Forward Prize. In 2014 she moved back to her home-city of Sulaimani to take up a post at the American University of Iraq (AUIS), becoming chair of the department of English in 2015.

Between 23 February and 6 September 1988 the Iraqi state launched
a genocide campaign against rural Kurdistan. The campaign targeted
six geographical regions, destroying over 2000 villages, killing
100,000 civilians and displacing many more. Besides conventional
bombing, 281 locations were gassed during the campaign. The
majority of the victims ended up in mass graves. Some civilians
died of starvation and illness in the prison camps while others
died during the bombardments and gassing or during their flight
to Iran and Turkey.

Dibs Camp, the Women's Prison
Nabat Fayaq Rahman

You do not die! Not when you want to.
Not when you see your strong husband, the big
brother in his own family, kicked bloody by a group
of men equipped with loaded guns and hatred.

Not when your beautiful teenage daughter
is handpicked by soldiers, never comes back.
And for the rest of your life you are left to wonder:
was she sold to prostitution? Does she still live?

Not when your son withers in your lap
and he cries until he can no more, when the last thing
he asks of you is 'cucumber', and you give him
a green slipper to suckle on, because he is beyond

knowing the difference. No. Not even when
the rest of your children grow fed up with
your black garments, secret tears, headaches
when you smell cucumber. You do not die.

The Gas Survivor
Badria Saeed Khidir, Nakhsheen Saeed Osman and Rabia Muhamad Ibrahim

My body is blooming. Every night leaking flowers,
I turn my mattress into a bed of roses – black,
cherry-red, pink and gold. By day I hand-wash
the towels, recall the stillborn after the gassing.

Who would have thought there are weapons
that turn every part of your body against you?
Every bruise, cough, or nosebleed seeming like
the final betrayal? Weapons that turn you into

a despised being in your own village, no one
daring to visit you, thinking you are contagious.
Weapons that kill you years after being exposed,
leaving you unable to blame anyone for your death?

Dispute Over a Mass Grave

The one you have finished examining
is my son. That is the milky coloured Kurdish
suit his father tailored for him, the blue shirt
his uncle gave to him. Your findings prove
that it is him – he was a tall fifteen year old,
was left handed, had broken a rib.

I know she too has been looking for her son
but you have to tell her that this is not him.
Yes the two of them were playmates and fought
the year before. But it was my son who broke
a rib, hers only feigned to escape trouble.

That one is mine! Please give him back to me.
I will bury him on the verge of my garden –
the mulberry tree will offer him its shadow,
the flowers will earnestly guard his grave,
the hens will peck on his gravestone,
the beehive will hum above his head.

The Angry Survivor

I am fed up with documentations of my grief –
journalists asking me to sing a lullaby for my
dead children, to broadcast during commemorations,
government officials using my story as propaganda
during elections, women activists forcing me to talk
about rape only to prove that women are oppressed,
researchers claiming to record history when
all they do is pick my wounds.

This is my story, not yours. Long after you
turn off your recorder I stay indoors and weep.
Why don't people understand? I am neither hero,
nor God, cannot stand the talk of forgiveness.
For years I went to every wake. Wept at every man's
funeral. Kept asking: Why? Realised I will never
understand. Now I just endure the days, by planting
cucumbers which you interrupted, by believing

in another world where there is justice, by watching my
remaining children as they sleep. Spare me your despair
and understanding. You can't resurrect the dead, feed
my hungry children, bring me recognition and respect.
Take history with you and go. Don't come here
again, I just don't want to know.

Researcher's Blues

Every day I try to lose them in the streets,
leave them behind in a bend in the road and keep on
walking. But they follow me everywhere, their voices
combining into a hum from which sentences rise and fall.
The woman I never interviewed cut the string of my sleep
at dawn, whispering: 'I am not well'. Why didn't I listen
to her story? Why didn't I realise that she was dying?
The one widowed at 26 told me, 'Imagine twenty
years of loneliness.' I remember her in the middle of
an embrace and start weeping. The pleading voice

of the woman who was raped echoes in my head:
'I only wanted bread for my son.' I wish I had told her
that she is good, she is pure, not spoiled as she thinks she is.
Then I remember the old couple in their mud-brick house,
surrounded by goats and chickens. I remember their tears
when they talk about their children, when they remember
a woman who had been rich and powerful in her own village
but in Nugra Salman 'she was stinking, abandoned,
worm-stricken'. What was the dead woman's name?
Why didn't I try to find her family? I keep walking away.
All I want is to walk without crying, without being
pitied by people who think that I have problems
with love, without the homeless man telling me that he is
sorry. I want to disappear, be unnoticed, unpitied.
Sometime ago when I started, it was all clear. I knew
what had to be done. All I can do now is keep walking,
carrying this sorrow in my soul, all I can do is
pour with grief which has no beginning and no end.

*   *   *

A Day for Love

Translated from Kurdish

CONSIDERING THE WOMEN (2015)

This is the day for love, the day not to think
of wars, to tell violence: 'we have had enough,
stand in the corner on one foot', give poverty
a loaf of bread so that it can snooze, warn oppression
to be careful: 'An oppressor is on the way.'

This is the day to remember
our first kiss, the first whisper,
the smell of your hands in the lavender garden,
the youthful rain, lush behind you and your oblivion
as you drenched yourself in the colour of my eyes.

We have this day for gratitude
so that I can thank you, thank God that you
are mine. Thanks for all the mornings when we
enclose our daughter like closed brackets
and I want to cry.

Please don't steal the day from us. Don't
tell us about the girl who was murdered in her sleep.
Don't show images of the foetus, shot dead inside
her mother. Don't tell us about the stupidity of leaders,
the folly of politicians, the brutality of humans.

We want to hold on to this moment today,
to think about love's voice, colour and taste.
Please leave this day to us. And don't worry,
tomorrow we will roll up our sleeves once again,
we will listen out. We will be here

to write another letter against oppression,
to sign another petition against injustice.
But today, let us be, to consider our love.

4 | KERRY HARDIE

Filmed by Neil Astley at Dookinella, Achill Island,
Co. Mayo, Ireland, 23 April 2012

Born in Singapore and raised in County Down, Kerry Hardie is an Irish writer who has published eight books of poetry and two novels. Often following the annual round of rural life, her poetry questions, celebrates and challenges all aspects of life and experience, exploring the mystery of 'why we are here', but is ultimately concerned with the quiet realisation that 'there is nothing to do in the world except live in it'. A number of her poems are narratives or parables in which experience yields a spiritual lesson and consolation; others chart a coming to terms with death or continuing illness and an acceptance of inevitability or flux. Human life quivers in consort with other lives in these seasons of the heart. 'In many of these poems, illness opens into a compassionate understanding of suffering and death, familial and historical [...] she finds in nature a redemptive power for the body, prompting the big questions of human and divine purpose.' (Selina Guinness, *The New Irish Poets*)

'Hardie's poetry is brave, steadily confronting both the deaths of her loved ones and her own experiences with illness as an ME sufferer. Her collections contain gentle, but insistent, works of memento mori... What makes her work exceptional is how skilfully she illustrates the connection between humanity and the cycles in the natural world. Poems and lives move through the unstoppable clockwork of seasons in her collections... A unique aspect of Hardie's poetry is the hope that is present in all her collections. She guides us through tragedy, reassuring us but never romanticising the true nature of life.' (Jennifer Matthews, *Poetry International*)

All the poems she reads in the film are included in her *Selected Poems* (2011), published in Ireland by the Gallery Press and in Britain by Bloodaxe, which draws on five earlier Gallery collections. *The Ash and the Oak and the Wild Cherry Tree* (2012) was later published by Gallery, and *The Zebra Stood in the Night* (2014) by Bloodaxe and shortlisted for the *Irish Times*–Poetry Now Award.

She lives in Co. Kilkenny with her husband Seán Hardie. They were staying in a cottage on Achill Island, Co. Mayo, a favourite place of retreat, when we made our filming arrangements.

271

Ship of Death

A FURIOUS PLACE (1996) | SELECTED POEMS (2011)

Watching you, for the first time,
turn to prepare your boat, my mother;
making it clear you have other business now –
the business of your future –
I was washed through with anger.

It was a first survey,
an eye thrown
over sails, oars, timbers,
as many a time I'd seen that practised eye
scan a laden table.

How can you plan going off like this
when we stand at last, close enough, if the wind is right,
to hear what the other is saying?
I never thought you'd do this, turning away,
mid-sentence, your hand testing a rope,

your ear tuned
to the small thunder of the curling wave
on the edge of the great-night sea,
neither regretful nor afraid –
anxious only for the tide.

May

(for Marian)

A FURIOUS PLACE (1996) | SELECTED POEMS (2011)

The blessèd stretch and ease of it –
heart's ease. The hills blue. All the flowering weeds
bursting open. Balm in the air. The birdsong
bouncing back out of the sky. The cattle
lain down in the meadow, forgetting to feed.
The horses swishing their tails.
The yellow flare of furze on the near hill.
And the first cream splatters of blossom
high on the thorns where the day rests longest.

All hardship, hunger, treachery of winter
forgotten.
This unfounded conviction: forgiveness, hope.

After My Father Died

THE SKY DIDN'T FALL (2003) | SELECTED POEMS (2011)

The sky didn't fall.

It stayed up there,
luminous, tattered with crows,
all through
January's short days,
February's short days.

Now the year
creeps towards March.
Damp days, grass springing.
The poplars' bare branches
are fruited with starlings and thrushes.
The world is the body of God.
And we –
you, me, him, the starlings and thrushes –
we are all buried here,

mouths made of clay,
mouths filled with clay,
we are all buried here, singing.

Avatars

A FURIOUS PLACE (1996) | SELECTED POEMS (2011)

Listen, this is the trinity, he said, tramping the wet road
in the thin well-being of a winter morning:
God the curlew, God the eider,
God the cheese-on-toast.
To his right a huddle of small blue mountains
squatted together discussing the recent storm.
To his left the sea washed.

I thought it was whimsical, what he said,
I condemned it as fey.
Then I saw that he meant it; that, unlike me,
he had no quarrel
with himself, could see his own glory
was young enough for faith still in flesh and in being.
He was not attracted by awe

or a high cold cleanness
but imagined a god as intimate
as the trickles of blood and juice that coursed about inside him,
a god he could eat or warm his hands on,
a low god for winter:
belly-weighted, with the unmistakable call
of the bog curlew or the sea-going eider.

Flesh

THE SILENCE CAME CLOSE (2006) | SELECTED POEMS (2011)

Sitting in a doorway,
in October sunlight,
eating
peppers, onions, tomatoes,
stale bread sodden with olive oil –

and the air high and clean,
and the red taste of tomatoes,
and the sharp bite of onions,
and the pepper's scarlet crunch –

the body
coming awake again,
thinking,
maybe there's more to life than sickness,
than the body's craving for oblivion,
than the hunger of the spirit to be gone –

and maybe the body belongs in the world,
maybe it knows a thing or two,
maybe it's even possible
it may once more remember

sweetness,
absence of pain.

Samhain

ONLY THIS ROOM 2009 | SELECTED POEMS 2011

You can feel the dead crowding.
In the fierce, low sun they've kept their distance:
light-fade and they flock like small brown moths
that dart and fall and crawl and rise and settle,
cloaking my shoulders with their soft, drab wings.

The great saints have their high appointed ritual.
This is a congregation of the parish dead,
local to these scattered fields and farms.

Sheep Fair Day

THE SKY DIDN'T FALL (2003) | SELECTED POEMS (2011)

> The real aim is not to see God in all things, it is that God,
> through us, should see the things that we see.
> SIMONE WEIL

I took God with me to the sheep fair. I said, 'Look
there's Liv, sitting on the wall, waiting;
these are pens, these are sheep,
this is their shit we are walking in, this is their fear.
See that man over there, stepping along the low walls
between pens, eyes always watching,
mouth always talking, he is the auctioneer.
That is wind in the ash trees above, that is sun
splashing us with running light and dark.
Those men over there, the ones with their faces sealed,
are buying or selling. Beyond in the ring
where the beasts pour in, huddle and rush,
the hoggets are auctioned in lots.
And that woman with the ruddy face and the home-cut hair
and a new child on her arm, that is how it is to be woman
with the milk running, sitting on wooden boards
in this shit-milky place of animals and birth and death
as the bidding rises and falls.'

Then I went back outside and found Fintan.
I showed God his hand as he sat on the rails,
how he let it trail down and his fingers played
in the curly back of a ewe. Fintan's a sheep-man
he's deep into sheep, though it's cattle he keeps now,
for sound commercial reasons.
                              'Feel that,' I said,
'feel with my heart the force in that hand
that's twining her wool as he talks.'
Then I went with Fintan and Liv to Refreshments,
I let God sip tea, boiling hot, from a cup,
and I lent God my fingers to feel how they burned
when I tripped on a stone and it slopped.
'This is hurt,' I said, 'there'll be more.'
And the morning wore on and the sun climbed
and God felt how it is when I stand too long,
how the sickness rises, how the muscles burn.

Later, at the back end of the afternoon,
I went down to swim in the green slide of river,
I worked my way under the bridge, against the current,
then I showed how it is to turn onto your back
with, above you and a long way up, two gossiping pigeons,
and a clump of valerian, holding itself to the sky.
I remarked on the stone arch as I drifted through it,
how it dapples with sunlight from the water,
how the bridge hunkers down, crouching low in its track
and roars when a lorry drives over.

And later again, in the kitchen,
wrung out, at day's ending, and empty,
I showed how it feels
to undo yourself,
to dissolve, and grow age-old, nameless:

woman sweeping a floor, darkness growing.

The Hunter Home from the Hill

A FURIOUS PLACE (1996) | SELECTED POEMS (2011)

Quiet by the window of the train
watching the blanched skies, the bleaching stubble,
a breaking down of colour
to something matte and porous and not at the heart of vision –

watching the winter lying down in the fields
as a horse lies – bone following bone –
the long ridge, the sheep, the blue note of the beet fields,

the bungalows on rutted patches starting awake
out of wild dreams in which they are gardens,

Carlow, the ugly here and there of it, the damp-stained houses,
the sky over the beet plant sausaged with fat round smoke,

all as it is,

like watching him in the kitchen in the morning,
his vest, his thinning slept-in hair, the way he is in your life,
and you content that he be there.

After Rage

THE SILENCE CAME CLOSE (2006) | SELECTED POEMS (2011)

It was only
when I had carried the seedlings
out into the cold day,
when I had sat myself down
in the damp grass
and pricked out
hollyhocks, poppies, lavender, pinks –
the young plants,
the fibrous trail of their webby roots –
firming them
into their new places;
only then
did I quiet enough
for the great winds to die down
in the whitethorns of my being,
for the magpies to leave off their rattling
in the grace of the silver birch.

5 | ROBERT HASS

Filmed by Neil Astley in Ledbury, 9 July 2014

From the beginning, Robert Hass's poems have seemed entirely his own: a complex hybrid of the lyric line, with an unwavering fidelity to human and non-human nature, and formal variety and surprise, and a syntax capable of thinking through difficult things in ways that are both perfectly ordinary and really unusual. Over the years, he has added to these qualities a range and a formal restlessness that seem to come from a sceptical turn of mind, an acute sense of the artifice of the poem and of the complexity of the world of lived experience that a poem tries to apprehend.

Hass's work is grounded in the beauty of the physical world. His familiar landscapes – San Francisco, the northern California coast, the Sierra high country – are vividly alive in his work. His themes include art, the natural world, desire, family life, the life between lovers, the violence of history, and the power and inherent limitations of language. He is a poet who is trying to say, as fully as he can, what it is like to be alive in his place and time.

His style – formed in part by American modernism, in part by his long apprenticeship as a translator of the Japanese haiku masters and Czesław Miłosz – combines intimacy of address, a quick intelligence, a virtuosic skill with long sentences, intense sensual vividness, and a light touch.

Born in 1941 in San Francisco, he lives in northern California with his wife, the poet Brenda Hillman, and teaches at the University of California at Berkeley. He served as US Poet Laureate in 1995-97. I was able to film him reading a selection of his poems when he was poet-in-residence at Ledbury Poetry Festival in 2014.

His retrospective *The Apple Trees at Olema* was published by Bloodaxe in 2011, featuring work from five collections – *Field Guide, Praise, Human Wishes, Sun Under Wood* and *Time and Materials* – as well as a substantial gathering of new poems, including a suite of elegies, a series of poems in the form of notebook musings on the nature of storytelling, a suite of summer lyrics, and two experiments in pure narrative that meditate on personal relations in a violent world and read like small, luminous novellas. This was followed in 2013 by *The Essential Haiku: versions of Basho, Buson and Issa*, the first UK edition of a modern classic published 20 years earlier in the US.

Meditation at Lagunitas

PRAISE (1979) | THE APPLE TREES AT OLEMA (2010/2011)

All the new thinking is about loss.
In this it resembles all the old thinking.
The idea, for example, that each particular erases
the luminous clarity of a general idea. That the clown-
faced woodpecker probing the dead sculpted trunk
of that black birch is, by his presence,
some tragic falling off from a first world
of undivided light. Or the other notion that,
because there is in this world no one thing
to which the bramble of *blackberry* corresponds,
a word is elegy to what it signifies.
We talked about it late last night and in the voice
of my friend, there was a thin wire of grief, a tone
almost querulous. After a while I understood that,
talking this way, everything dissolves: *justice,*
pine, hair, woman, you and *I.* There was a woman
I made love to and I remembered how, holding
her small shoulders in my hands sometimes,
I felt a violent wonder at her presence
like a thirst for salt, for my childhood river
with its island willows, silly music from the pleasure boat,
muddy places where we caught the little orange-silver fish
called *pumpkinseed.* It hardly had to do with her.
Longing, we say, because desire is full
of endless distances, I must have been the same to her.
But I remember so much, the way her hands dismantled bread,
the thing her father said that hurt her, what
she dreamed. There are moments when the body is as numinous
as words, days that are the good flesh continuing.
Such tenderness, those afternoons and evenings,
saying *blackberry, blackberry, blackberry.*

Human Wishes

HUMAN WISHES (1989) | THE APPLE TREES AT OLEMA (2010/2011)

This morning the sun rose over the garden wall and a rare blue sky leaped from east to west. Man is altogether desire, say the Upanishads. Worth anything, a blue sky, says Mr Acker, the Shelford gardener. Not altogether. In the end. Last night on television the ethnologist and the cameraman watched with hushed wonder while the chimpanzee carefully stripped a willow branch and inserted it into the anthill. He desired red ants. When they crawled slowly up the branch, he ate them, pinched between long fingers as the zoom lens enlarged his face. Sometimes he stopped to examine one, as if he were a judge at an ant beauty contest or God puzzled suddenly by the idea of suffering. There was an empty place in the universe where that branch wasn't and the chimp filled it, as my wife, finding no back on an old Welsh cupboard she had bought in Saffron Walden, imagined one there and imagined both the cupboard and the imagined back against a kitchen wall in Berkeley, and went into town looking for a few boards of eighteenth-century tongue-and-groove pine to fill that empty space. I stayed home to write, or rather stayed home and stared at a blank piece of paper, waiting for her to come back, thinking of the phrase tongue-and-groove, as if language were a kind of moral cloud chamber through which the world passed and from which it emerged charged with desire. The man in the shop in Cambridge said he didn't have any old pine, but when my wife went back after thinking about it to say she was sure she had seen some, the man found it. Right under his feet, which was puzzling. Mr Acker, hearing the story, explained. You know, he said, a lot of fiddling goes on in those places. The first time you went in, the governor was there, the second time he wasn't, so the chap sold you some scrap and he's four quid in pocket. No doubt he's having a good time now with his mates in the pub. Or he might have put it on the horses at Newmarket. He might parlay it into a fortune.

Ezra Pound's Proposition

TIME AND MATERIALS (2007) | THE APPLE TREES AT OLEMA (2010/2011)

Beauty is sexual, and sexuality
Is the fertility of the earth and the fertility
Of the earth is economics. Though he is no recommendation
For poets on the subject of finance,
I thought of him in the thick heat
Of the Bangkok night. Not more than fourteen, she saunters up to you
Outside the Shangri-la Hotel
And says, in plausible English,
'How about a party, big guy?'

Here is more or less how it works:
The World Bank arranges the credit and the dam
Floods three hundred villages, and the villagers find their way
To the city where their daughters melt into the teeming streets,
And the dam's great turbines, beautifully tooled
In Lund or Dresden or Detroit, financed
By Lazares Frères in Paris or the Morgan Bank in New York,
Enabled by judicious gifts from Bechtel of San Francisco
Or Halliburton of Houston to the local political elite,
Spun by the force of rushing water,
Have become hives of shimmering silver
And, down river, throw that bluish throb of light
Across her cheekbones and her lovely skin.

Privilege of Being

HUMAN WISHES (1989) | THE APPLE TREES AT OLEMA (2010/2011)

Many are making love. Up above, the angels
in the unshaken ether and crystal of human longing
are braiding one another's hair, which is strawberry blond
and the texture of cold rivers. They glance
down from time to time at the awkward ecstasy –
it must look to them like featherless birds
splashing in the spring puddle of a bed –
and then one woman, she is about to come,

282

peels back the man's shut eyelids and says,
look at me, and he does. Or is it the man
tugging the curtain rope in that dark theater?
Anyway, they do, they look at each other;
two beings with evolved eyes, rapacious,
startled, connected at the belly in an unbelievably sweet
lubricious glue, stare at each other,
and the angels are desolate. They hate it. They shudder pathetically
like lithographs of Victorian beggars
with perfect features and alabaster skin hawking rags
in the lewd alleys of the novel.
All of creation is offended by this distress.
It is like the keening sound the moon makes sometimes,
rising. The lovers especially cannot bear it,
it fills them with unspeakable sadness, so that
they close their eyes again and hold each other, each
feeling the mortal singularity of the body
they have enchanted out of death for an hour or so,
and one day, running at sunset, the woman says to the man,
I woke up feeling so sad this morning because I realised
that you could not, as much as I love you,
dear heart, cure my loneliness,
wherewith she touched his cheek to reassure him
that she did not mean to hurt him with this truth.
And the man is not hurt exactly,
he understands that life has limits, that people
die young, fail at love,
fail of their ambitions. He runs beside her, he thinks
of the sadness they have gasped and crooned their way out of
coming, clutching each other with old, invented
forms of grace and clumsy gratitude, ready
to be alone again, or dissatisfied, or merely
companionable like the couples on the summer beach
reading magazine articles about intimacy between the sexes
to themselves, and to each other,
and to the immense, illiterate, consoling angels.

A Story About the Body

HUMAN WISHES (1989) | THE APPLE TREES AT OLEMA (2010/2011)

The young composer, working that summer at an artist's colony, had watched her for a week. She was Japanese, a painter, almost sixty, and he thought he was in love with her. He loved her work, and her work was like the way she moved her body, used her hands, looked at him directly when she made amused and considered answers to his questions. One night, walking back from a concert, they came to her door and she turned to him and said, 'I think you would like to have me. I would like that too, but I must tell you that I have had a double mastectomy,' and when he didn't understand, 'I've lost both my breasts.' The radiance that he had carried around in his belly and chest cavity – like music – withered very quickly, and he made himself look at her when he said, 'I'm sorry. I don't think I could.' He walked back to his own cabin through the pines, and in the morning he found a small blue bowl on the porch outside his door. It looked to be full of rose petals, but he found when he picked it up that the rose petals were on top; the rest of the bowl – she must have swept them from the corners of her studio – was full of dead bees.

6 | JOHN HEGLEY

Filmed at home in London by Pamela Robertson-Pearce,
11 January 2014

Poet, comic, singer, songwriter and glasses-wearer, John Hegley
has captivated and devastated audiences all over the country, in
theatres and festivals, at gigs at the Edinburgh Festival, and with
numerous appearances on radio and television. Bloodaxe published
his *New & Selected Potatoes* in 2013, a greatest hits, best of gold-
en oldies compilation (with some new stuff) from 'Comedy's poet
laureate' (Independent). This shows the breadth of his appeal, with
seriously funny, cleverly comic poems on everything from love,
family, France, art and the sea to dogs, dads, gods, taxidermy,
carrots, spectacles and – of course – potatoes. For 'John Hegley is
to potatoes what Wordsworth has been to daffodils' (*Observer*). The
book includes work from a dozen collections, from *Visions of the
Bone Idol* (1984) to *Peace, Love & Potatoes* (Serpent's Tail, 2012),
plus a generous helping of *New Potatoes* (2013).

Born in Newington Green, London, in 1953, he grew up in
Luton and Bristol. After attending Bradford University he returned
to London and joined the community arts collective Interaction; he
has continued their interactive ethos ever since. During the early
1980s he was a regular performer at London's Comedy Store and
also recorded with The Popticians, including two sessions for John
Peel's BBC Radio One programme. He has worked regularly on
radio and television and remains a popular performer across the
UK and abroad, blending poetry, comedy and song. In 2012 he
was Writer in Residence at Keats House, in Hampstead, London.

No Hegley performance is ever the same. If he doesn't remem-
ber the words to a poem or song, he improvises, making up new
lines as he goes along. Thus when he treated us to two poems sung
with mandolin in our home recording session at Hegley Mansions
in Stoke Newington, a carved wooden dog lying on the table
became part of 'A Declaration of Need', and 'Say It Now' wasn't
said or sung exactly how it was/is printed in the book but how it
needed to be sung then, in that moment.

Some Resolutions

BEYOND OUR KENNEL (1998) | NEW & SELECTED POTATOES (2013)

Some resolve to give up on the smoking
some resolve to cut out all the meat
some resolve to get their trunks more regularly soaking
and some resolve to stop all the deceit.
Some resolve to solve financial problems
by taking up a life involving crime
and some resolve to give their ageing parents
more than just the fag end of their time.
Some resolve to have a hobby
some resolve to join a lobby
some resolve to clear up every jobbie
that their doggie does
and not go hosepipe crazy in the drought
and some of the aforesaid resolutions
dissolve before the Christmas tree's been put outside the door,
especially resolutions one and four.

Taking Out the 'in it' and Putting 'innit' In It

PEACE, LOVE & POTATOES (2012) | NEW & SELECTED POTATOES (2013)

This clock has still got a lot of mileage in it.
This clock is well-stocked with mileage, innit.

This society has still got deep class divisions in it.
Class wise, this society is still deeply divided, innit.

This potato has the possibility of the most delightful bloom in it.
This potato is bloomful of possible delight, innit.

This gap between the floorboards has got some little bits of old cheese in it.
Have you thought about doing some hoovering, innit.

Peace, Love and Potatoes

PEACE, LOVE & POTATOES (2012) | NEW & SELECTED POTATOES (2013)

Wed in 1944,
my mother
kept on peeling from the pick
of the potato sack,
with the occasional knack
of getting their jackets off
all in one piece.
Quite a trick. A quiet feat.
Like her and dad's feeling for each other:
uninterruptedly alive
and complete.

Glasses Good, Contact Lenses Bad

FIVE SUGARS PLEASE (1995) | NEW & SELECTED POTATOES (2013)

In the embrace of my glasses,
I openly accept my vulnerability
and affirm my acceptance of outside help.
As well as providing open acknowledgment
of the imperfection in my eyesight,
my glasses are a symbolic celebration
of the wider imperfection that is the human condition.
In contrast, contact lenses are a hiding of the fault;
they pretend the self-sufficiency of the individual
and minister unto the cult of stultifying normality.
They are that which should be cast out of your vision:
they are a denial of the self,
they are a denial of the other,
they are a betrayal of humanity.

I Wouldn't Say My Brother-in-Law Was Fat, Because He Is Quite Thin

THE BROTHER-IN-LAW AND OTHER ANIMALS (1986) | NEW & SELECTED POTATOES (2013)

He's as miserable as sin
but not as interesting.
He's as open as the pub is at twenty past four
in the morning,
and as welcome as an open sore
on your eye,
but he thinks he's great.
He isn't beautiful,
he's horrible.
He eats crisps in the cinema as a matter of principle.
In a previous incarnation he was a beer crate.
If he does you a favour then you know that you're in debt.
If you want someone to help you, he's a very outside bet.
If you were in a lifeboat and someone had to go
and my brother-in-law was there,
you wouldn't exactly need a ballot.
He's ten stone in his pyjamas
and that's ten stone overweight.
He's not exactly an artist
but they should hang him in the Tate.
He was an adult from the age of eight,
and whatever age he dies at it will be far too late.
I don't like him.

His Heart's in the Wrong Place, It Should Be in the Dustbin

THE BROTHER-IN-LAW AND OTHER ANIMALS (1986) | NEW & SELECTED POTATOES (2013)

The other night I went to see my brother-in-law for a chat.
After five minutes he went and sat in the garage.
After ten minutes he came back in saying
Here, John, are you staying the night?
If that's all right, I said.
Then he was gone,
up to the spare bedroom
to change the sheets,
to put the dirty ones back on.

A Dog and a Pigeon

THE BROTHER-IN-LAW AND OTHER ANIMALS (1986)

In a shocking flurry of feathers,
a seemingly pleasant dog attacked a pigeon in the park.
The badly-shaken owner tethered the attacker,
who began to bark.
If that dog can kill, I said,
you should let it finish the job.
No, said another witness,
it's not our job to interfere with nature.
The owner looked.
The pigeon bled.
It's your dog – your decision, I said.
I'll let him go, said the owner,
and then it's up to Fred.
So Fred is freed
and the bleeding bird
is shaken and left, but still not dead.
It's even worse now, the owner whimpers.
A brick on the head, then, I say.
I can't, says the owner, beginning to weep.
Can you – can you do it?
Then my brother-in-law comes over
with half a paving stone.
I'll do it, he says,
for ten quid.

Max

(likes to be with people but people don't like to be with Max)

VISIONS OF THE BONE IDOL (1984) | NEW & SELECTED POTATOES (2013)

Max is a dog with a problem.
The sort of problem it's a job to ignore.
The first time they all thought it was funny,
but not any more.
Picture the scene. This home-loving hound
is sleeping by the fire with the family round.
He wakes up and makes a little sound.

289

Little Albert gets it first,
he's nearest the ground.
Albert's mum gets wind of it
and she says open the door.
And whatever we've been feeding him,
I don't think we should give him no more.
Max does another one, like old kippers,
wakes up daddy in his fireside slippers.
Daddy wakes up and says, open the door.
Albert says, it's open dad, I did it when he did it before.
Then mum says, it's hard to relax with Max about.
Yesterday it happened while we were out in the car.
And it's a small car.
And granny, she was sick.
She's not used to it like we are.
Maybe we should swap him for a budgerigar.
Max is smelly,
he can spoil your telly.
But luckily
he's not and elephant.

A Declaration of Need

BEYOND OUR KENNEL (1998) | NEW & SELECTED POTATOES (2013)

I need you like a novel needs a plot.
I need you like the greedy need a lot.
I need you like a hovel needs a certain level of grottiness
to qualify.
I need you like acne cream needs spottiness.
Like a calendar needs a week.
Like a colander needs a leek.
Like people need to seek out what life on Mars is.
Like hospitals need vases.
I need you.
I need you like a zoo needs a giraffe.
I need you like a psycho needs a path.
I need you like King Arthur need a table
that was more than just a table for one.
I need you like a kiwi needs a fruit.
I need you like a wee wee needs a route out of the body.

I need you like Noddy needed little ears,
just for the contrast.
I need you like bone needs marrow.
I need you like straight needs narrow.
I need you like the broadest bean needs something else on the plate
before it can participate
in what you might describe as a decent meal.
I need you like a cappuccino needs froth.
I need you like a candle needs a moth
if it's going to burn its wings off.

Say It Now

DOG (2000) | NEW & SELECTED POTATOES (2013)

Don't hold on till it's time to go
before you let your emotional side show,
don't hold on until tomorrow,
don't hold on for another moment.
Saying I love you's not original,
but nor is never letting someone know.
Why leave it till it's almost time to say the last goodbye
before you get to say the big hello?
Don't hang on till the gate is closing,
don't hang on till the daisies grow.
Why wait until it's nearly far too late.
Why wait for another moment?
Do you feel at home with a heart that's hardly ever open?
Why keep it bottled up
when there's a genie hoping to get out,
to shout it out,
the thing you really should have spoken about by now.
Why keep it bottled up until that heart is broken?
Say it now, it's not a moment too soon,
say it now, don't wait until next July or June.
Say it now, don't wait for the next eclipse of the moment.
One wish: no feeling will dilly-dally.
One wish: no lagging with love to show.
One wish: don't be an emotional scallywag,
you silly so-and-so.

7 | RITA ANN HIGGINS

Filmed at home in Galway by Neil Astley,
26 April 2012

Rita Ann Higgins is a gutsy, anarchic chronicler of Irish lives and foibles who writes provocative and heart-warming poems of high jinx, jittery grief and telling social comment, mischievous and playful in their portrayal of feckless folk and outcasts, flirts and weasels, gasbags and scallywags. Giving readings throughout the country, and appearing on radio and TV shows, she became the laureate of the Irish dispossessed and disregarded, before as well as since the demise of the Celtic tiger, firstly through the poems from books included in *Throw in the Vowels: New & Selected Poems* (2005), and latterly with two Celtic zeitgeist collections, *Ireland Is Changing Mother* (2011) and *Tongulish* (2016).

Reviewing the first of those collections in *The Irish Times*, Fintan O'Toole wrote: 'It shouldn't be unusual to hear a smart, sassy, unabashed, female working-class voice in Irish writing. But it is. Higgins's achievement doesn't depend on that rarity value, but it is certainly amplified by it. Higgins is, quite consciously, an artistic outsider...a unique fusion of wry, deadpan humour on the one side and absolute sincerity on the other... She has made what is still the most direct and powerful statement of the class divide in Irish society... The boom years had no great effect on Higgins's voice, on her point of view or on her style. She had a manic linguistic energy long before the hysteria of the Tiger era quickened the pulse of the culture as a whole: Higgins could be regarded, in one of her guises, as Ireland's first rapper... Her political satire hasn't lost its edge, but it no longer reads as a cry in the wilderness... Now the bubble's burst, we're left with our real treasures, and Rita Ann Higgins is one of them.'

Born in 1955 in Galway, where she still lives, she left school at 14, and was in her late 20s when she started writing poetry. She has since published eleven books of poetry, five with Bloodaxe and six with her first publisher, Salmon Poetry. *Throw in the Vowels* was reissued in 2010 with an audio CD of her reading her poems. She has written several plays, and is is a member of Aosdána.

God-of-the-Hatch Man

(for Community Welfare Officers everywhere)

GOD ON THE MERVUE BUS (1986) | THROW IN THE VOWELS (2005)

Smoking and yes mamming,
snoozing in the fright
of his altered expression,
caused always by the afternoon.

Tepid water sipper, coffee glutton,
pencil pointer, negative nouner,
God-of-the-hatch man, hole in the wall.

We call religiously every Thursday,
like visiting the holy well,
only this well purports to give you things
instead of taking them away.

Things like scarlatina, schizophrenia,
migraine, hisgraine but never your grain,
lockjaw and wind, silicosis,
water on the knee, hunger in the walletness.

We queue for an hour or three,
we love to do this,
our idea of pleasure,
Then whatever-past what-past he likes,
he appears.

Tepid water sipper, coffee glutton,
pencil pointer, negative nouner,
God-of-the-hatch man, hole in the wall.

He gives us money and abuse,
the money has a price,
the abuse is free.

'Are you sure your husband isn't working?'
'Are you sure grumbling granny is quite dead?'
'Are you sure you're not claiming for de Valera?'
'Are you sure you count six heads in every bed?'

Hummer of Andy Williams' tunes,
most talked about man in the waiting-room,
tapper of the pencil on the big brown desk.

God-of-the-hatch man, hole in the wall.
God-of-the-hatch man, hole in the wall.

The Did-You-Come-Yets of the Western World

WITCH IN THE BUSHES (1988) | THROW IN THE VOWELS (2005)

When he says to you:
You look so beautiful
you smell so nice –
how I've missed you –
and did you come yet?

It means nothing,
and he is smaller
than a mouse's fart.

Don't listen to him…
Go to Annaghdown Pier
with your father's rod.
Don't necessarily hold out
for the biggest one;
oftentimes the biggest ones
are the smallest in the end.

Bring them all home,
but not together.
One by one is the trick;
avoid red herrings and scandal.

Maybe you could take two
on the shortest day of the year.
Time is the cheater here
not you, so don't worry.

Many will bite the usual bait;
they will talk their slippery way
through fine clothes and expensive perfume,
fishing up your independence.

These are
the did-you-come-yets of the western world,
the feather and fin rufflers.
Pity for them they have no wisdom.

Others will bite at any bait.
Maggot, suspender, or dead worm.
Throw them to the sharks.

In time one will crawl
out from under thigh-land.
Although drowning he will say,
'Woman I am terrified, why is this house
shaking?'

And you'll know he's the one.

Some People

(for Eoin)

WITCH IN THE BUSHES (1988) | THROW IN THE VOWELS (2005)

Some people know what it's like,

to be called a cunt in front of their children
to be short for the rent
to be short for the light
to be short for school books
to wait in Community Welfare waiting-rooms full of smoke
to wait two years to have a tooth looked at
to wait another two years to have a tooth out (the same tooth)
to be half strangled by your varicose veins, but you're
198th on the list
to talk into a banana on a jobsearch scheme
to talk into a banana in a jobsearch dream

to be out of work
to be out of money
to be out of fashion
to be out of friends
to be in for the Vincent de Paul man
to be in space for the milk man
(sorry, mammy isn't in today she's gone to Mars for the weekend)
to be in Puerto Rico this week for the blanket man
to be in Puerto Rico next week for the blanket man
to be dead for the coal man
(sorry, mammy passed away in her sleep, overdose of coal
in the teapot)
to be in hospital unconscious for the rent man
(St Judes ward 4th floor)
to be second-hand
to be second-class
to be no class
to be looked down on
to be walked on
to be pissed on
to be shat on

and other people don't.

An Awful Racket

AN AWFUL RACKET (2001) | THROW IN THE VOWELS (2005)

In the winter
we don't light a fire everyday,
three days a week max
always on a Saturday night though.

Me and the kids sit around the fire
and sing songs, the twins clap,
they play Baker's Man
we have great craic,
except for Justin
I nearly had him in a taxi
that's why we called him Justin.

He's fourteen now, he's always angry.
'What good is looking into the fire like spas,
what's fuckin wrong with ye?' he says.

Then all hell breaks loose.
I don't allow fowl language,
I didn't bring them up like that,
then the twins start bawling
and I can't shut them up.
The eldest starts first,
he was born ten seconds before Paul.
I say to Peter, 'If you don't shut that
fucking cake hole, I'll throttle ya.'
Then Paul starts,
he has lungs like a broken exhaust.

Last year when things
were a bit slack
we burned their father's wardrobe.
We split up two years ago,
we parted on amiable grounds though.
I couldn't aim
And he couldn't miss.

The kids thought it was a howl
me taking a hatchet to the wardrobe
on Christmas Day.
There was nothing much in it anyway,
only a couple of his shirts
I'd forgotten to put in the mincer,
old papers where the cat had kittens
and a banjaxed tennis racket.

That racket caused more trouble;
one day no one wanted it,
the next day they all wanted it.
I ended up throwing it on the fire.

It crackled like lard.

Grandchildren

THROW IN THE VOWELS (2005)

It's not just feasible at the moment
one daughter tells me.
What with Seamus still robbing banks
and ramming garda vans when he gets emotional
on a fish-free Friday in February.

Maybe the other daughter could deliver.
She thinks not, not at the moment anyway
while Thomas still has a few tattoos to get,
to cover any remaining signs that might link him
with the rest of us.

Just now a B52 bomber flies over
on its way from Shannon
to make a gulf in some nation's genealogy.

The shadow it places on all our notions is crystal clear
and for a split of a second helping
it juxtaposes the pecking order.
Now bank robbers and tattooers
have as much or as little standing
as popes and princes
and grandchildren become another lonely utterance
impossible to pronounce.

Tongued and Grooved

(for C)

IRELAND IS CHANGING MOTHER (2011)

The look
was longing
was lustful
was lasting.

The kiss
was luscious
was lazy
was luptuous.

She staggered away
was woozy
was wanton
was wet.

It's Platonic

PHILOMENA'S REVENGE (1992) | THROW IN THE VOWELS (2005)

Platonic my eye,

I yearn
for the fullness
of your tongue
making me
burst forth
pleasure after pleasure
after dark,

soaking all my dreams.

He Was No Lazarus

(for Niall MacMonagle)

IRELAND IS CHANGING MOTHER (2011)

In the newsagents cum bric-à-brac
days were spent gawking out
hoping the girls would come in for a chat
or any old gossip that would help throttle
a jaded afternoon.

I smoked nearly as many cigarettes as I sold
and what I didn't sell, I gave away.
The Shantalla gang came in ones and twos
'give us a fag loveen' and I'd give them twenty.

Once I gave Elvis Kelly a yo-yo
to pass the time until he went to England.
I'll give you one long snake kiss for it, he said.
They all went to England on the half three out of Galway.
We were like banshees crying over them
then we lived for the S.W.A.L.K. letters.

Harlesden got him and plenty more besides;
he drowned his sorrows in The Green Man.
A right yo-yo, he fell under his own weight and broke his skull.
A maverick blood vessel made the same noise as a cork,
pop went his flash lights and he all fell down.

When he went down he stayed down, ton of bricks style,
he was no Lazarus, no shape-changing Greek or Roman God
no comic book super villain who could say,
Abra Kadabra now you see me now you don't.

He was no Zossima either, though he wore the brown
scapular of our lady of Mount Carmel around his neck.
He came home in a box, spartan no frills
just a shiny plate with his name, his date of birth.

I was one long snake kiss out of pocket.

No One Mentioned the Roofer

(for Pat Mackey)

IRELAND IS CHANGING MOTHER (2011)

We met the Minister,
we gave him buns, we admired his suit.
The band played, we all clapped.

No one mentioned the roofer;
whose overtime was cut
whose under time was cut
whose fringe was cut
whose shoelaces were cut
whose job was lost.

We searched for his job
but it had disappeared.
One of us should have said:

Hey Minister, we like your suit
have a bun, where are our jobs?
But there was no point,
he was here on a bun eating session
not a job finding session.

His hands were tied.
His tongue a marshmallow.

Ireland Is Changing Mother

IRELAND IS CHANGING MOTHER (2011)

Don't throw out the loaves
with the dishes mother.
It's not the double-takes so much
it's that they take you by the double.
And where have all the Nellys gone
and all the Missus Kellys gone?
You might have had
the cleanest step on your street

301

but so what mother,
nowadays it's not the step
but the mile that matters.

Meanwhile the Bally Bane Taliban
are battling it out over that football.
They will bring the local yokels
to a deeper meaning of over the barring it.
And then some scarring will occur –
as in cracked skull for your troubles.
They don't just integrate, they *limp-pa-grate*,
your sons are shrinking mother.

Before this mother,
your sons were Gods of that powerful thing.
Gods of the apron string.
They could eat a horse and they often did,
with your help mother.
Even Tim who has a black belt in sleepwalking
and border lining couldn't torch a cigarette,
much less the wet haystack of desire,
even he can see, Ireland is changing mother.
Listen to black belt Tim mother.

When they breeze onto the pitch
like some Namibian Gods
the local girls wet themselves.
They say in a hurry, O-Ma-God, O-Ma-God!
Not good for your sons mother,
who claim to have invented everything
from the earwig to the *sliothar*.
They were used to seizing Cynthia's hips
looking into her eyes and saying
I'm Johnny come lately, love me.

Now the Namibian Gods and the Bally Bane Taliban
are bringing the local yokels
to their menacing senses
and scoring more goals than Cú Chulainn.
Ireland is changing mother
tell yourself, tell your sons.

sliothar: hurling ball

8 | TONY HOAGLAND

Filmed at home in Wellfleet, Cape Cod, USA,
by Pamela Robertson-Pearce, 26 August 2008

Tony Hoagland's zany poems poke and provoke at the same time as they entertain and delight. He is American poetry's hilarious 'high priest of irony', a wisecracker and a risktaker whose disarming humour, self-scathing and tenderness are all fuelled by an aggressive moral intelligence. He pushes the poem not just to its limits but over the edge.

Bloodaxe published his first UK edition in 2005, *What Narcissism Means to Me*, a selection drawing on three collections, *Sweet Ruin* (1992), *Donkey Gospel* (1998) and *What Narcissism Means to Me* (2003). He has since produced two later collections, *Unincorporated Persons in the Late Honda Dynasty* (2010) and *Application for Release from the Dream* (2015/2016). Born in 1953 in Fort Bragg, North Carolina, he grew up on various military bases throughout the South where his father was stationed as an army doctor. He now teaches at the University of Houston, and lives in Santa Fe, New Mexico. We filmed him when he was still on Cape Cod.

Henry Shukman said of him (*Poetry London*) that 'he belongs to that wagon-circle of American poets who believe in a "common reader"... Hoagland is a poet of a ragged, half-satirical, half-lyrical intensity. If Billy Collins is Updike, Hoagland is Salinger, or perhaps Holden Caulfield...making us think we know the ground we are on, then showing us that we don't... For me, he not only pulls the rug from under my feet when it comes to the moral complacencies and platitudes that I don't notice I live by, he does the same with my given poetic certainties.'

In the film, the ending of 'Romantic Moment' is different from the published text: 'Then she suggests that it is time for us to / do something personal, hidden and human.' When giving readings now, Hoagland prefers his character to say it's time 'to get some ice cream cones and eat them', just as he did when reading to us from the original manuscript of what was to become *Unincorporated Persons*. The pre-publication version he reads includes another phrase revised for book publication, 'the mock orange' in the third line becoming 'the orange trees'. He also reads the manuscript version of another poem from that collection, which then began: '"Poor Britney Spears" / is not the beginning of a sentence / you hear often uttered in my household', and ends 'in a tired voice', rather than 'in a quiet way'.

Lawrence

DONKEY GOSPEL (1998) | WHAT NARCISSISM MEANS TO ME (2005)

On two occasions in the past twelve months
I have failed, when someone at a party
spoke of him with a dismissive scorn,
to stand up for D.H. Lawrence,

a man who burned like an acetylene torch
from one end to the other of his life.
These individuals, whose relationship to literature
is approximately that of a tree shredder

to stands of old-growth forest,
these people leaned back in their chairs,
bellies full of dry white wine and the ova of some foreign fish,
and casually dropped his name

the way that pygmies with their little poison spears
strut around the carcass of a fallen elephant.
'O Elephant,' they say,
'you are not so big and brave today!'

It's a bad day when people speak of their superiors
with a contempt they haven't earned,
and it's a sorry thing when certain other people

don't defend the great dead ones
who have opened up the world before them.
And though, in the catalogue of my betrayals,
this is a fairly minor entry,

I resolve, if the occasion should recur,
to uncheck my tongue and say, 'I love the spectacle
of maggots condescending to a corpse,'
or, 'You should be so lucky in your brainy, bloodless life

as to deserve to lift
just one of D.H. Lawrence's urine samples
to your arid psychobiographic
theory-tainted lips.'

304

Or maybe I'll just take the shortcut
between the spirit and the flesh,
and punch someone in the face,
because human beings haven't come that far

in their effort to subdue the body,
and we still walk around like zombies
in our dying, burning world,
able to do little more

than fight, and fuck, and crow:
something Lawrence wrote about
in such a manner
as to make us seem magnificent.

Benevolence

DONKEY GOSPEL (1998) | WHAT NARCISSISM MEANS TO ME (2005)

When my father dies and comes back as a dog,
I already know what his favorite sound will be:
the soft, almost inaudible gasp
as the rubber lips of the refrigerator door
unstick, followed by that arctic

exhalation of cold air;
then the cracking of the ice-cube tray above the sink
and the quiet *ching* the cubes make
when dropped into a glass.

Unable to pronounce the name of his favorite drink, or to express
his preference for single malt,
he will utter one sharp bark
and point the wet black arrow of his nose
imperatively up
at the bottle on the shelf,

then seat himself before me,
trembling, expectant, water pouring
down the long pink dangle of his tongue

as the memory of pleasure from his former life
shakes him like a tail.

What I'll remember as I tower over him,
holding a dripping, whiskey-flavored cube
above his open mouth,
relishing the power rushing through my veins
the way it rushed through his,

what I'll remember as I stand there
is the hundred clever tricks
I taught myself to please him,
and for how long I mistakenly believed
that it was love he held concealed in his closed hand.

Romantic Moment

UNINCORPORATED PERSONS IN THE LATE HONDA DYNASTY (2010)

After seeing the nature documentary we walk down Canyon Road,
into the plaza of art galleries and high end clothing stores

where the orange trees are fragrant in the summer night
and the smooth adobe walls glow fleshlike in the dark.

It is just our second date, and we sit down on a bench,
holding hands, not looking at each other,

and if I were a bull penguin right now I would lean over
and vomit softly into the mouth of my beloved

and if I were a peacock I'd flex my gluteal muscles to
erect and spread the quills of my Cinemax tail.

If she were a female walkingstick bug she might
insert her hypodermic proboscis delicately into my neck

and inject me with a rich hormonal sedative
before attaching her egg sac to my thoracic undercarriage,

and if I were a young chimpanzee I would break off a nearby tree limb
and smash all the windows in the plaza jewelry stores.

And if she was a Brazilian leopard frog she would wrap her impressive
tongue three times around my right thigh and

pummel me lightly against the surface of our pond
and I would know her feelings were sincere.

Instead we sit awhile in silence, until
she remarks that in the relative context of tortoises and iguanas,

human males seem to be actually rather expressive.
And I say that female crocodiles really don't receive

enough credit for their gentleness.
Then she suggests that it is time for us to go

to get some ice cream cones and eat them.

'Poor Britney Spears'

UNINCORPORATED PERSONS IN THE LATE HONDA DYNASTY (2010)

is not a sentence I expected
to utter in this lifetime.

If *she* wants to make a career comeback,
so her agent gets a spot on the MTV awards show
but she can't lose the weight beforehand

so looks a little chubby in a spangled bikini
before millions of fanged, spiteful fans and enemies
and gets a little drunk beforehand
so misses a step in the dance routine,

making her look, one critic says,
like a 'comatose piglet',

well, it wasn't by accident, was it?
That she wandered into the late-twentieth-century glitterati party
of striptease American celebrity?

First we made her into an object of desire,
then into an object of contempt,
now we want to turn her into an object of compassion?

Are you sure we know what the hell we're doing?

Is she a kind of voodoo doll
onto whom we project
our vicarious fantasies of triumph and humiliation?

Is she a pink, life-size piece of chewing gum
full of non-FDA approved additives
engineered by the mad scientists
of the mainstream dream machine?

Or is she nothing less than a gladiatrix
who strolls into the coliseum
full of blinding lights and tigers

with naught but her slim javelin of talent
and recklessly little protective clothing?

Oh my adorable little monkey,
prancing for your candy,

with one of my voices I shout, 'Jump, jump, you little whore!'
With another I say,

in a tired voice that turns down the lights,
'Put on some clothes and go home, Sweetheart.'

9 | MATTHEW HOLLIS

Filmed by Pamela Robertson-Pearce at Highgreen Manor,
Tarset, Northumberland, 28 July 2007

The poems of Matthew Hollis's debut collection *Ground Water* (2004) immerse us in the undercurrents of our lives. Love and loss are buoyed by a house full of milk, an orchard underwater, the laws of walking on water. Rainwater, floodwater, flux – the liquid landscapes which shift relentlessly through the book – threaten and comfort by turns. *Ground Water* is brimming with courage in adversity as well as the promise of renewal, culminating in a powerful sequence about a father's struggle with terminal illness.

Born in 1971 in Norwich, he now lives in London and is Poetry Editor at Faber & Faber. He won an Eric Gregory Award in 1999. He is co-editor of *101 Poems Against War* (Faber, 2003) and *Strong Words: Modern Poets on Modern Poetry* (Bloodaxe Books, 2000), and editor of the *Selected Poems of Edward Thomas* (Faber, 2011). *Ground Water* was shortlisted for the Guardian First Book Award (the first time for a poetry book), the Whitbread Poetry Award and the Forward Prize for Best First Collection. His beautifully written and expertly researched biography, *Now All Roads Lead to France: The Last Years of Edward Thomas* (Faber, 2011), won the Costa Biography Award, the H.W. Fisher Biography Award and a Royal Society of Literature Jerwood Award for Non-Fiction, and was BBC Radio 4 Book of the Week and *Sunday Times* Biography of the Year. In 2016 he published two limited letterpress and handmade pamphlets, *Stones* (Incline Press) and *East* (Clutag Press).

He was teaching a residential poetry course with Anthony Dunn for Highgreen Arts next door to Bloodaxe in the summer of 2007 when we managed to grab him during a break in proceedings to read us the four poems included on the film.

Wintering

GROUND WATER (2004)

If I close my eyes I can picture him
flitting the hedgerow for splints
or a rib of wood to kindle the fire,

or reading the snow for whatever
it was that came out of the trees
and circled the house in the night;

if I listen I can hear him out
in the kitchen, scudding potatoes,
calling the cat in; if I breathe

I can smell the ghost of a fire,
a burning of leaves that would fizz
in the mizzle before snow.

There is in this house now
a stillness of cat fur and boxes,
of photographs, paperbacks, waste-

paper baskets; a lifetime
of things that I've come here
to winter or to burn.

There is in this world one snow fall.
Everything else is just weather.

The Fielder

(for Kim Walwyn)

GROUND WATER (2004)

The day is late, later than the sun.
He tastes the dusk of things and eases down,
and feels the shade set in across the yard.
He never thought there'd be so much undone,

so much in need of planing: the haugh unmown
with its fist of bracken, the splinting of the cattle bar,
the half-attended paddock wall
scribbled with blackthorn and broke-wool.

Perhaps he could have turned the plough for one last till,
be sure, or surer, of where the seeding fell.
But then it's not the ply that counts, but the depth of furrow,
knowing the take was deep and real, knowing the change was made.
And field by field the brown hills harvest yellow.
And few of us will touch the landscape in that way.

And let us say

(for Emma McKiernan, on her birth, 8/9/99)
GROUND WATER (2004)

That if the linen flapped too loud
The washing line was taken down

And if a shopdoor bell was rung
Its tongue was held with cotton thumbs

And if a milkfloat tattled by
It was flagged down and held aside

And should the rivers drown us out
We had them dammed at every mouth

And coughed our engines gently off
And wrapped our tyres in woollen socks

And sat awhile on silent roads
Or dawdled home in slippered shoes

And did not sound but held our tongues
And watched our watches stop, and startle on.

The Sour House

GROUND WATER (2004)

Through the frost-hole of the passenger window
your tenant's house is ringed in winter.
He's turning the snow from the path

that lay in the night. He can far less
handle a spade than you, dipping the lug
as though the shovel itself was unbalanced.

And what you found inside you would not forget:
room on room of bottled milk, gagging
the stairwell, the hallway, bookshelves,

like a stumbled-on ice world, a sweep of winter.
For years he maintained the world his parents left,
taking in milk he never drank. Evenings spent out

in the yard, piecing apart the Ford his father drove –
sill-lines, cogwheels, dippers fanned round him,
working each burr to a touch.

For years I coloured your world in hues
you didn't recognise; never your island,
always your skerry – 'unable to see

the romance of the thing for the thing itself'.
That, airing his house, the rancour
would catch as far as the common;

and what you found in the garage was scrap:
not the showpiece I'd imagined but the pin
pulled out, a car returned to the sum of its parts.

Driving now through the cloughs at dusk
I am struck by the things *I* can't let go;
that some things weal on the body like braille –

the sight of you just home from the milk-house
matted and choking, your raw nose streaming,
gutting the fridge in two clean strokes –
like a swimmer striking out for land.

312

10 | ESTHER JANSMA

Filmed by Neil Astley in Ledbury, 5 July 2011

Esther Jansma is a leading Dutch poet as well as an influential archaeologist. Interweaving a dazzling variety of strands, her poetry explores time and memory, past and present, death, loss, decay and legacy, and yet draws fresh power from these perennial themes because she writes from two opposite but complementary viewpoints.

As an archaeologist she refined a technique for establishing the age of wooden artefacts from growth-rings in the wood which could be applied to timber from the Netherlands. Lending a voice to the past, making time visible in all its aspects, is also what she does in her poetry. The philosophical is earthed in the everyday, the mythic intertwines with the mundane, the word with the world.

In her early work, the voices of the past are heard from bewildering years: as a child, the death of a father, then as a mother, the loss of a child ('That she was there and then no more...'). Her later poetry is less personal but more compelling as her poetic universe expands, embracing the whole world.

Born in 1958 in Amsterdam, she studied philosophy at the University of Amsterdam, obtaining her doctorate for research in dendrochronology. Now a professor in Dendrochronology and Palaeo-Ecology at Utrecht University, she is also senior researcher at the Cultural Heritage Agency of the Netherlands and Director of the Netherlands Centre for Dendrochronology/ RING Foundation.

In 2004 she took part in the Writing on the Wall project, a five-year international programme involving writers from the north of England, Scotland and the countries which originally garrisoned Hadrian's Wall. Translated by Francis R. Jones, *What It Is: Selected Poems* (Bloodaxe Books, 2008) was the first English translation of her work, drawing on all the collections she had published in the Netherlands and including poems inspired by parts of the Wall where Friesian and Schelt Auxiliaries were stationed.

She reads her poems in Dutch and in Jones's English translation in the film, made during her visit to Ledbury Poetry Festival in 2011. Her introductions help illuminate the background to many of the poems, including an explanation of how the hare (*haas*) in the poem 'Uitzicht' became a swift in English.

The Dutch texts are from *Altijd vandaag* (De Arbeiderspers, 2006).

Schrödingers vangst

WAAIGAT (1993) | ALTIJD VANDAAG (2006)

Lang is de zeemeermin in het ruisende
ruim onder de wereld van de visser
in een onzichtbaar net van kansen
niet verstrikt, maar wordt ze waar.

Wat doet ze bij haar ontstaan?
Weet ze van het naderend einde en
slaat ze haar staart en koralen nagels
vergeefs in haar wereld van water?

Hoe bang is ze nu het water meegeeft?

De visser keert zijn boot. 'Deze avond
is anders. Zie hoe de wolken als handen
over de horizon hangen, het laatste
zonlicht door die vingers scheert.
Vreemd stil is het.'

'Dat ze er was en toen niet meer...'

BLOEM, STEEN (1990) | ALTIJD VANDAAG (2006)

Dat ze er was en toen niet meer
en wat daartussen ligt – verhalen
ontstaan uit hoe we ons herhalen
die nacht door, en weer –

zoals lamplicht takken kaal
in kringen legt, legt taal ons
om niets – het gaat maar door,
hoofd aan hoofd, voet aan voet,
geluiden in een broze hoepel.

Schrödinger's catch

BLOWHOLE (1993) | WHAT IT IS (2008)

The mermaid in the gurgling hold
below the fisherman's world
is no longer tangled in invisible
nets of chance, but turning true.

What does she do as she comes into being?
Does she know of the approaching end
and beat her tail and claw her coral nails
to no avail in her world of water?

How afraid is she now the waters give way?

The fisherman turns his boat. 'This evening's
different. See those clouds dangling
like hands above the horizon, the last of
the sunlight flitting between those fingers.
It's strangely still.'

'That she was there and then no more...'

FLOWER, STONE (1990) | WHAT IT IS (2008)

That she was there and then no more
and what lies in between – tales
take hold as we retell the told
all through that night, and again –

as streetlight lays branches bare
in rings, language lays us out
round nothing – never letting up,
head to head, foot to foot,
sounds in a flimsy hoop.

Uitzicht

HIER IS DE TIJD (1998) | ALTIJD VANDAAG (2006)

Zoals wijd bijna
in weiland past,
de koe woont in
zijn koele manieren
van grazen, breekt

uit de taal de haas:
frontaal, waarna
het staartje t
zich uit het zicht
dat dit gedicht is
haast.

Archeologie

HIER IS DE TIJD (1998) | ALTIJD VANDAAG (2006)

Als we ons dan toch moeten kleden
tegen kou bijvoorbeeld of in naam van iets
in resten van dit of dat verleden
verhalen en geheugensteuntjes die niets

vertellen dan dat we er al waren
in de tijd die bestond voor dit heden –
als wij onszelf alleen in het nu kunnen bewaren
door onszelf voortdurend uit te vinden in het nu

dan liefst eenvoudig, aan de hand van kleding.
Je zit aan tafel. Opeens zie je hoe iemand
ijs overstak, hoe hem de kou beving

of een ander einde en je zegt: kijk,
hier heb je zijn schoenen, leren mantel, wanten.
'Waar is de tijd? Hier is de tijd.'

Swift

TIME IS HERE (1998) | WHAT IT IS (2008)

The way that grand
goes round grassland
and cow lies
in her cowl of flies,
swiftwings flit with a sigh

into sight: then, swifter
than the telling, a tail
ineffably
light in flight v-
eers out of this
verse.

Archaeology

TIME IS HERE (1998) | WHAT IT IS (2008)

If we have to dress, when all is said at last
against the cold or in something's name
in what remains of this or another past
tales and aides-memoire which simply claim

that we were here and nothing more
in time which existed before today –
if we can only stay in this now for sure
by constantly inventing ourselves in this now

let's keep it simple, by using clothes.
You sit at table. You suddenly see
someone crossing ice, and how the cold

or some other end overcame him and you say: look,
here you have his mittens, shoes, and leather cloak.
'Where is time? Time is here.'

Aanwezigheid

VAN *Hebben*

DAKRUITERS (2000) | ALTIJD VANDAAG (2006)

Ik ben uitgevraagd. Vanaf nu ga ik dingen weten.
Vanaf nu is zij geen roos maar julia

en is haar slaap niet de slaap van de dingen.
Vanaf nu kan zij gekend worden, ga ik heel lang

met haar in een huis wonen en haar eten geven,
leer ik haar praten en vertelt zij me hoe het is

terwijl ze steeds verandert. Steeds gebruikt ze andere woorden.
Soms knip ik haar haren. Dan verandert haar hoofd.

Zelf verander ik zo langzaam dat zij niets merkt,
wanneer zij groot is

ben ik altijd al oud en blij geweest.

Alles is nieuw

ALLES IS NIEUW (2005) | ALTIJD VANDAAG (2006)

Wat zou gebeuren was er altijd al, volmaakt
gespeld door een beker die stukviel
scherven waarin de afdrukken van duimen
het rilschrift van naalddunne takjes staan.

Het is geen verhaal dat wij maakten maar iets
wat er was en er is in de sporen van greppels
en staanders en lang gedoofd houtvuur.
Het hoefde alleen maar gevonden te worden.

iemand moest ernaar kijken en zeggen: wat is het
dit is het, en daar was het, een huis met een haard-
plaats, mensen die daar zoals altijd en altijd
voor het eerst in het nu zichzelf zijn en zitten

Presence

FROM *Having*

SKYLIGHTS (2000) | WHAT IT IS (2008)

I'm done with questions. From now on I'm going
to know things. From now on she is not rose but julia

and her sleep is not the sleep of things.
From now on she can be known, I'm going to live

a long long time with her in a house and feed her,
I'll teach her to speak and she will tell me how it is

while she keeps changing. She keeps using different words.
Sometimes I cut her hair. Then her head changes.

As for me, I change so slowly she won't notice.
When she's grown-up

I'll always have been old and happy.

Everything is new

EVERYTHING IS NEW (2005) | WHAT IT IS (2008)

What would happen was always there, perfectly
spelt by a cup which shattered, shards
marked with the imprints of thumbs
the shiver-script of pinsharp twigs.

It's not a tale we made up but something
that was here and is here in the traces of ditches
and posts and wood fires long gone cold.
It just needed finding, that's all.

Someone had to look at it and say: what is it
it's this, and there it was, a house with a hearth
people as ever and ever being themselves
the first time in this now and sitting

met warme handen die een beker vasthouden
bij het vuur en ze praten en de tiktak van regen
is een cirkel geluid en het deert niet, de nacht
de onzichtbare wolken, de stilte van alles

wat buiten in slaap is of wacht op de dag
zijn het dak en de wanden om het dak en de muren
van het huis dat al oud is maar nieuw
want opnieuw in dit heden gevonden.

De verzamelaar

ALLES IS NIEUW (2005) | ALTIJD VANDAAG (2006)

Dit is niet op zolder gevonden maar in de grond
van de zaak hetzelfde als spullen die resten
na een moderne dood, verkommerd slap afval
in de handen van de erfgenaam, ik, verzamelaar.

Het is geen verlangen naar iets hogers dat me drijft
naar de diepte, het is klein en schaamteloos, het is kleertjes
die de vuilnisman liet liggen – oneffen plaveisel geworden,
verregend – oprapen om te weten hoe het was.

Het is rotzooien, het verdwijnen achterna, de mensen
van vroeger, brokjes van het denken, volgordes
die tot handelen leidden – het schaven van hout

het knippen van kleertjes – momenten, lang geleden
die er echt zijn geweest en die echt zijn
verdwenen tot iemand ze vasthoudt, terugleest.

Original poems in Dutch from *Altijd vandaag* (Uitgeverij De Arbeiderspers, 2006)

with warm hands which clasp a cup
by the fire and talking and the tick-tick of rain
is a circle of sound and nothing matters, the night
the invisible clouds, the silence of all

outside that's sleeping or waiting for day
are the roof and the walls round the roof
and the bricks of the house that is already old
but new, being found again today.

The collector

EVERYTHING IS NEW (2005) | WHAT IT IS (2008)

This was not found in some attic but down
at rock bottom like things left after
a modern death, limp neglected tat
in the hands of the heir, myself, collector.

What drives me into the depths is not a desire for
something higher, it's little and insolent, picking up
clothes the dustman left behind – turned to uneven
paving, rain-stained – to know what it was like.

It's rummaging after what vanishes, people
of the past, bits of thinking, sequences
which led to action – the planing of wood

the cutting out of little clothes – moments, long ago
which really were and which really are
vanished till someone holds them, reads them back.

All poems translated from the Dutch by Francis R. Jones

11 | JENNY JOSEPH

Filmed by Pamela Robertson-Pearce in Ledbury, 8 July 2008

Jenny Joseph's poems explore the duality of existence, a track that runs through all her work, whether for children or adults, in poetry or prose. She views them as attempts to present 'how things work' at the core, at the edge.

Robert Nye said that she 'writes poems full of mist and reason, poems strange in what they say but plain in the way they say it, poems rooted in an English tradition of passionate but quiet exactness...careful craftsmanship, an honest exploration of the human heart, and statement after statement that nags at the memory' (*The Times*).

She is best-known for her poem 'Warning', a dramatic monologue in which a young woman talks of her fantasies of old age, voted Britain's favourite modern poem in a BBC poll in 2006. The second line of this poem inspired the formation of America's Red Hat Society, one of the largest women's social groups in the world (which has over 70,000 members and almost 24,000 chapters in the US and 25 other countries) and encourages fun, friendship, freedom and fulfilment.

Born in Birmingham in 1932, she was first published by John Lehmann in the 1950s. She lived in London for many years and then for much of her life in Gloucestershire before moving to Swansea. Her first book of poems, *The Unlooked-for Season* (1960), won her an Eric Gregory Award, and she won a Cholmondeley Award for her second collection, *Rose in the Afternoon* (1974). Two further collections followed from Secker & Warburg, *The Thinking Heart* (1978) and *Beyond Descartes* (1983). Her *Selected Poems* was published by Bloodaxe Books in 1992, drawing on these four books. Her other books include four other titles from Bloodaxe: *Persephone* (1986), *Ghosts and other company* (1995), *Extended Similes* (1997), and *Extreme of things* (2006).

Pamela filmed her reading a set of poems she had scripted for the occasion before her reading at Ledbury Poetry Festival in 2008.

from Fables

ROSE IN THE AFTERNOON (1974) | SELECTED POEMS (1992)

1

The gentleman that my black hen lays eggs for
Has diamond links joining impeccable cuffs
And a suit and a voice and a smile of exquisite finish,
But has never been known to express a liking for eggs –
Which is all that my black hen can lay for him.

9

Stay close, little tortoise, dig in.
Put on the coffee pot fourteen times a day
Day and night intermingled with much slow pottering.
Put your nose out rarely

So that in the spring
There will be someone calm to note the spot
Where my beautiful friend the hare
Died galloping across the frozen hills.
Stay close, little tortoise, stay alive,
Collect your strength, drip, drip, through months, in a phial,
To sing a dirge for our beautiful friend the hare.

Another Story of Hare and Tortoise

ALL THE THINGS I SEE (2000) | EXTREME OF THINGS (2006)

There was something I forgot to tell you when I told you the story
Of the hare and the tortoise. You remember,
How the one animal, splendid, desirable, eager
Life tingling in its limbs, was admired by all
And how the other
Arrived when nobody was actually looking.

They said it was his desire to win – obstinacy,
Nobody else was there. He said he got there.
We were all gathered round the starry hare
Succouring his weakness.
(His faint was only a lapse; he was a splendid runner).

But even if it's true what tortoise said
We were not there to greet him at his win.
The world had gone elsewhere
We wanted to be with hare.

The loneliness of saying 'I won' to nothing but emptiness!
He wasn't liked. He worked for what he got
And always so damned fair.
It was much more fun with hare.

Patriotic poem against nationalism
for a newborn child
GHOSTS AND OTHER COMPANY (1995)

1

Is it too bright for you, darling?
Under the yews in the churchyard
Inland from the town, into the hills, up the lanes
It is cool and green-shadowed and quiet;   and there

LYETH the Bodi of Ann David
Who died the 21st January 1784
Aged one month – so born just about Christmas.
And you are two days, born into flaming June.

2

Many the infant children buried here
Beneath elaborate tiles, and graved slate
Polished hard and clean with the lettering
As clear as the day it was done.

Memorials, important, memories solid
For each little scrap of throwaway life
Slate thick and heavy as marble, but dimmer
And, absorbing the light, seeming more part of the earth.
The hillside sleeps in the morning sun, in the years
Of sleep that has come to this place.
Beyond the shaded porch-path, out in the field
Light pours unwinking on the bright new graves.

3

'Genth' I shall call you, who have no Welsh in you.
Little Welsh girl, little scrap born in Wales.
We have no Welsh in us, and I no drop of Celtic.
But I more than you likely to learn these stones
And I, for no reason, more likely to learn this language.

4

To the traveller
Any place they come to can be home
Even for a day or two
And any language learnt can be our own
For as long as we care to use it, can be
In that we all are strangers somewhere.
Everything we know
We have to learn, even what we are,
Become the part we practise.

You come from wandering people much attached
To places here and there, and fed by roots
(What that lives isn't?) but like water lilies
Floating in moving streams
That take and give back wherever they find themselves;
               from people attached to the day
Wherever it fades or opens. The same light
Flowing round somewhere else will make you blink,
As you do now, gossamer, so frail, so silken,
Force you to come to terms, force you to stir.

5

Later you will get
Particulars: names nationalities opinions,
A history, and be pulled along the track
Your people make to travel on.
                              Now
It is just life and air and the June sun
Shining by the sea on Wales,
A morsel of flesh and its light breathing,
Gossamer-light for life, durable,
Tough as thistle-down or the fair hair of the dandelions
Seeding to make the inextirpable roots
That fill the banks with flowers.

6

I drive from dark shadows up into light again
The sun hitting my mirror
Plunged into dazzle of darkness I continue half blind
Until sight settles.
We swing from dark to light to dark, swaying
Between the Poles
We clutch, we scream   and you, tiny slip,
Take it all so quietly. You are so calm
Blinking, adjusting, your blood settling no doubt
To pulse at its own speed now, in its separate world.
It has been dark where you have come from
Dark and quiet like the churchyard on the hill
Drowsing in noontide, dark surrounded by light.

7

Too much is put on children by our wishes:
To carry the banner, to forge and protect the nation,
To make Utopia, which we could not do.
We really should not wish you anything
Except good luck and health and the wit to use them.
But – old ritualist – I want my wishes.
I wish you may
Avoid being mired by the past or the claim of sects;
Not lose the sense of history, but loose
The clutch of the bitter ghosts unsettled people
Feed with acrid blood, as some keep dogs
Hungry on the highway.
It is for such as you who everywhere
Turn to their mother's milk, try out the air,
Move away from the glare, that if we could
We would change nations into geography.

I hope you will love whatever place you live in
Because you love it, not because commanded
By joyless people gritting their teeth for power;
Welcomed everywhere, and safe enough
To welcome others and like them for their strangeness.
This is for later,
                                    for now
Welcome, strange darling, into this new place
Where you have lighted, soft and quiet as thistledown
To thrive wherever you land, Madog, my girl from Wales.

Such is the sea

EXTREME OF THINGS (2006)

Such is the sea you cannot catch and keep it.
It never will be old, though it's always there.
Stand at the edge and throw a pebble in it
The heaving waves are the same as they ever were.

And such the land that, go to where the earth is –
Leaving the beach, scrambling across the sand –
There's a track between ditches, houses, then a river,
Flints in the ground you can take into your hand.

And you might find a place where something in it –
Shards that you finger – were the very ones
Discarded by the people who made tools
With delicate cutting edges, from the stones.

Such is the sea nothing can mark or map it.
Veined with time's tracks and remnants, such the land.

. . . .

It was a rather empty stretch of heath
I came to once, a slope up from a wood,
Pits with flints in the walls, an uneven wind,
The setting sun in cloud, and an anxious mood

You cannot hold time, for time is like the sea
Washing all round us, but can hold a stone;
And you might feel the same as someone thought
Who, wanting not to be caught by the dark, alone,

Went scuttering down this track, and suddenly stooped
To pick a shining black bit from the ground,
Ground that holds vestiges of what has lived
Solid with time, itself to transience bound.

Such seems the sea to those who are not of it
But are the stuff of earth,
                              and such the land.

Warning

ROSE IN THE AFTERNOON (1974) | SELECTED POEMS (1992)

When I am an old woman I shall wear purple
With a red hat which doesn't go, and doesn't suit me.
And I shall spend my pension on brandy and summer gloves
And satin sandals, and say we've no money for butter.
I shall sit down on the pavement when I'm tired
And gobble up samples in shops and press alarm bells
And run my stick along the public railings
And make up for the sobriety of my youth.
I shall go out in my slippers in the rain
And pick the flowers in other people's gardens
And learn to spit.

You can wear terrible shirts and grow more fat
And eat three pounds of sausages at a go
Or only bread and pickle for a week
And hoard pens and pencils and beermats and things in boxes.

But now we must have clothes that keep us dry
And pay our rent and not swear in the street
And set a good example for the children.
We must have friends to dinner and read the papers.

But maybe I ought to practise a little now?
So people who know me are not too shocked and surprised
When suddenly I am old, and start to wear purple.

12 | LULJETA LLESHANAKU

Filmed by Neil Astley at Tibradden, Rathfarnham,
Co. Dublin, 26 March 2010

Luljeta Lleshanaku belongs to the first "post-totalitarian" generation of Albanian poets. Born in 1968, she grew up under family house arrest, forbidden to attend college or to publish her poetry until the weakening and eventual collapse of Enver Hoxha's Stalinist dictatorship. She later studied Albanian philology at the University of Tirana, and has worked as a schoolteacher, literary magazine editor and journalist. Her first UK publication, *Haywire: New & Selected Poems* (2011), translated by Henry Israeli and others, was shortlisted for the Corneliu M. Popescu Prize.

In *Haywire*, Lleshanaku turns to the fallout of her country's past and its relation to herself and her family. Through intense, powerful lyrics, she explores how these histories intertwine and influence her childhood memories and the retelling of her family's stories. Sorrow, death, imprisonment and desire are some of the themes that echo deeply in her hauntingly beautiful poems.

In his introduction to *Haywire*, Peter Constantine calls Lleshanaku 'a pioneer of Albanian poetry' who 'speaks with a completely original voice, her imagery and language always unexpected and innovative. Her poetry has little connection to poetic styles past or present in America, Europe, or the rest of the world. And, interestingly enough, it is not connected to anything in Albanian poetry either. We have in Lleshanaku a completely original poet.'

The citation for the Crystal Vilenica Prize (2009) includes this comment: 'Luljeta Lleshanaku's poems take place in a melancholy landscape of mountain villages, chestnut trees, and collapsing futures where "spring kills solitude with its solitude" and the only emotional expression not considered a sign of weakness is impatience. The place of her poems is like a zero point that can only look out from itself in all directions at once. But the poet looks inward beyond paradox, and, instead of judgment, she finds recognition. In Lleshanaku's work, geography and soul are charted on the same map. The rhythms of her new poems are expertly managed to enact vulnerability and withdrawal. Her lines stretch out and suddenly retract into fragments with the sensitivity of snail horns.' (Forrest Gander)

I met her for the first time in 2010, when she visited Ireland to read at DLR Poetry Now in Dún Laoghaire, and filmed her at Selina Guinness's house in Rathfarnham, reading some of the poems which would appear in the Bloodaxe edition the following year.

Me fatin e shkruar në fytyrë

Shoku im i bangës në shkollën fillore
kishte gishta blu, buzët blu dhe një vrimë të pariparueshme blu në zemër.
I shënuar me vdekje. I padukshëm. Ai vetëm ruante rrobat
i ulur mbi një gur, jashtë fushës së lojës,
asaj alkimie djerse dhe pluhuri.

I shënuari për të qenë mbret
është i ftohtë, i gatshëm për një rënie të lire,
i lindur parakohe nga një mitër e palumtur.

Gruaja flokëkuqe që pret përnatë burrin e pirë
do të vazhdojë ta presë kështu edhe njëqind vjet.
Nuk është faji i alkoolit. Ajo ka pritjen t'vulosur në fytyrë.
Dhe ai ndodhet krejt rastësisht në këtë akt
sa spektatori i rastit
që shiu e futi nga rruga në sallë.

Po kështu nuk është faji i luftës që i merr jetën djaloshit
me sy të trishtë. Ai ishte i prerë për listat e rekrutimit.
Melankolia është arsenali bazë i ushtrive.

Kurse ai që është vulosur me mbijetesë
do të vazhdojë të ushqehet me këlyshët e tij, si ariu polar,
pa e marrë kurrë vesh se moti është ngrohur.

Te gjithë të mbyllur si teoremat. Qielli i tyre
është një shtëpi e marrë me qera,
ku nuk mund të ngulësh as edhe një gozhdë më tepër.

Në pritje të një një urdhëri të dytë,
të cilin do ta injorojnë gjithsesi,
me krahët lidhur pas lopatave dhe veshët zënë më dyllë,
si njerëzit e Odiseut, në shtegun e sirenave.

Marked

CHILD OF NATURE (2010) | HAYWIRE (2011)

My deskmate in elementary school
had blue nails, blue lips, and a big irreparable hole in his heart.
He was marked by death. He was invisible.
He used to sit on a stone
guarding our coats
as we played in the playground, that alchemy of sweat and dust.

The one marked to be king
is cold, ready for a free fall
born prematurely from a sad womb.

And the redheaded woman waiting for her drunk husband to return
will go on waiting for one hundred years.
It isn't the alcohol; she is marked by 'waiting.'
And he only as guilty as an onlooker
pushed indoors by rain.

What's more, it isn't the war
that took the life of the young boy
with melancholy eyes. He was marked as well, born to be on the recruiter's list.
Melancholy is the standard arsenal of war.

And then there is one marked for survival
who will continue to eat his offspring like a polar bear
that never notices the warming climate.

All of them are as closed as theorems, their sky
a rental home
where hammering even a single nail of change is forbidden.

They are waiting for their next command, which they will ignore anyway
like the Argonauts who filled their ears with wax
and rowed on through the sirens' path.

The Mystery of Prayers

CHILD OF NATURE (2010) | HAYWIRE (2011)

In my family
prayers were said secretly,
softly, murmured through sore noses
beneath blankets,
a sigh before and a sigh after
thin and sterile as a bandage.

Outside the house
there was only a ladder to climb
a wooden one, leaning against a wall all year long,
ready to use to repair the tiles in August before the rains.
No angels climbed up
and no angels climbed down –
only men suffering from sciatica.

They prayed to catch a glimpse of Him
hoping to renegotiate their contracts
or to postpone their deadlines.

'Lord, give me strength,' they said
for they were descendants of Esau
and had to make do with the only blessing
left over from Jacob,
the blessing of the sword.

In my house praying was considered a weakness
like making love.
And like making love
it was followed by the long
cold night of the body.

from Monday in Seven Days

CHILD OF NATURE (2010) | HAYWIRE (2011)

5

Broken toys were my playthings:
zebras, wind-up Chinese dolls, ice-cream carts
given to me as New Year's presents by my father.

But none was worth keeping whole.
They looked like cakes whose icing had been
                    licked off by a naughty child

until I broke them, cracked and probed their insides, the tiny
                              gears, the batteries,
not aware then that I was rehearsing
                    my understanding of freedom.

———

When I first looked at a real painting
I took a few steps backward instinctively
                    on my heels
finding the precise place
where I could explore its depth.
It was different with people:
I built them up,
loved them, but stopped short of loving them fully.
None were as tall as the blue ceiling.
As in an unfinished house, there seemed to be a plastic sheet
                    above them instead of a roof
at the beginning of the rainy autumn of my understanding.

   9

Medio tutissmus ibis, the middle is the safest ground.
The embroidered tablecloth in the middle of the table.
The table in the middle of the carpet.
The carpet in the middle of the room.
The room in the middle of the house.
The house in the middle of the block.
The block in the middle of the town.
The town in the middle of the map.
The map in the middle of the blackboard.
The blackboard in the middle of nowhere.

Lola is an angel. Her forehead hasn't grown since she was eight,
her centre of gravity unchanged. And she likes edges, corners,
although she always finds herself
in the middle of the bus
where people rush toward the doors at either end.

My neighbours never went to school
nor have they heard of aesthetics
and hardly ever have they read anything
about the Earth's axes, symmetry, or absolute truth.
But instinctively they let themselves drift toward the middle
like a man laying his head on a woman's lap,
a woman who, with a pair of scissors
will make him more vulnerable than ever
before the day is done.

Memory

FRESCO (2002) | HAYWIRE (2011)

There is no prophecy, only memory.
What happens tomorrow
has happened a thousand years ago
the same way, to the same end –
and does my ancient memory
say that your false memory
is the history of the featherhearted bird
transformed into a crow atop a marble mountain?
The same woman will be there
on the path to reincarnation
her cage of black hair
her generous and bitter heart
like an amphora full of serpents.

There is no prophecy, things happen
as they have before –
death finds you in the same bed
lonely and without sorrow, shadowless
as trees wet with night.

There is no destiny, only laws of biology;
fish splash in water
pine trees breathe on mountains.

*These poems were all translated from the Albanian by Henry Israeli, the first three
with Shpresa Qatipi and 'Memory' with Albana Lleshanaku.*

13 | NIKOLA MADZIROV

Filmed by Neil Astley in Ledbury, 6 July 2012

Macedonia's Nikola Madzirov is one of the most powerful voices in contemporary European poetry. Born in a family of Balkan War refugees in Strumica in 1973, he grew up in the Soviet era in the former Republic of Yugoslavia ruled by Marshall Tito. When he was 18, the collapse of Yugoslavia prompted a shift in his sense of identity – as a writer reinventing himself in a country which felt new but was still nourished by deeply rooted historical traditions. The example and work of the great East European poets of the postwar period – Vasko Popa, Czesław Miłosz, Zbigniew Herbert – were liberating influences on his writing and thinking. The German weekly magazine *Der Spiegel* compared the quality of his poetry to Tomas Tranströmer's. There is a clear line from their generation, and that of more recent figures like Adam Zagajewski from Poland, to Nikola Madzirov, but Madzirov's voice is a new 21st-century voice in European poetry and he is one of the most outstanding figures of the post-Soviet generation.

Remnants of Another Age, his first book of poetry in English, translation, was published in a bilingual edition by BOA Editions in the US in 2011 and by Bloodaxe in Britain in 2013, translated by Peggy and Graham W. Reid, Magdalena Horvat and Adam Reed. In her introduction, Carolyn Forché writes that 'Madzirov calls himself "an involuntary descendant of refugees", referring to his family's flight from the Balkan Wars a century ago: his surname derives from *mazir* or *majir*, meaning "people without a home". The ideas of shelter and of homelessness, of nomadism, and spiritual transience serves as a palimpsest in these Remnants' – while Madzirov himself tells us in one of his poems, 'History is the first border I have to cross.'

He has read his work at many literature festivals around the world, including Poetry Parnassus at London's Southbank Centre followed by Ledbury Poetry Festival in July 2012, when I was able to film him away from the public platform.

The order of poems in the book differs from that in the film so that those read in Macedonian as well as in English translation can appear on facing pages. On the film he reads the poems in this order (those in Macedonian are asterisked): 'I Don't Know',* 'Separated', 'Home',* 'After Us', 'Shadows Pass Us By',* 'Before We Were Born', 'Many Things Happened' and 'Fast Is the Century'.

Не знам

Далечни се сите куќи што ги сонувам,
далечни се гласовите на мајка ми што на
вечера ме повикува, а јас трчам кон полињата со жито.

Далечни сме ние како топка што го промашува голот
и оди кон небото, живи сме
како термометар кој е точен само тогаш кога
ќе погледнеме кон него.

Далечната стварност секој ден ме испрашува
како непознат патник што ме буди на половина пат
со прашање „Тој ли е автобусот?“,
а јас му велам „Да“, но мислам „Не знам“,
не знам каде се градовите на твоите дедовци
што сакаат да ги напуштат сите откриени болести
и лековите што содржат трпеливост.

Сонувам за куќа на ридот од нашите копнежи,
да гледам како брановите на морето го исцртуваат
кардиограмот на нашите падови и љубови,
како луѓето веруваат за да не потонат
и чекорат за да не бидат заборавени.

Далечни се сите колиби во кои се криевме од дождот
и од болката на срните што умираа пред очите на ловците
кои беа повеќе осамени, отколку гладни.

Далечниот миг секој ден ми поставува прашање
„Тој ли е прозорецот? Тој ли е животот?“, а јас му велам
„Да“, а всушност „Не знам“, не знам кога
птиците ќе прозборат, а да не кажат „Небо“.

I Don't Know

Distant are all the houses I am dreaming of,
distant is the voice of my mother
calling me for dinner, but I run towards the fields of wheat.

We are distant like a ball that misses the goal
and goes towards the sky, we are alive
like a thermometer that is precise only when
we look at it.

The distant reality every day questions me
like an unknown traveller who wakes me up in the middle of the journey
saying *Is this the right bus?*,
and I answer *Yes*, but I mean *I don't know*,
I don't know the cities of your grandparents
who want to leave behind all discovered diseases
and cures made of patience.

I dream of a house on the hill of our longings,
to watch how the waves of the sea draw
the cardiogram of our falls and loves,
how people believe so as not to sink
and step so as not to be forgotten.

Distant are all the huts where we hid from the storm
and from the pain of the does dying in front of the eyes of the hunters
who were more lonely than hungry.

The distant moment every day asks me
Is this the window? Is this the life? and I say
Yes, but I mean *I don't know*, I don't know if
birds will begin to speak, without uttering *A sky*.

Дом

Живеев на крајот од градот
како улично светло на кое никој
не му ја менува светилката.
Пајажината ги држеше ѕидовите заедно,
потта нашите споени дланки.
Во преобразбите на невешто соѕиданите камења
го криев плишаното мече
спасувајќи го од сонот.

Деноноќно го оживував прагот
враќајќи се како пчела што
секогаш се враќа на претходниот цвет.
Беше мир кога го напуштив домот:

гризнатото јаболко не беше потемнето,
на писмото стоеше марка со стара напуштена куќа.

Кон тивките простори од раѓање се движам
и под мене празнини се лепат
како снег што не знае дали на земјата
или на воздухот припаѓа.

Home

I lived at the edge of the town
like a streetlamp whose light bulb
no one ever replaces.
Cobwebs held the walls together,
and sweat our clasped hands.
I hid my teddy bear
in holes in crudely built stone walls
saving him from dreams.

Day and night I made the threshold come alive
returning like a bee that
always returns to the previous flower.
It was a time of peace when I left home:

the bitten apple was not bruised,
on the letter a stamp with an old abandoned house.

From birth I've migrated to quiet places
and voids have clung beneath me
like snow that doesn't know if it belongs
to the earth or to the air.

Сенките нѐ одминуваат

Еден ден ќе се сретнеме,
како бротче од хартија и
лубеница што се лади во реката.
Немирот на светот ќе
биде со нас. Со дланките
ќе го помрачиме сонцето и со фенер
ќе се доближуваме.

Еден ден ветрот нема
да го промени правецот.
Брезата ќе испрати лисја
во нашите чевли пред прагот.
Волците ќе тргнат по
нашата невиност.
Пеперутките ќе го остават
својот прав врз нашите образи.

Една старица секое утро
ќе раскажува за нас во чекалната.
И ова што го кажувам е
веќе кажано: го чекаме ветрот
како две знамиња на граничен премин.

Еден ден сите сенки
                ќе нѐ одминат.

Shadows Pass Us By

We'll meet one day,
like a paper boat and
a watermelon that's been cooling in the river.
The anxiety of the world will
be with us. Our palms
will eclipse the sun and we'll
approach each other holding lanterns.

One day, the wind won't
change direction.
The birch will send away leaves
into our shoes on the doorstep.
The wolves will come after
our innocence.
The butterflies will leave
their dust on our cheeks.

An old woman will tell stories
about us in the waiting room every morning.
Even what I'm saying has
been said already: we're waiting for the wind
like two flags on a border.

One day every shadow
                    will pass us by.

Separated

I separated myself from each truth about the beginnings
of rivers, trees, and cities.
I have a name that will be a street of goodbyes
and a heart that appears on X-ray films.
I separated myself even from you, mother of all skies
and carefree houses.
Now my blood is a refugee that belongs
to several souls and open wounds.
My god lives in the phosphorus of a match,
in the ashes holding the shape of the firewood.
I don't need a map of the world when I fall asleep.
Now the shadow of a stalk of wheat covers my hope,
and my word is as valuable
as an old family watch that doesn't keep time.
I separated from myself, to arrive at your skin
smelling of honey and wind, at your name
signifying restlessness that calms me down,
opening the doors to the cities in which I sleep,
but don't live.
I separated myself from the air, the water, the fire.
The earth I was made from
is built into my home.

After Us

One day someone will fold our blankets
and send them to the cleaners
to scrub the last grain of salt from them,
will open our letters and sort them out by date
instead of by how often they've been read.

One day someone will rearrange the room's furniture
like chessmen at the start of a new game,
will open the old shoebox
where we hoard pyjama-buttons,
not-quite-dead batteries and hunger.

One day the ache will return to our backs
from the weight of hotel room keys
and the receptionist's suspicion
as he hands over the TV remote control.

Others' pity will set out after us
like the moon after some wandering child.

Before We Were Born

The streets were asphalted
before we were born and all
the constellations were already formed.
The leaves were rotting
on the edge of the pavement,
the silver was tarnishing
on the workers' skin,
someone's bones were growing through
the length of the sleep.

Europe was uniting
before we were born and
a woman's hair was spreading
calmly over the surface
of the sea.

Many Things Happened

Many things happened
while the Earth was spinning on
God's finger.

Wires released themselves
from pylons and now
they connect one love to another.
Ocean drops

deposited themselves eagerly
onto caves' walls.
Flowers separated
from minerals and set off
following the scent.

From the back pocket pieces of paper
started flying all over our airy room:
irrelevant things which we'd
never do unless
they were written down.

Fast Is the Century

Fast is the century. If I were wind
I would have peeled the bark off the trees
and the facades off the buildings in the outskirts.

If I were gold, I would have been hidden in cellars,
into crumbly earth and among broken toys,
I would have been forgotten by the fathers,
and their sons would remember me forever.

If I were a dog, I wouldn't have been afraid of
refugees, if I were a moon
I wouldn't have been scared of executions.

If I were a wall clock
I would have covered the cracks on the wall.

Fast is the century. We survive the weak earthquakes
watching towards the sky, yet not towards the ground.
We open the windows to let in the air
of the places we have never been.
Wars don't exist,
since someone wounds our heart every day.
Fast is the century.
Faster than the word.
If I were dead, everyone would have believed me
when I kept silent.

14 | JENNIFER MAIDEN

Filmed at home in Penrith, NSW, Australia,
by Pamela Robertson-Pearce, 18 February 2010

Jennifer Maiden has never travelled outside Australia but her poetry reflects an intimate awareness of world events, thanks to a massive, almost house-high satellite dish installed in her backyard which was beaming in global news long before the internet gave everyone else 24/7 coverage. Responding to international conflicts and crises, many of her poems probe moral dilemmas, confronting the existential, ethical problem of evil: why people commit inhuman acts. Watching the progress of a war, day by day, hour by hour, via satellite television, she experiences 'that singular oddness of feeling' of being always 'at a tangent to it somehow albeit / with despair's edgy wit' and there is 'too much passion in the evil'. Just as 'One needs the private voice / to balance a public terror', so the public focus sharpens the private perspective of her poems.

Two characters keep appearing in her books, George Jeffreys and his companion, Clare Collins. In her novel *Play With Knives* George was a probation officer and Clare a young girl released from prison after murdering her three younger siblings as a nine-year-old. When they reappear in her poems – now working as observers for human rights organisations – they are deeply involved in an ethical analysis which extends to 9/11, the Iraq War, Afghanistan, the Middle East, Hurricane Katrina and the World Financial Crisis.

Always pointedly serious, her poems can also be flamboyant or risqué, outrageously witty or daringly provocative. They blur, challenge and cross boundaries between real and imagined, fact and fiction, inner lives and the outside world. Politicians appear as themselves, including Hillary Clinton (talking to Eleanor Roosevelt), George W. Bush and Madeleine Albright. But at the centre of all these satellite lives, mapping their intimate geography, is Jennifer Maiden herself: questioning, engaging, pouncing and processing to create defiantly humane poetry of impassioned moral witness.

Jennifer Maiden was born in 1949 in Penrith, NSW, where she still lives and where we filmed her in 2010. Plans for her first UK publication, *Intimate Geography: Selected Poems 1991-2010*, were agreed with her then, prior to publication by Bloodaxe in 2012. Her later books include *Liquid Nitrogen* (2012), shortlisted for the International Griffin Poetry Prize, *Drones and Phantoms* (2014), *The Fox Petition* (2015) and *The Metronome* (2016/2017).

George Jeffreys Woke Up in Kabul

FRIENDLY FIRE (2005) | INTIMATE GEOGRAPHY (2012)

George Jeffreys woke up in Kabul.
George Bush Junior was on the TV, obsessed
as usual with Baghdad.
            George Jeffreys hummed an old
border ballad which haunted him
often now: 'What's that
that hirples at my side?
The foe that you must fight, my Lord.
That rides as fast as I might ride?
The shadow of your might, my Lord.'
Was George Bush Junior mad?
A plausible US spokesman for one
of those countless right-wing thinktanks
argued on the BBC that W
only pretended to be mad, 'like Nixon',
to intimidate his foes. But
Nixon, thought Jeffreys, was mad,
surely?   Is that the price perhaps
for pretending too long? Certainly
on the TV now, W
had the quality of an animal
pretending – as you can see animals
pretend when maintaining
uneasy pack position, and he had
an animal's absence of self-parody,
                        one lack
which Jeffreys (who had seen
Ronald Reagan) thought Reagan had not.
            As with Alzheimer's itself,
there was some self-parody in Reagan.
None in Nixon. None in either Bush.
            George Jeffreys looked out
at a paved alhambra of pain,
at the latticed dust of Kabul, which
looked back and pretended to be sane.

Clare and Paris

PIRATE RAIN (2010) | INTIMATE GEOGRAPHY (2012)

Clare Collins woke up in the Paris Hilton. Paris
Hilton was on the TV. Fox News, having disastered
on Iraq, retrained its sites
on Paris Hilton, more in its scope, but its
obscene joy at her suffering, her crying for
her mother, filled Clare with horror.
                            The hotel
was as smooth, clean and confident with light
as Paris herself once. The city itself, however,
seemed to Clare the world's most terrible.
She had thought at first it would be like
a metaphor for herself, who had killed
her younger siblings as a child, in what
she was forced to acknowledge had been
a type of revolution. The Catacombs of skeletons,
now tourist attractions, might be like
the way the haunted have to treat their lives
and deaths as over-crowded commodities. Poor
Paris the woman in prison reminded
Clare of grief. At an early age, Clare
had been warned by George Jeffreys that any
emotion she showed about her crimes – especially
remorse – would seem obscene, so she'd
just shrugged her soul back into the normal,
felt the usual things about most things, with some
relief. And one of the more normal things she always
felt was grief. Paris the city was grief,
                            so grey
and sparkling in its rigid overfocus.
Grief had made Clare careless with her life
if still organising others with that other
big-sisterly carefulness in grief. It seemed as if
her dead flocked beneath her wings
upholding her in danger and she never
cared at all if they should let her fall
to be with them again.
                            But now she left the Hilton
and found the right address. Where suddenly
was fire:

347

real fire not metaphor danced up
about the old hotel become a refuge
for women and their children from abuse.
Clare was here because the Human Rights
unit she represented had followed up that
Amnesty report condemning maltreatment
of women in France. Perhaps some angry
husband had heard that she was visiting.
                              A crowd
below watched and videoed but no one
appeared on the landing above. Was
the woman in 32 trapped alive waiting?
Whole as usual only in a crisis,
Clare climbed the fire escape. No one
seemed to see her. I have been a ghost
since I was nine, she thought, in terror. Jeffreys
in her head accused her of melodrama. The metal
was hot but the flames were uneven:
sometimes mountainous then skirting
back wider like a pack of wolves. Clare
knew to focus on the horizon, if one
were scared of heights. The Eiffel
Tower obsessed the horizon. The window
to 32 was open. Inside, a woman
was tied to a couch and a baby shrieked. Clare
crept in and untied the lady's washing line
from her arms. The lady quietly rubbed
the blood back as Clare led her out onto
the fire escape, holding the baby, which
breathed now quickly, like a kitten. The crowd
at the bottom of the stairs for some reason
assumed the women lived together. The lady,
who looked like Paris Hilton: fair, fragile, calm
and childlike in inviting conversation,
said, 'I'm Sophie', politely. Clare asked,
'Do you want to tell the police?', was relieved
when Sophie said, 'You bet', in careful English.
The wolves of flame were rushing at the roof now.
One heard their howl and then the sirens.
Clare swayed giddily and in her head Jeffreys
said by now she should be used to conflict.
Get back, she smiled. Old super-ego, you.
                        With Sophie and the baby,

walking back in the Paris of Sarkozy, this
Bastille Day when he had just refused
to grant the traditional Amnesty in prisons,
Clare said, 'The only really beautiful parts
of Paris are the new concrete suburbs.
They remind me of Mount Druitt: small
trees in grouted tubs and that same eerie
green tinge light has on long concrete malls.'
She texted Jeffreys: 'Darling, as you know,
quite practically, one can't save anyone
at all if one is saving one's own soul.'

GEORGE JEFFREYS 7

George Jeffreys Woke Up in New Orleans

PIRATE RAIN (2010) | INTIMATE GEOGRAPHY (2012)

George Jeffreys woke up in New Orleans.
George Bush Junior was on the TV, obsessed
as usual with Baghdad. The TV should not
have been working, thought Jeffreys, as the street
below flashed with powerlines in water.
   Hiss.   He looked at black
water already blacker with blood, shit and all
the opals of oil. The TV changed to a group of women
wailing in funereal harmony:
         'Kiss me mother, kiss your darlin'.
Lay my head upon your breast... I am weary,
let me rest...' George Jeffreys was weary and
so, anyway, had been New Orleans. Weary.
       He was searching
for Clare, his not-quite-girlfriend, who herself sought
some victim or other in a local prison. George had driven
in on the Highway next to the Mississippi, where
the levees were okay. The storm had started,
was now keening like a train around the building.
Another keening noise outside the window, George
saw was a thin black man clinging
upright to a lamppost. At first he had looked
as if testing how long he could stand in a storm –

but now, George thought, the guy could not let go
for fear of flying debris, powerlines. George felt that
Bourbon Street was probably undamaged and a bar
seemed more attractive than this, so he left
the room and the TV, ploughed over to the lamppost,
helped the man that much further down the road.
In a brothel's bar full of candelabras, George
and the black man drank Southern Comfort. On
the wall was a photo of Robert Johnson, the
guitarist-singer who was sometimes not mentioned
around here, being said to have traded
his soul to the Master of the Crossroads. Jeffreys's
impressions of Voodoo had usually been benign,
however, involving much dancing, trancing and
a gorgeous goddess Ezili, clad in blue. For such
a weary town, this was not a tired religion. A TV
in the corner blurted on, the same
group of singing women: 'I am standing by the river
Angels wait to take me home...'
        In the sixth hour of the storm,
George left the Southern Comfort with his friend,
forced open the door
and walked back towards the nightflood, easily
for the wind walked for him. Soon a broken angel
in stone floated past, and too distant a tiny
nightdress or a child. Waiting-weariness will lead
always, he thought to violence. As a child,
Clare had killed her younger siblings
          for no-reason
          for some reason
that seemed to have significance tonight.
        The water
was black salt. Ezili was a seawater spirit
from ancient Dahomey. He focused on
her and not the crossroads, the sighing black street,
        but suddenly there was
Clare liquid with rain, in a blue dress
like Ezili with trance eyes, walking.
        Jeffreys
touched her with both hands and the electricity
numbed him to his spine. She held a white, purring
kitten she had somehow pulled from some
electric wires, and George soon guessed

she had spoken with the Master of the Crossroads
of whom he no longer felt afraid. She said,
'If you do want to meet him, you should probably
do it now, before the flood.'
'The flood?', asked George, puzzling biblically, but she
added dryly, 'Just the levees – when the waters
"stabilise" tomorrow it means that this whole city
will have become part of Lake Pontchartrain.'
                    So Jeffreys
followed her back down through deeper water
to a place near the Garden District. They could hear
the Mississippi singing like a choir. The Master
of the Crossroads leaned back smoking
a roll-your-own, his face thought George, that of
that photo in the bar of Robert Johnson,
looking slim and black and much-too-young,
in a hat.   Clare whispered,
'He's obsessed with George Bush, Junior. I told him
you'd met Bush, didn't mention that
you probably saved his life', the last fact still
clearly made her bitter. George didn't fancy
a dark night analysing Bush but the Master
drowned his cigarette under
his neat shoe in floodwater with an odd
pink smell of jasmine and said, 'I will
tell you about the buses, Mr Jeffreys,
do you understand about the buses?'
George said, 'Yes'. But the Master continued,
'The buses don't come, but to Bush
the buses exist and are moving people
out in an orderly fashion. To him, they're as
real as his chain-of-command. Iraq, he thought,
was to prove him his chain-of-command. I know
how this man thinks, Mr Jeffreys. He experiences
nothing but an ideal, or the chaos of the real,
                    he can't combine
the two into a bus that transports people.'
                    George nodded: 'That
I find is the problem of evil.'   The Master
held another cigarette from somewhere, offered
it to Clare, who declined it,
with her lovely, polite blue eyes. He said,
'And you don't smoke either, do you, Mr Jeffreys?

351

Sorry

I can't offer you any wine and my bourbon
is in storage for some time. So your impression
of the President is much the same as mine?'

Clare's expression

dared George to relent a second time, but he said,
'He doesn't have to face a new election.' Then the Master
said, 'There are more than two elections', with a tone
of sentimental satisfaction, and was gone.
As they walked up. Clare said, 'You know I was quite
nervous to go there, after everything I've done.'

For some reason,

George kept expecting
the cat to become a baby, but it sat
as still as a statue in her arms.

HILLARY AND ELEANOR 1:

The Companion

PIRATE RAIN (2010) | INTIMATE GEOGRAPHY (2012)

Hillary Clinton has said that she talks with Eleanor Roosevelt when stressed.

Hillary Clinton woke up in Michigan
in the GM plant strike of 1936. Eleanor
Roosevelt stood at a steaming stewpot, filled
containers to pass up to the men. She smiled, 'After
44 days, they'll be members of a union. Franklin
wouldn't let troops in and I've financed the strike
...my dear, you look naughty and lovely as ever,
not wronged-wife or riled-mother-of-a-nation',
smoothed Hillary's gamin fringe back, with a hand
smelling damply of potatoes. Hillary said,
'I've missed you. God, I voted for the Iraq War.
I'm threatening Iran, my Health Insurance
plans went down the gutter and my campaign
angels are capitalists from Delhi. Eleanor,
I've outsourced my integrity. Put down that spoon:
you were never a nurturer either.' 'You didn't
invent image', retorted Eleanor, but still pleased

352

that her visitor was so pretty. Would, however,
anyone elect her? McCain would win
if they just wanted someone deadly, with
a sheen of compromise. She laughed, 'Being a woman
is as good for the imagination
as being crippled like Franklin, don't forget.
Don't throw in your cards just yet.'
It was after Christmas and the factory frozen.
The two gripped hands together for protection,
knowing that the only friend can die within.

15 | SAMUEL MENASHE

(1925-2011)

Filmed at home in Greenwich Village, New York City,
by Pamela Robertson-Pearce, 9 September 2008

Samuel Menashe's poetry has a mysterious simplicity, a spiritual intensity and a lingering emotional force. Like Kay Ryan's similarly short poems, each poem is packed with meaning, its wit released through quirky wordplay. They are often so short that they're over before you know it, and you have to re-read them several times for their brilliance to become fully apparent. Like Kay Ryan again, he would often read or rather say his poems twice, to give you a second chance of taking them in. They are brief in form but profound in their engagement with ultimate questions. As Stephen Spender wrote in an early review, Menashe 'compresses thought into language intense and clear as diamonds'. Derek Mahon referred to his art of 'compression and crystallisation'. Both those comments are from the 1960s, when Menashe's poetry was briefly noticed in reviews. He was always a solitary figure in American poetry, not writing like anyone else, not part of any clique, not supported by a teaching post and not published for decades.

Intensely musical and rigorously constructed, Menashe's work stands apart in its solitary meditative power, but it is equally a poetry of the everyday. The humblest of objects, the minutest of natural forms, here become powerfully suggestive, and even the shortest of the poems are spacious in the perspectives they open.

In 2004 he became the first winner of the Poetry Foundation's Neglected Masters Award, a prize that both paid tribute to his excellence and made reparation for the years in which his achievements were overlooked. His *New and Selected Poems* was published by the Library of America in 2005. We were fortunate to meet him and to hear his phenomenal performance at Ledbury Poetry Festival in July 2008. I quickly made arrangements for Bloodaxe to publish a UK edition of his book, and that September we filmed him in the tiny New York apartment where he lived from the 1950s until 2009. Even in his 80s, Menashe still knew all his poems by heart, and between engaging digressions on poetry, life and death, he recites numerous examples with engaging humour, warmth and zest. The short video included here is an excerpt from Pamela's film *Life is IMMENSE: visiting Samuel Menashe* released on DVD with the expanded Bloodaxe edition of *New & Selected Poems* published in 2009.

'Pity us...'

Pity us
By the sea
On the sands
So briefly

Daily Bread

I knead the dough
Whose oven you stoke
We consume each loaf
Wrapped in smoke

Family Silver

That spoon fell out
Of my mother's mouth
Before I was born,
But I was endowed
With a tuning fork

Night Music
(pizzicato)

Why am I so fond
Of the double bass
Of bull frogs
(Or do I hear the prongs
Of a tuning fork,

Not a bull fiddle)
Responding—
In perfect accord—
To one another
Across this pond
How does each frog know
He is not his brother
Which frog to follow
Who was his mother
(Or is it a jew's harp
I hear in the dark?)

Improvidence

Owe, do not own
What you can borrow
Live on each loan
Forget tomorrow
Why not be in debt
To one who can give
You whatever you need
It is good to abet
Another's good deed

Voyage

Water opens without end
At the bow of the ship
Rising to descend
Away from it

Days become one
I am who I was

Salt and Paper

Here and there
White hairs appear
On my chest—
Age seasons me
Gives me zest—
I am a sage
In the making
Sprinkled, shaking

Scissors

Sharpen your wit—
Each half of it—
Before you shut
Scissors to cut
Shear skin deep
Underneath wool
Expose the sheep
Whose leg you pull

'A pot poured out...'

A pot poured out
Fulfills its spout

16 | ESTHER MORGAN

Filmed at home near Bungay, Norfolk,
by Neil Astley, 10 November 2009

The main themes of Esther Morgan's poetry are loss, loneliness and what remains unspoken. She describes her subject-matter as being 'family and ancestry, the domestic space, the secrets of hidden lives'. Reviewing her work in the *TLS*, Stephen Knight wrote of how 'erasure, absence and isolation are explored in a voice so ingenuous, its language and syntax so plain, that it takes a while to notice quite how disturbing the poetry is'.

Some poems travel great distances across huge landscapes, both real and metaphorical: the big skies and endless horizons of the English Fens, the dust and rock of the Moon, the seas and deserts of dreams, in her debut collection, *Beyond Calling Distance* (2001), winner of the Aldeburgh First Collection Prize. Out of these distances, voices speak, or try to speak, wanting to bridge the gap, to connect, to be heard as well as to listen. Many of her characters are isolated people: the woman taken in adultery, a suicide waiting to be discovered, the survivors of war. Balancing doubt with faith in language, these figures in a landscape depict themselves and the strange worlds they inhabit in sensuous detail.

Her second collection, *The Silence Living in Houses* (2005), was largely inspired by her time caretaking a run-down Edwardian house in Oxfordshire. Here she unlocks the doors to houses of secrets and dreams where ghosts of the past are more real than the living. In unsettling poems rich with intrigue, she traces the presence of those whose stories are fading like the wallpaper: the servant girl who smashed the dinner service and disappeared; the sisters whose macabre end is still spoken of in whispers; the mistress who breathes sweet nothings from behind the roses.

Her third collection, *Grace* (2011), was shortlisted for the T.S. Eliot Prize. In poems of lyric concentration, *Grace* examines our need for purpose, for the signs that might help us decide what to do with our lives. It's a desire that makes for restless spirits – like the woman who keeps shifting her furniture around or the invisible subjects of an early photograph, moving too fast to be captured.

She started writing poetry while working as a volunteer at the Wordsworth Trust in Cumbria, and has since worked as an editor and teacher, at the University of East Anglia and Edith Cowan University in Perth, Australia, and for the Poetry Archive.

The Reason

BEYOND CALLING DISTANCE (2001)

It's because you never left
these endless fields

where an oak tree sails the horizon
like a lost galleon

where rabbits crouch in mad-dog heat
under a sky full of eyes

where a gunshot scatters acres of birds
leaving wires like empty staves

where a road runs straight for hours
towards a shimmering spire

where a man can live all his life
beyond calling distance.

Bone China

THE SILENCE LIVING IN HOUSES (2005)

I want to leave something behind
like the maid who cracked one night
the length of her heart,
who crept shaking down the staircase
to where the service shone on the dresser,
plates pale as a row of moons.

She stacked them in her arms –
a weight greater than all she owned –
bore their white tower to the kitchen garden
where she stood between the soft fruit beds
and smashed each one against the wall
with a planetary anger.

That dawn she walked out of her story forever,
though her flavour salted the servants' tongues for months,
and clearing the ground a hundred years later
of this self-seeded scrub of ash
I can still piece bits of her together – white and sharp –
as if the earth were teething.

At the parrot sanctuary

THE SILENCE LIVING IN HOUSES   (2005)

our presence disturbs their sleep:
heads bob and weave,
beaks biting the wire.

Some have plucked the feathers
from their tails,
their breasts,
as if trying to find out love.

Bright eyes stare out
from circles of wizened skin,
fix us,

and then the dead begin to speak:

a chorus of greetings and goodbyes,
nicknames, profanities,
the ghost of a woman's laugh.

No one can live long
with this ventriloquy,
voices thrown from the dark.

Not us,
who leave them quickly to their cages,
to the silence that only comes
when we are gone.

Grace

GRACE (2011)

You've been living for this for weeks
without knowing it:

the moment the house empties like a city in August
so completely
it forgets you exist.

Light withdraws slowly
is almost gone before you notice.

In the stillness, everything becomes itself:
the circle of white plates on the kitchen table
the serious chairs that attend them

even the roses on the papered walls
seem to open a little wider.

It looks simple: the glass vase holding
whatever is offered –
cut flowers, or the thought of them –

simple, though not easy
this waiting without hunger in the near dark
for what you may be about to receive.

Among Women

GRACE (2011)

One evening I came back home
and everything was just as I'd left it –

except the bowls gleamed with a new knowledge,
the cat wore his yellow gaze like a mask,

and I sensed the house had been visited –
wings unfurling like ferns in the quiet air.

I was blessed with children anyway,
I shook my life out like a cloth,

and perhaps there is a purpose after all
in not being chosen:

the minute my clock has never regained,
sunlight in the guest room climbing its ladder of dust.

I want to go back to The Angel
GRACE (2011)

Why won't somebody take her?
It's only a short walk away

    across the late summer allotments
    where the dill must already be running to seed.

Meanwhile, here are *Tunes from the War* –
her head grows feathery with voices

    in a room bright as a kindergarten.
    A meal appears out of nowhere and is frightening.

Then it's time for undressing again,
though nothing's been done, nothing that should have been –

    the takings not counted and locked in the safe,
    the tables still sticky with rings.

Tomorrow they croon
like the daughter who'll always come later

    Tomorrow promises the wind across the river
    Tomorrow sing the creaking wings.

What Happens While We Are Sleeping

GRACE (2011)

Frost. Foxes. Owl-kills.
The wheel of stars.
Thundering lorries with somewhere
to get to by dawn.

Beads of dew forming
along the telegraph wires.
A red deer delicately eating
each closed tulip like a prayer.

After Life

GRACE (2011)

As far back as great, great, great
        names and faces
                are scoured away

like plates scraped clean
        of painted flowers
                by daughters wanting more.

What remains
        after voice and gesture are lost,
                is less love

than force of habit:
        the angle of a peeler's
                thinning blade,

the battered wisdom of the pan
        you boil the morning milk in,
                its patina of burnt lace.

If only I could learn to be
    this fit for purpose:
        the passed-down smoothness

of handled ash, a dailyness
    like prayer or bread
        and the mouth's need of them.

Risen

GRACE (2011)

Like the woman who wakes at dawn
to find herself three fields from home
my body is given to me like a flower –

the kind that stars the hedgerow every spring,
the kind I used to pick as a child
without thinking.

Perhaps if I keep very still and empty
I too will grow into stem, leaf, corona,
become the common wayside name for love.

The thought opens up in this early morning light
with such a wild sweetness
it could fill the whole house for a day.

17 | JULIE O'CALLAGHAN

Filmed by Pamela Robertson-Pearce in the Long Room Gallery,
Trinity College Dublin, 24 April 2008

Julie O'Callaghan is a singularly acute observer of human behaviour, with a sharp Swiftian eye and an alert ear that have made her one of the finest and funniest practitioners of the monologue in poetry. Yet, notably in the poems charting her father's illness and death, she can also strike an elegiac and heartbreaking note, while her poems set in the court of Heiain Japan unscroll with great poignancy and delicacy.

Born in Chicago in 1954, she has lived in Ireland since 1974, most of that time with her late husband, the poet and critic Dennis O'Driscoll. For many years she worked as a librarian at Trinity College Dublin, and Pamela's film was shot in one of her favourite places, Trinity's Long Room Gallery, the subject of the first poem she reads. Her selection ranges from the *Edible Anecdotes* her readers gorged on in the 1980s to later work confronting a very 'scary' 21st century with an armoury of lively and defiant language – as well as a baseball bat under the bed.

Writing in *The Irish Times*, Patrick Crotty praised 'O'Callaghan's subtle ear for the intonations of speech, her appalled delight in the things language is made to do in our consumer-crazed era... and her shrewd handling of line-endings mark her as a true poet, someone with an almost deranged interest in the possibilities and impossibilities of words'.

She received Ireland's Michael Hartnett Award in 2001 for poems which 'seem effortless and are immediately accessible and yet achieve great emotional weight by the lightest of means', while in Britain her work has been championed by poets as different as Wendy Cope, George Szirtes, Selima Hill and Carol Ann Duffy.

She has published three poetry books with Bloodaxe, one a Poetry Book Society Choice and two Recommendations, most recently, *Tell Me This Is Normal: New & Selected Poems* (2008), and three poetry collections for older children with Bloodaxe, Faber and Orchard Books. She is a member of the Irish academy of arts, Aosdána.

The Long Room Gallery

Trinity College Dublin

NO CAN DO (2000)

There is nothing to breathe
here in the Gallery
except old years.
The air from today
goes in one lung
and 1783 comes out the other.
As for spirits,
stand perfectly still
and you will feel them
carousing near your ear.
Tourists down below
think they've seen a ghost
when they spot you
floating through bookcases
over their heads.
On a creaky wooden balcony
you tunnel through centuries,
mountains of books
rising into the cumulus.
You could scale a ladder
up the rockface of knowledge
or search the little white slips
stuck in books
for a personal message
from Swift.
Ancient oxygen,
antique dust particles,
petrified wood...
Who are you kidding?
You belong down there:
baseball caps, chewing gum, videos.

No Can Do

NO CAN DO (2000)

I know I'm a total party-pooper.
But there's no way
I can go to Red Lobster.
I have to stay home.
I have to rest.
I can't move.

Chip is like:
'How come you don't want to
to go out anyplace?'

I'm this huge moose
with no hair,
a cheapo wig and cancer.
And I'm supposed to go
and eat a Seafood Platter?
No can do.

Home

NO CAN DO (2000)

The Illinois sunrise demonstrates
exactly what an alien you are
in your car on the prairie
heading north to Chicago
where some Irish guy
aimed a hundred years ago.
That's why you're going there
instead of somewhere else.

He is controlling your life
and the direction of your auto.
If he had decided on Boston –
you'd be driving there instead.
Funny how we let this geezer
place us here and give us an accent,

expecting us to live surrounded
by corn and soybean fields.

In a booth at the Dixie Truck Stop
you drink your bottomless coffee
and figure how the rustics to your left
and the military personnel to the rear
were similarly plonked down
in the middle of nowhere.
Simple souls that we are
we now call this region 'Home'.

from Edible Anecdotes

EDIBLE ANECDOTES (1983)

17

oh yeah, it's an all-you-can-eat
salad buffet all right
but did you notice that your rear-end
barely fits on these chairs
and to get past the other tables
you have to hold your breath?
not only that, but every time you get up
with your plate you're surrounded by mirrors
telling you that your spare tyre
and midriff bulge are thriving
and that everyone in the place
is watching your blubber ripple
to top it all off the waitresses are thin as sticks
oh yeah, all-you-can-eat my eye

18

life holds no more unpredictable delights for me
I know now that if he asks me out
on Friday night it means a meal at Gino's
nothing personal against Gino
but it isn't exactly romantic to line up outside
for half an hour with every sort of rowdy
and once inside have to scream at each other

while we pull apart our triangles of pizza
and slurp beer from mugs
not that we never scream at each other
he always carves our initials in a heart
on the woodwork at our table
just so I won't get angry
when we have to go and park
down at the beach afterwards
so he can smooch
there are no surprises for me
if he calls on a Saturday
it means a movie and a chocolate shake

The Great Blasket Island

WHAT'S WHAT (1991)

Six men born on this island
have come back after twenty-one years.
They climb up the overgrown roads
to their family houses
and come out shaking their heads.
The roofs have fallen in,
birds have nested in the rafters.
All the whitewashed rooms
all the nagging and praying
and scolding and giggling
and crying and gossiping
are scattered in the memories of these men.
One says, 'Ten of us, blown to the winds –
some in England, some in America, some in Dublin.
Our whole way of life – extinct.'
He blinks back the tears
and looks across the island
past the ruined houses, the cliffs
and out to the horizon.

Listen, mister, most of us cry sooner or later
over a Great Blasket Island of our own.

Lettergesh Strand

TELL ME THIS IS NORMAL (2008)

has all these ghosts
running through the
windy spray.
Wave after wave
of people I know
haunting the beach
like translucent jellyfish.
There goes my father
examining a rock pool
with a starfish floating.
I wish a handful of bleached sand
didn't remind me of that
plastic bag labelled
This package contains
the cremated remains of…

*

The ringing
gets louder.
I search everywhere:
I push aside soft
rounded rocks,
globs of seaweed,
pick up a tiny
curved shell
and hold it
to my ear.
Your voice
– a little distant –
is talking to me,
telling your old jokes,
gushing about
where you are now.
It's great to hear
from you.

I should have known
you'd be hanging out
on this chilly Connemara beach.
No – I'm not in a rush.
Keep talking.
I'm listening.

Problems

TELL ME THIS IS NORMAL (2008)

Take weeds for example.
Like how they will overrun
your garden and your life
if you don't obliterate them.
But forget about weeds
– what about leaves?
Snails use them as handy
bridges to your flowers
and hordes of thuggish slugs
will invade – ever thought about *that*?
We won't even go into
how leaves block up the gutters.
I sure hope you aren't neglecting
any puddles of water in your bathtub
– discoloration will set in.
There is the wasp problem,
the storms problem, the grass
growing-between-the-bricks-in-the-driveway problem.
Then there's the remembering to
lock-all-the-windows problem.
Hey, knuckleheads!
I guess you just don't appreciate
how many problems there are.

Scary

TELL ME THIS IS NORMAL (2008)

Journeys can be frightening
wouldn't you say?
When everyone on the plane
stops talking and grabs the arm rest
and you're over the North Atlantic,
what about that scenario?

Parties – scary.
Bosses – scary.
Reviews – scary.
Families – very scary.
Computers – scary.
Waiters and waitpersons – scary.

It is all so complicated to explain –
like the way my father used to ask me,
'How did you get to be so scared?'
Try being born, like me,
on Kafka's birthday
and you wouldn't need to ask.
People are terrifying, for one thing.
No way around
that sad and sorry fact.
Mr Hotshot is in a hurry
and happens to run you over ('by mistake').
Or if you're out strolling along
and somebody gets a yen
to stab somebody
then sees you?
I find that a little scary.

Houses – hope the foundation isn't faulty.
Water – hope it isn't sewage-laden.
Buses – hope the driver quits talking on his cell phone.
Diet Coke – hope those chemicals are OK.
Work – hope you don't get a nervous breakdown.
Aches – hope it isn't a tumour.

Hey, parents – do you worry yourself sick
whatwith sharp edges and open flames
and bullies and learning disabilities
and maniacs and drugs?
Scary.

Getting old – scary.
Money – scary.
The future – scary.
Burglars – scary.
Superbugs – scary.

Let's welcome in the New Year
hiding under the bed
with a baseball bat.
Scary.

18 | LEANNE O'SULLIVAN

Filmed at home in Beara, West Cork,
by Neil Astley, 17 February 2012

Leanne O'Sullivan comes from the Beara peninsula in West Cork. Her first collection, *Waiting for My Clothes* (2004), published when she was 21, traced a deeply personal journey, from the traumas of eating disorder and low self-esteem to the saving powers of love and positive awareness. Her focus switched in her second collection, *Cailleach: The Hag of Beara* (2009), to Irish mythology and the eternal feminine: *An Cailleach Bhéarra*, or the Hag of Beara, is a wise woman figure embedded in the physical and mental landscape of western Ireland. A large rock rests on the ridge overlooking Ballycrovane Harbour near her home on the Beara peninsula, said to be the petrified body of the Cailleach; she has had several lives, beginning each life with a birth from her stony form – and returning to stone at the end.

The Mining Road (2013), her third poetry collection, finds inspiration in the disused copper mines that haunt the rugged terrain around Allihies, also near her home at Beara. Like remnants of a lost world, the mines' ruined towers, shafts, man-engines and dressing floors, evoke an elemental landscape in which men and women laboured above as well as underground, and even mined in caverns below sea level. Mining promotes a sense of memory, and the riches embedded in the landscape are human as well as material. But things brought to the surface can have a startling ability to shine in the present, and O'Sullivan's poems move and provoke as they resonate with experiences at the heart of contemporary Ireland.

She reads nine poems in the film, which was shot in the kitchen of the O'Sullivan family farm at Beara, seven of these from *The Mining Road*. 'Safe House' relates a story from the Irish War of Independence, when "safe houses" were used to shelter men hiding from the British soldiers.

374

The Cord

WAITING FOR MY CLOTHES (2004)

I used to lie on the floor for hours after
school with the phone cradled between
my shoulder and my ear, a plate of cold
rice to my left, my schoolbooks to my right.

Twirling the cord between my fingers
I spoke to friends who recognised
the language of our realm. Throats and lungs
swollen, we talked into the heart of the night,

toying with the idea of hair dye and suicide,
about the boys who didn't love us, who
we loved too much, the pang of the nights.
Each sentence was new territory, a door

someone was rushing into, the glass shattering
with delirium, with knowledge and fear.
My mother never complained about the phone bill,
what it cost for her daughter to disappear

behind a door, watching the cord
stretching its muscle away from her.
Perhaps she thought it was the only way
she could reach me, sending me away

to speak in the underworld. As long as
I was speaking she could put my ear
to the tenuous earth, allow me to listen,
to decipher. And these were the elements

of my mother – the earthed wire,
the burning cable – as if she flowed
into the room with me to somehow say:
Stay where I can reach you, the dim room,

the dark earths. Speak of this
and when you feel removed from it
I will pull the cord and take you
back towards me.

Birth

CAILLEACH: THE HAG OF BEARA (2009)

Now comes November,
my birth time, and white ribs of tide
uproot the silence of the bay.

Today I break from stone onto sand,
motherless, my mother a stone
bedding the earth and dreaming my image.

I stretch like a snail from a deep sleep,
my flesh gathering its warm fabrics
and unknitting me from this womb.

I listen and mimic the flood-tide,
open my ears to the haul of shells,
sheer salts erupting my birth-cry.

My eyes lift as the day begins
to shape itself, light being emptied
into it as a soft fall of rain sweeps

my moss-lined palms. I tread
into this soaked brightness,
bogland and the air full of fuchsia.

This is the blood and bone of my mother,
sheets of grass and weed – all her flushing skins
I lean on with my hands and knees.

Feeling a thirst gently pull
I bring my mouth to the fall of water
from a leaf to taste the cool, plentiful drops.

I shake the drench from branches, my limbs
and lips moving fluently, the way a full throat
learns to move for its earliest swallowing.

Townland
THE MINING ROAD (2013)

A hankering in the skull, uttered and worked,
the stagger of heather beds cleaved in the throat;
Gorth and *Ahabrock*, and in the old stone walls
the swallows going like windborne rumours.
An ordinary night my father walking there
thought he'd heard the ghost of Norah Seer,
the border streams swelling to the sound
of her steel crutch tapping out the hours.

Old homes and a half remembered word of mouth;
we'd prowl the lanes ourselves calling her out,
the underground all moan and winnow
with disappearing streams and passages
that swept the yellowing furze. Unlistened for,
the roofless village a thousand times passed,
and beyond, the waning lift and turn of a gate,
the fall of banked moss, and all of us listening.

The Mining Road
THE MINING ROAD (2013)

Where moss is gold in the copper pools
my mother dreams her mother on the road,
sitting up ahead, among whistled reeds

and ocean steaming rocks. Up and out
of her hospital bed, her wound stitched
and silvering beneath her night-clothes.

Quietly, she slips her cardigan off and starts
to unravel it, both hands working and steady
until she has teased it apart completely.

And begins again. Famine road, mine road,
moss stitch; like grass swallowed down a shaft
the wool quivers up again towards her lap,

her eyes cast down, needles tapping out the work,
its strangeness, until it heals her, the old
movements long clenched and deep in her hands.

I dream them now together in mountain light
leading each other where the road winds down,
and carries on, past where they thought it would end.

Love Stories

THE MINING ROAD (2013)

And when they fought, my father said,
in those day-lit, lamp-lit rooms, him bowed
into the ceremonies of the newspapers,
the sound would be of her slamming
closed the cupboard doors, the front door,
cups and plates smashed into the deep sink
like a sudden downpour of hailstones.
He would turn the pages very slowly,
so as not to disturb her, mindful of knives
where buttery spuds still plumed on the blade.

And once peering over the rim of the page
he calmly offered, 'Would you prefer a hammer?'
so that the whole thing started up again.
For three days and nights hinges turned over
the world, soft mortar crumbled somewhere
down behind the dresser, and from the eaves
the nesting starlings darted and sprung in fright,
and raised the weathered roof like a sparking flare.

Antique Cabinets

THE MINING ROAD (2013)

So this is what I will marry into –
night drives to dig out cast-offs from a skip,
the long sweated haul, as if we had coaxed
and pulled a sleep-walked body back home
and set it up again in our own rooms.

Or another you saw at the back of a shop
found its own purchase and worked on you.
You said the shine off it was like looking
down through water, down past old wood,
a poplar sky or walnut's burred flower.

And what would I make of such an inheritance?
When you are gone and I am left wondering
what should keep of love and trees and shadows,
I imagine myself not surprised to find
the settled world steady among your things.

Sea Level

FROM *Man Engine*

THE MINING ROAD (2013)

We always knew
they were mining
below the sea,
under the great bellies

of the earth –
could hear sometimes
far out
beyond the pier

the inconsolable
hammering
of those workers
ossifying in the tides,

the fill
of their shovels
streaming above them
in candlelight

towards crescent moon
or starfish,
where I wade
in the grey water,

the drag of my feet
hauling clouds
of shingle and ore
along their dressing floors.

Safe House

THE MINING ROAD (2013)

When they were beginning to build a country
some of the men came to hide in a house
where there was a family, and a child upstairs,
listening. They told him what to say if anyone

ever asked. Say they were never there.
Say there was only a family in that house.
And during the night the boy went to the room
where their bags and belongings were hidden.

He felt along the canvases, the mouldy wet
and sag of the straps. His fingers touched on
papers and coins, and lifted out the revolver,
its coolness and the weight of it in his hands.

Then he felt nothing. His blood crept slowly
and dark along the floorboards, underneath them,
and the room shook, and stood still,
and seemed to hang for a moment in that night.

When they found him they cleaned him,
his face, gently and quickly, and his mother
wrapped him in a blanket and took him
out to a corner of the farm and buried him.

Back in the house they gathered his things,
and built up a fire again in the kitchen,
burning his clothes, his shoes, all the signs
and small, clumsy turnings of a child.

And afterwards, in the freezing dark, the father
went out to find the doctor and the parish priest
to tell them what had happened, and what they
should say if anyone ever asked.

Tell them there was never a child.
Say they were never there.
There was never a home
or the found, easy measures of a family.

There was never a map that could lead back to
or out of that place, foreknown or imagined,
where the furze, the dark-rooted vetch, turned
over and over with the old ground and disappeared.

The Glimmerman

THE MINING ROAD (2013)

Let the light burn down,
Love, the night falls now.
He's not on the road,
not yet in the town.
Come away from the door,
let the light burn down.

Or sit by the window
where the lamplight shone,
all of your beauty a-glimmer,
all of the darkness gone.
Let the light burn down, Love,
let the light burn down.

And there must be light enough
for I can just make do –
the sweeping of your footfall,
the softness of your mouth.
Let the light burn down, Love,
let the light burn out.

DVD 4

CLARE POLLARD – ROBERT WRIGLEY

1 | CLARE POLLARD

Filmed at home in London by Neil Astley, 24 June 2011

Born in Bolton in 1978, Clare Pollard has published five collections with Bloodaxe: *The Heavy-Petting Zoo* (1998), which she wrote while still at school; *Bedtime* (2002); *Look, Clare! Look!* (2005); *Changeling* (2011), a Poetry Book Society Recommendation; and *Incarnation* (2017). She published her translation, *Ovid's Heroines*, with Bloodaxe in 2013, and took it on the road as a touring theatre show.

In the film she introduces and reads from *Changeling*, a book steeped in folktale and ballads, which looks at the stories we tell about ourselves. From the Pendle witch-trials in 17th-century Lancashire to the gangs of modern-day east London, *Changeling* takes on our myths and monsters. These are poems of place that journey from Zennor to Whitby, Broadstairs to Brick Lane. Whether relocating the traditional ballad 'The Twa Corbies' to war-torn Iraq, introducing us to the bearded lady Miss Lupin, or giving us a glimpse of the 'beast of Bolton', *Changeling* is a book about our relationship with the Other: fear and trust, force and freedom.

Reviewing the book in the *Yorkshire Post*, Frances Leviston wrote that 'The themes are ancient – guilt, grief, the almost unbearable commingling of beauty and suffering – but shown through contemporary globalised life in all its grossness and glory... Pollard's wit, honesty and recklessness'.

Tam Lin's Wife

CHANGELING 2011

They sat us in a pale and private place,
quietly conveyed the worst –
explained the curse that was your fate
and how for one long, ill-starred night
you'd turn and burn, become all beasts
you could dream up.
I think that I cried out. They said
that if I want to have you
then I have to hold,
to hang on tight and not let go,
and not let go,
until you wake entire again within my arms –
pale skin, dark tufts of hair, long bones –
in crumpled daylight.
And now the sun has sunk, dark taken hold,
and in my hug you jolt
to sudden adder, X-marked, zigzagged, venom-
quick, then rear to brute-necked dog,
as black as forests and spume-jawed.
I tell myself that you are still my love
although I'm wet with blood, and you're a lynx
filthy with fingerprints, clean pink mouth snapping teeth
near heart, my throat.
I keep you caught and don't let go,
and don't let go,
and feel your skull become a bleach December sun,
your eyes hot coals, you burst to blaze: a wicker-man.
You're searing through my fingers,
molten lead.
Dear husband, all those things I prize in you –
your beauty, kindness, laugh –
are stripped off one by one
but even with them gone
my boy stares out from stricken shapes,
and love has no conditions. None.

Pendle

CHANGELING 2011

When you must climb the hill, a woman's back bruised tender
with heather, & frozen puddles are fingernails gone bad,
then someone is to blame.

When you must wade for miles through ragged-robin, the rain-knives
& bog-rosemary to beg alms, when the neighbours owe you oats,
then someone is to blame.

When your children curdle like milk & turn one by one to clay dolls,
& your husband's fledgling-weak & you're a good Christian woman,
then someone is to blame.

When you dream of a woman fucking goats or men with horns;
of waking the witch, swimming her – lime-scalded & vice-tight,
then someone is to blame.

When you imagine her face yoked in a bridle & you want to slit
below her heart & suck there; weigh her weight against a bible,
then someone is to blame.

When the merlin steals hen-chicks & your fields are blighted
like a mouthful of black teeth, & your cow stark mad
then someone is to blame.

The Two Ravens

(a ballad)

CHANGELING 2011

As I walked down a street alone,
I heard two ravens make a plan,
one bird unto the other said:
'Which shall we dine on of the dead?'

'Out there upon a dirty track
     way down a down, way down
a woman's spread upon her back,
     in the mud.
her throat cut and her body raped,
for bags of books, a glimpse of face.
     O down, derry derry, if she's bad they're good.

The bird said: 'no one cares she lies
In dust near dogs in smears of flies,
the army's led by fear and oil,
the husband's had his honour spoiled,

'her son's stood in a hood of black
     way down a down, way down
a donkey, ridden, told to crack,
     in the blood.
and other women fear to speak,
which means she'll waste if not for beaks.'
     O down, derry derry, if they're bad she's good.

So low as planes they did swoop down,
to chew on unveiled eyes of brown,
they pecked out clumps of her dark hair
to line their nests when they grew bare.

And many commentators moaned,
     way down a down, way down
but armoured cars drove past the bones.
     and I stood
I watched the ravens feed on war,
and knew I'd watch for evermore.
     O down, derry derry, if she's bad we're good.

The Caravan

CHANGELING 2011

We were alive that evening, on the north Yorkshire moors,
in a valley of scuffed hills and smouldering gorse.
Pheasants strutted, their feathers as richly patterned
as Moroccan rugs, past the old Roma caravan –
candles, a rose-cushioned bed, etched glass –
that I'd hired to imagine us gipsies
as our bacon and bean stew bubbled,
as you built a fire, moustached, shirt-sleeves rolled.
It kindled and started to lick, and you laughed
in your muddy boots, there in the wild –
or as close as we can now get to the wild –
skinning up a joint with dirty hands, sloshing wine
into beakers, the sky turning heather with night,
the moon a huge cauldron of light,
the chill wind blasting away our mortgage,
emails, bills, TV, our broken washing machine.
Smoke and stars meant my thoughts loosened,
and took off like the owls that circled overhead,
and I knew your hands would later catch in my hair,
hoped the wedding ring on them never seemed a snare –
for if you were a traveller I would not make you settle,
but would have you follow your own weather,
and if you were a hawk I would not have you hooded,
but would watch, dry-mouthed, as you hung above the fields,
and if you were a rabbit I would not want you tame,
but would watch you gambolling through the bracken,
though there is dark meat packed around your ribs,
and the hawk hangs in the skies.

2 | ADÉLIA PRADO

Filmed with Ellen Doré Watson in Newcastle by Neil Astley,
13 November 2014

Adélia Prado was "discovered" when she was nearly 40 by Brazil's foremost modern poet, Carlos Drummond de Andrade, who was astonished to read her 'phenomenal' poems, launching her literary career with his announcement that St Francis was dictating verses to a housewife in the provincial backwater of Minas Gerais. Psychiatrists in droves made the pilgrimage to Divinópolis to delve into the psyche of this devout Catholic who wrote startlingly pungent poems of and from the body; they were politely served coffee and sent back to the city. After publishing her first collection, *Baggage*, in 1976, she went on to become one of Brazil's best-loved poets.

Adélia Prado's poetry combines passion and intelligence, wit and instinct. Her poems are about human concerns, especially those of women, about living in one's body and out of it, about the physical but also the spiritual and the imaginative life; about living in two worlds simultaneously: the spiritual and the material. She also writes about ordinary matters, insisting that the human experience is both mystical and carnal. For her these are not contradictory: 'It's the soul that's erotic,' she writes.

Born in 1935, she has lived all her life in the provincial, industrial city of Divinópolis. She was the only one in her family of labourers to see the ocean, to go to college, or to dream of writing a book. In June 2014 she received the Griffin Lifetime Achievement Award in Canada. In November 2014 her first UK edition, *The Mystical Rose: Selected Poems*, was published by Bloodaxe Books. This drew on on Ellen Doré Watson's translations from her two US titles, *The Alphabet in the Park: Selected Poems* (Wesleyan University Press, 1990) and *Ex-Voto* (Tupelo Press, 2013). Adélia Prado visited Britain then for the first time to launch *The Mystical Rose* with Ellen Doré Watson at Aldeburgh Poetry Festival, followed by further readings in London, Hull, and Newcastle, where I was able to film them before their NCLA event. *The Mystical Rose* was later shortlisted for the Popescu European Poetry Translation Prize 2015 for Ellen Doré Watson's translations from Brazilian Portuguese.

Dia

O CORAÇÃO DISPARADO (1978) | POESIAS REUNIDA (2015)

As galinhas com susto abrem o bico
e param daquele jeito imóvel
– ia dizer immoral –,
as barbelas e as cristas envermelhadas,
só as artérias palpitando no pescoço.
Uma mulher espantada com sexo:
mas gostando muito.

A rosa mística

O PELICANO (1987) | POESIAS REUNIDA (2015)

A primeira vez
que tive a consciência de uma forma,
disse à minha mãe:
dona Armanda tem na cozinha dela uma cesta
onde põe os tomates e as cebolas;
começando a inquietar-me pelo medo
do que era bonito desmanchar-se,
até que um dia escrevi:
'neste quarto meu pai morreu,
aqui deu corda ao relógio
e apoiou os cotovelos
no que pensava ser uma janela
e eram os beirais da morte.'
Entendi que as palavras
daquele modo agrupadas
dispensavam as coisas sobre as quais versavam,
meu próprio pai voltava, indestrutível.
Como se alguém pintasse
a cesta de d. Armanda
me dizendo em seguida:
agora podes comer as frutas.
Havia uma ordem no mundo,
de onde vinha?

Day

THE HEADLONG HEART (1978) | THE MYSTICAL ROSE (2014)

The chickens open their beaks in alarm
and stop, with that knack they have,
immobile – I was going to say immoral –
wattles and coxcombs stark red,
only the arteries quivering in their necks.
A woman startled by sex,
but delighted.

The Mystical Rose

THE PELICAN (1987) | THE MYSTICAL ROSE (2014)

The first time
I was conscious of form,
I said to my mother:
'Dona Armanda has a basket in her kitchen
where she keeps tomatoes and onions'
and so began fretting that even lovely things
don't last forever,
until one day I wrote:
'It was here in this room that my father died,
here that he wound the clock
and rested his elbows
on what he thought was a windowsill
but was the threshold of death.'
I saw that words grouped a certain way
made it possible to live without
the things they described,
my father was coming back, indestructible.
It was as if someone painted a picture
of Dona Armanda's basket and said:
'Now you can eat the fruit.'
There was order in the world
– where did it come from?

E por que contristava a alma
sendo ela própria alegria
e diversa da luz do dia,
banhava-se em outra luz?
Era forçoso garantir o mundo
da corrosão do tempo, o próprio tempo burlar.
Então prossegui: 'neste quarto meu pai morreu...
Podes fechar-te, ó noite,
teu negrume não vela esta lembrança.'
Foi o primeiro poema que escrevi.

Desenredo

O CORAÇÃO DISPARADO (1978) | POESIAS REUNIDA (2015)

Grande admiração me causam os navios
e a letra de certas pessoas que esforço por imitar.
Dos meus, só eu conheço o mar.
Conto e reconto, eles dizem 'anh'.
E continuam cercando o galinheiro de tela.
Falo de espuma, do tamanho cansativo das águas,
eles nem lembram que tem o Quênia,
nem de leve adivinham que estou pensando em Tanzânia.
Afainosos me mostram o lote: aqui vai ser a cozinha,
logo ali a horta de couve.
Não sei o que fazer com o litoral.
Fazia tarde bonita quando me inseri na janela, entre meus tios,
e vi o homem com a braguilha aberta,
o pé de rosa-doida enjerizado de rosas.
Horas e horas conversamos inconscientemente em português
como se fora esta a única língua do mundo.
Antes de depois da fé eu pergunto cadê os meus que se foram,
porque sou humana, com capricho tampo o restinho de molho na panela.

Saberemos viver uma vida melhor que esta,
quando mesmo chorando é tão bom estarmos juntos?
Sofrer não é em língua nenhuma.
Sofri e sofro em Minas Gerais e na beira do oceano.

And why does order – which is joy itself,
and bathes in a different light
than the light of day –
make the soul sad?
We must protect the world
from time's corrosion, we must cheat time itself.
And so I kept writing:
'It was here in this room that my father died…
O Night, come on down,
your blackness can't erase this memory.'
That was my first poem.

Dénouement

THE HEADLONG HEART (1978) | THE MYSTICAL ROSE (2014)

I have great admiration for ships
and for certain people's handwriting which I attempt to imitate.
Of my entire family, I'm the only one who has seen the ocean.
I describe it over and over; they say 'hmm'
and continue circling the chicken coop with wire.
I tell about the spume, and the wearisome size of the waters;
they don't remember there's such a place as Kenya,
they'd never guess I'm thinking of Tanzania.
Eagerly they show me the lot: this is where the kitchen will be,
that's where we'll put in a garden.
So what do I do with the coast?
It was a pretty afternoon the day I planted myself in the window, between uncles,
and saw the man with his fly open,
the trellis angry with roses.
Hours and hours we talked unconsciously in Portuguese
as if it were the only language in the world.
Faith or no, I ask where are my people who are gone;
because I'm human, I zealously cover the pan of leftover sauce.

How could we know how to live a better life than this,
when even weeping it feels so good to be together?
Suffering belongs to no language.
I suffered and I suffer both in Minas Gerais and at the edge of the ocean.

Estarreço de estar viva. Ó luar do sertão,
ó matas que não preciso ver pra me perder,
ó cidades grandes, estados do Brasil que amo como se os tivesse inventado.
Ser brasileira me determina de modo emocionante
e isto, que posso chamar de destino, sem pecar,
descansa meu bem-querer.
Tudo junto é inteligível demais e eu não suporto.
Valha-me noite que me cobre de sono.
O pensamento da morte não se acostuma comigo.
Estremecerei de susto até dormir.
E no entanto é tudo tão pequeno.
Para o desejo do meu coração
o mar é uma gota.

Responsório

O PELICANO (1987) | POESIAS REUNIDA (2015)

Santo António,
procurai para mim a carteira perdida,
vós que estais desafadigado,
gozando junto de Deus a recompensa dos justos.
Estão nela a paga do meu trabalho por um mês,
documentos e um retrato
onde apareço cansada, com uma cara
que ninguém olhará mais de uma vez
a não ser vós, que já em vida
vos apiedáveis dos tormentos humanos:
sumiu a agulha da bordadeira,
sumiu o namorado,
o navio no alto-mar,
sumiu o dinheiro no ar.
Tenho que comprar coisas, pagar contas,
dívidas de existir neste planeta convulso.
Prometo-vos uma vela de cera,
um terço do meu salário
e outro que rezarei
pra entoar vossos louvores, ó Martelo dos Hereges,
cuja língua restou fresca
entre vossos ossos, intacta.

I stand in awe of being alive. Oh, moon over the backlands,
oh, forests I don't need to see to get lost in,
oh, great cities and states of Brazil that I love as if I had invented them.
Being Brazilian places me in a way I find moving
and this, which without sinning I can call fate,
gives my desire a rest.
Taken all at once, it's far too intelligible; I can't take it.
Night! Make yourself useful and cover me with sleep.
Me and the thought of death just can't get used to each other.
I'll tremble with fear until the end.
And meanwhile everything is so small.
Compared to my heart's desire
the sea is a drop.

Responsory

THE PELICAN (1987) | THE MYSTICAL ROSE (2014)

Saint Anthony,
please find my lost wallet,
you who are tireless,
there with God enjoying your just rewards.
A whole month's pay is in that wallet,
plus my I.D.'s and a photo
of me, exhausted, a face
no one would look at twice
except for you, since even when you were alive
you had compassion for human anguish:
the disappearing embroidery needle,
boyfriend gone without a trace,
ship on the high seas,
money into thin air.
I have a shopping list, bills to pay,
dues for living on this tumultuous planet.
I promise I'll light a fancy candle,
give a third of my paycheck
pray a third of the rosary,
intoning your praises, O Hammer of Heretics,
whose tongue remained fresh
among your bones, intact.

Servo do Senhor, procurai para mim a carteira perdida
e se tal não aprouver a Deus para a salvação da minha alma,
procurai antes me ensinar
a viver como vós,
como um pobre de Deus.
Amém!

Sedução

BAGAGEM (1976) | THE MYSTICAL ROSE (2014)

A poesia me pega com sua roda dentada,
me força a escutar imóvel
o seu discurso esdrúxulo.
Me abraça detrás do muro, levanta
a saia pra eu ver, amorosa e doida.
Acontece a má coisa, eu lhe digo,
também sou filho de Deus,
me deixa desesperar.
Ela responde passando
língua quente em meu pescoço,
fala pau pra me acalmar,
fala pedra, geometria,
se descuida e fica meiga,
aproveito pra me safar.
Eu corro ela corre mais,
eu grito ela grita mais,
sete demônios mais forte.
Me pega a ponta do pé
e vem até na cabeça,
fazendo sulcos profundos.
É de ferro a roda dentada dela.

Servant of the Lord, please find my lost wallet
and if God doesn't think this best for my soul
then teach me instead
to live like you,
like a poor wretch of God,
Amen!

Seduction

BAGGAGE (1976) | THE MYSTICAL ROSE (2014)

Poetry catches me with her toothed wheel
and forces me to listen, stock-still,
to her extravagant discourse.
Poetry embraces me behind the garden wall, she picks up
her skirt and lets me see, loving and loony.
Bad things happen, I tell her,
I, too, am a child of God,
allow me my despair.
Her answer is to draw her hot tongue
across my neck;
she says *rod* to calm me,
she says *stone*, *geometry*,
she gets careless and turns tender,
I take advantage and sneak off.
I run and she runs faster,
I yell and she yells louder,
seven demons stronger.
She catches me, making deep grooves
from tip to toe.
Poetry's toothed wheel is made of steel.

A treva

O PELICANO (1987) | POESIAS REUNIDA (2015)

Me escolhern os claros do sono
engastados na madrugada,
a hora do Getsêmani.
São cruas claras visões,
às vezes pacificadas,
às vezes o terror puro
sem o suporte dos ossos
que o dia pleno me dá.
A alma desce aos infernos,
a morte tem seu festim.
Alé que todos despertem
e eu mesma possa dormir,
o demônion come a seu gosto,
o que não é Deus pasta em mim.

Direitos humanos

ORÁCULOS DE MAIO (1999) | THE MYSTICAL ROSE (2014)

Sei que Deus mora em mim
como sua melhor casa.
Sou sua paisagem,
sua retorta alquímica
e para sua alegria
seus dois olhos.
Mas esta letra é minha.

The Dark of Night

THE PELICAN (1987) | THE MYSTICAL ROSE (2014)

I'm singled out by flashes
embedded in half-sleep,
pre-dawn, Gethsemane hour.
These visions are raw and clear,
sometimes peaceful,
sometimes pure terror
without the bone structure
daylight provides.
The soul descends to hell,
death throws its banquet.
Until everyone else wakes up
and I can doze,
the devil eats his fill.
Not-God grazes on me.

Human Rights

ORACLES OF MAY (1999) | THE MYSTICAL ROSE (2014)

I know God lives in me
as in no other house.
I am His countryside,
His alchemical vessel,
and, to His joy,
His two eyes.
But this handwriting is mine.

3 | SALLY READ

Filmed by Neil Astley in London, 24 March 2010

Born in Suffolk in 1971, Sally Read trained and worked as a psychiatric nurse in London while completing a BA with the Open University, and went on to earn her MA at the University of South Dakota in the US. She received an Eric Gregory Award in 2001, and has published three poetry collections with Bloodaxe: *The Point of Splitting* (2005), *Broken Sleep* (2009) and *The Day Hospital* (2012).

Living mostly in Santa Marinella, Rome, she is poet in residence at the Hermitage of the Three Holy Hierarchs. Her memoir, *Night's Bright Darkness*, the story of her conversion to Catholicism, was published by Ignatius Press in 2016, and she has recently translated the spiritual diary of the Blessed Maria Crocifissa Curcio into English for the Carmelite Missionary Sisters of Saint Thérèse of the Child Jesus.

She reads from her first two collections in the film. *The Point of Splitting* ranges from London's hospital wards to rural Italy and the Great Plains, eulogising the emotional and physical borders we cross, whether in sexual surrender, the squeezing of a trigger, or the point at which skin is pierced by a needle. What results appeals to the thresholds at which we succumb to desire, love, or grief. Yet, ultimately, there is tenderness and acceptance as she considers what breaks us, and what binds.

The intimate and truthful poems in *Broken Sleep* move from the very earliest and most delicate stages of life to the many adjustments of adulthood. Always startlingly honest, the pains of closeness and separation, love and mortality are dealt with in unflinching and transforming ways, notably in a cycle of poems from a mother to her baby, moving from the uncertainty and awe at the discovery of a pregnancy, through the ecstasy of early motherhood.

Instruction

THE POINT OF SPLITTING (2005)

Check: water, soap, a folded sheet, a shroud.
Close cubicle curtains; light's swallowed
in hospital green. Our man lies dense
with gravity: an arm, his head, at angles
as if dropped from a great height. There is
a fogged mermaid from shoulder to wrist,
nicotine-stained teeth, nails dug with dirt –
a labourer then, one for the women.
A smooth drain to ivory is overtaking
from the feet. Wash him, swiftly, praising
in murmurs like your mother used,
undressing you when asleep. Dry carefully.
If he complained at the damp when alive, dry
again. Remove teeth, all tags, rip off elastoplast –
careful now, each cell is snuffing its lights,
but black blood still spurts. Now,
the shroud (opaque, choirboy ruff), fasten
it on him, comb his hair to the right. Now
he could be anyone. Now wrap in the sheet,
like a parcel, start at his feet. Swaddle (not
tight nor too loose) – it's an art, sheafing
this bundle of untied, heavy sticks. Hesitate
before covering his face, bandaging warm
wet recesses of eyes, mouth. Your hands
will prick – an animal sniffing last traces
of life. Cradle the head, bind it with tape
and when it lolls, lovingly against your chest,
lower it gently as a bowl brimmed with water.
Collect tags, teeth, washbowl. Open
the window, let the soul fly. Through
green curtains the day will tear: cabs, sun-
glare, rain. Remember to check:
tidied bed, emptied cabinet, sheeted form –
observe him recede to the flux between seconds,
the slowness of sand. Don't loiter. Slide
back into the ward's slipstream; pick up
your pace immediately.

The Reflex

BROKEN SLEEP (2009)

Then we had to undress the new patient.
We freed her thin arms from her top, passed
her hands from one of ours to the other,

guided her scarred wrists as she pulled
down her jeans. Like suitors we preserved
a fine electricity of contact, and I noted

the slow curves of a 14-year-old girl –
muted waist, bare scoops of breasts;
the drugged grease of her gaze, as though this

new growth were salted for us.
She was malleable. So slack
we could have rolled her in water

like silk and pegged her to dry.
She snaked down the bath-tub
to condensation and sweat; the wet

weed of hair bothering her face,
her hands too doped to connect.
I rested my arms on the side;

the steam rose; her starved pelvis
emerged in a crisp bluish line;
and she dove. She slipped, hard,

through our grasp. We grabbed
water; hit flesh, porcelain; fingered
the newly breathing hair. She threw

her legs high, and as they broke
to the astonishing lightness of air,
she almost wheeled over. Her mind's

one living note riffled the world
for an exit as a prisoner is alert
to any envelope of sun.

But her lungs smarted and wrung
themselves like hands; and her legs,
as we cradled her and the bath

swallowed its load, kicked
like a newborn lamenting
the apparent desertion of gravity.

The Soldier's Girl
THE POINT OF SPLITTING (2005)

I've never held a gun, but knew
if I did it would be like this:
in a red nightdress in a foreign town,
a smell of chicken clinging
in the curtains, a man standing over me
saying *Never touch it*,
                              then taking me through it.
Stiff with gold buttons and starch, you slide
the magazine in, draw the barrel, cock,
slick as a dealer's shuffle, part brag,
part second nature, hand it to me, packed
like a dead man's head. I raise, pull
the trigger. It's slight as a key turning,
the high click carrying the relief
of every Russian roulette scene. But I let
the safety-catch lecture, mechanical
breakdown, count of sixteen bullets (strapped
ready for action) wash over.
                              I'm afraid
of fluency. Take standing in a bar,
a stranger's mouth dry and silent,
so close you see pupils crawl open
like ink on cartridge paper, the tremors
of each hair, feel the pull of heat inches
from you.
              This childish giving in to instinct
could squeeze fingers round a gun, engulfing
as a blush. And take that scene: me worse for wear,
unable to see a line, let alone draw it.

You in the doorway; the hot recognition
of my white arms sprawled across another
man's neck kick-starting fury, easy
as a light switch, and jarring your eyes'
membrane for seconds before black.

Mafia Flowers

BROKEN SLEEP (2009)

4 A.M., you're called to the blindness of a country night
where you only tell the mute space of your eyes,
awkward step, formless breath.

The farmhouse is lit: a cage of day. Every lamp
and overhead jammed on, the unshakeable light
of a hundred suns. The white haired man's

vertical in the middle of the room, eyes popped
of meaning like a baked fish. Red hands covering
his mouth in the first fresh jump of shock,

though the florist's van came in daylight, innocent,
at the regular hour of eight. *'Why'd you wait so long
to call?' 'There were more than I'd reckoned.'*

The room's bright as a butcher's shop with blooms.
Not blooms, not flowers. Wrought, dyed, compressed
funeral wreaths. Dense, satin-sashed circles,

and one spelling his name in rusty chrysanths.
It's propped on his straight chair, another's laid
on the bed, another on the sports section

at the folding table, more overwhelm the floor.
Tight daisies in fanciful blue, salmony pink,
hawkish yellow, heaving the scent and stickiness

of God's nature, amassed beyond wonder.
The colours of Gabriel's miraculous, oily wings
(as fleshed out by men). You take your cap off,

bedazzled at the light, at this man's funeral
and the man not dead. You walk the creaking wreaths,
pretending notes, pour grappa to restore his voice,

bag them like bodies, flick switches one by one
to a dim bedside lamp, so as you step out into the cold
the moon reasserts itself calmly on stones,

the natural order of things. But as you drive,
you can't shake the image of the man slunk in his chair
– crazy – refusing to wake his brothers or tell a soul

of this visitation. The daylight and angels and wreaths
are his – whatever crime he may or may not have done –
as if he conjured each flower himself; he stinks of them.

The same as if 14-year-old Mary had gone running
to Elizabeth, broad-sided by her elaborate tale, saying
it was nothing of her idea and she'd as soon forget it.

Too late. Already the gold congeals above her head,
and Elizabeth's eyeing her warily, her flesh
and blood womb leaping in fear.

On the main road the dawn develops, grey
as sanity, the town is a host of cool witnesses
waking, and as you turn into your lane

there's an almighty rightness you're still
clinging to a month on
when news of his death is delivered.

Peony

BROKEN SLEEP (2009)

The room dim behind fly-screens.
Cicadas ratcheting their waves of itch,
scratch, itch. Your face is swollen
like an unsprung peony. Asleep

on my arm it bobs and tinkers
gravity like a bud barely able
to support its neck in a glass jar.
Even in this heat your skin

is smooth. It has a dull light,
and your lashes score your cheeks,
your face so full your eye-lids
belie their sockets. You slide

between my arms, your parted lips
hovering at my breast's tip.
Dry thrill. Your mouth smacks
and dreams of milk. I think

of the five peonies I kept on my desk
last year and how I yearned
to bin them when they broke
their rash of swiftly browning secrets.

I couldn't stand the recklessness;
the deep pink and the fancy layers;
the exhaustion of promise – blasé
as the neck of a woman out of love.

4 | LAWRENCE SAIL

Filmed at home in Exeter by Pamela Robertson-Pearce,
8 November 2009

Lawrence Sail's poems balance dream and history, delight and
unease: they weigh the art of the possible against the encroach-
ment of time. His characteristic themes are the border country
between belief and doubt; the interplay of memory and imagina-
tion; the possibilities of art; and the context of silence. Attentive
to the often alluring details of the material and natural world,
many of them reflecting a lifelong love of the sea, his poems also
contemplate the relationship between appearance and essence.

His Bloodaxe retrospective *Waking Dreams: New & Selected
Poems* (2010), covers work written over four decades, drawing on
poems from ten collections, from *Opposite Views* (1974) to the
New Poems (2010) first collected in this volume. It includes poems
from four books previously published by Bloodaxe, *Out of Land:
New & Selected Poems* (1992), *Building into Air* (1995), *The World
Returning* (2002), and *Eye-Baby* (2006). In Pamela's film he reads
and introduces a selection of poems from this body of work. A
later collection, *The Quick*, was published by Bloodaxe in 2015.

Reviewing his work for *PN Review*, Peter Scupham wrote that
'There is a shimmering quality to Sail's sensibility which moves
easily between sharply focused observations of the particulars of
object and place, the play of light on the locally loved and known,
and a constant alertness to larger climates and movements...close
and subtle looking and a rich, playful use of language are the tools
by which discoveries are made.'

Born in 1942 in London and brought up in Exeter, he studied
French and German at Oxford University, then taught for some
years in Kenya, before returning to teach in the UK. He is now a
freelance writer and lives in Exeter. His other books include *Cross-
currents: essays* (Enitharmon, 2005), a memoir of childhood, *Sift*
(Impress Books, 2010), *Songs of the Darkness*, a selection of his
Christmas poems with illustrations by his daughter, Erica Sail
(Enitharmon, 2010), and several anthologies.

The Cablecar

THE WORLD RETURNING (2002) | WAKING DREAMS (2010)

The silver box rose lightly up from the valley,
ape-easy, hanging on by its one arm;
in minutes, it had shrunk the town to a diagram,
the leaping river to a sluggish leat of kaolin,
the fletched forests to points it overrode.
It had you in its web of counterweights,
of circles evolved to parallel straight lines.

Riding the long slurs, it whisked you over
the moraine's hopeless rubble. It had your heart
in your mouth at every pylon, where it sagged,
leaned back, swooped on. It had you hear how ice
cracked on the cable. It had you watch it throw
an already crumpled shadow of bent steel
onto the seracs. It made you think of falling.

By the time it lowered you back to the spread valley,
to the broad-roofed houses decorated with lights,
you could think only of what it was like to step
out, at the top, onto the giddy edge
of snowfields still unprinted, that pure blaze;
to be robbed of your breath by the thin air, by a glimpse
of the moon's daytime ghost on solid blue.

Departures

OUT OF LAND (1992) | WAKING DREAMS (2010)

Set in a floral arcade,
These are the dreams of departures, in which
The ancient climbing roses are always
In bloom beneath the shivering glass
Of the station's forcing-house. Although
Figures must dwindle and twined fingers
Have to unclasp, the backward look
Stays for ever. On cheeks high-toned
With grief, a single frozen tear.

But dreams are dreams – already
The first bend has removed the station
From view, and the shapely words of thanks
And farewell no longer make sense as the engine
Rattles through landscapes to which they belong
Not at all. Accept, nonetheless,
This real ghost train of gratitude, of words
Marshalled before, to be printed after,
As the lights of the carriages shrink into darkness.

The Enclosures

THE WORLD RETURNING (2002) | WAKING DREAMS (2010)

Four unexpected meadow flowers slide out from
the sky-blue letter you sent from Kyrgyzstan –
a clover with pink bristles, a blue vetch
faded to light mauve, a yellow crucifer,
a white chickweed. They lie here, tiny, flattened,
intact – as delicate as any of the wreaths
found buried with the ithyphallic boy-king
and all his rubble of riches: the collarette
with little love-apples and berries of woody nightshade
strung on strips of palm; or the farewell garland
of olive leaves, blue water-lily petals
and cornflowers, which someone left on the dark threshold.
  These, too, paling with absence, recast love's spell
  as open pathos, and time as immortelles.

Rain at Sea

AQUAMARINE (1988) | WAKING DREAMS (2010)

It rings the raddled waves, pocking
The long troughs with icy shot,
Replacing the horizon deftly
With its cold, sea-rain ghosts –

Of the captain pinned in the tall wheelhouse,
His pinched and bearded face that peers
Onto sheer disasters, the oncoming truth
Of irrefutable, house-high crests;

Of the green cabin-boy, so pale
And pretty, felled by sea fever,
Tipped from under the ensign, in the lee
Of the Horn, the crew on deck, grim-faced;

Of the ship that steers through every weather,
Doubling the Cape of Immoderate Hope,
Wheel lashed, bound for the shores of
Dark Narragonia, Never-Never...

The rain, the seething rain that falls
Knows more of soft corruption than any
Churning depth. The sea's decks,
Awash, grow wormy as any wreck.

Snooker Players

DEVOTIONS (1987) | WAKING DREAMS (2010)

They whistle the fine smoke
Of blue dust from the cue,
Suave as gunslingers, never
Twitching one muscle too few.
At ease, holstering their thumbs
In trimmest waistcoats, they await
Their opponent's slip, the easiest
Of shots miscalculated.
Their sleek heads shine, spangled
With the sure knowledge of every angle.

Once at the table, they bend
In level reverence to squint
At globe after globe, each
With its window of light glinting
On cushioned greener than green,
The rounded image of reason.

One click and cosmology thrives,
All colours know their seasons
And tenderly God in white gloves
Retrieves each fallen planet with love.

Watching them, who could believe
In the world's lack of balance?
Tucked in this pocket of light
Everything seems to make sense –
Where grace is an endless break
And justice, skill repaid,
And all eclipses are merely
A heavenly snooker displayed.
Yet all around, in the framing
Darkness, doubt dogs the game.

At the Bedside

FROM EYE-BABY (2006) | WAKING DREAMS (2010)

Perhaps it is not, after all,
the whole story which races
through the heads of the dying, with the gloss
of last words in waiting –
but some inconsequential detail
which just happens to have stuck.

Say, for instance, the taste
of a boiled egg eaten, when a child,
in St Austell, by a window looking
out over kaolin mountains.
The sweetness of the yolk against
the tangy bread and butter.

Or the perfect round of apples
at the foot of a tree in Brittany
so scrawny as to make fruit seem
miraculous. It looked as if
it had shed them all at once
as a single golden earth-halo.

411

Or the view of the old bridge
at Mostar, its high brow
soaring and swooping above
the Neretva. Or the drugging smell
of red valerian, or the feel
of silk rubbed between the fingers.

But perhaps such images are only
the journeys of wishing and warding
for those who wait by the bed,
for whom also it is late,
and who cannot ignore the tut
and sigh of the morphine shunt.

5 | CAROLE SATYAMURTI

Filmed at home in London by Neil Astley,
22 March 2010

Carole Satyamurti's poetry explores love, attachment and the fragility of personal survival, charting the tension between connected and separate lives. With an unflinching eye, she takes on complex and often painful subject-matter – cancer for instance or raising a disabled child. Many of her poems hinge on a turning-point or a place where one life touches another, bearing witness to the way we imagine – or fail to imagine – the otherness of others.

Her Bloodaxe retrospective *Stitching the Dark* (2005) draws on four previous books plus a new collection featuring poems with a deeper engagement with the universal predicament of how to live in the face of mortality – of what it means to exist, and to cease existing. Her title suggests that the act of writing – the search for the right words – is an attempt to repair, illuminate, and give form to what is unknown, fearful, perplexing. But these poems are by no means solemn. There is also wit and celebration, dark humour and a fine sense of the absurd.

The central theme of her later collection, *Countdown* (2011), is the shifting relationship between loss and gain. It explores the varied ways in which that relationship is played out in day-to-day experience. The poems range from personal to the political, the psychological to the scientific, many addressing the human cost of war and terror, most notably in 'Memorial', written after a visit to Oradour-sur-Glane, the still desolate French village where six hundred innocent people were massacred in 1944.

Her whole of her sequence 'Changing the Subject' is included in this anthology, but on the film she reads six of its 13 sections (2, 3, 6, 9, 12, 13).

Carole Satyamurti is a sociologist as well as a poet, and taught for many years at the Tavistock Clinic, where her main academic interest was in the relevance of psychoanalytic ideas to an understanding of the stories people tell about themselves, whether in formal autobiography or in social encounters. She co-edited *Acquainted with the Night: psychoanalysis and the poetic imagination* (2003). Her other books include *Mahabharata: A Modern Retelling* (W.W. Norton, 2015), joint winner of the inaugural Roehampton Poetry Prize.

Changing the Subject

CHANGING THE SUBJECT (1990) | STITCHING THE DARK (2005)

1 *The Word*

It started with my grandmother
who, fading unspeakably,
lay in the blue room; disappeared
leaving a cardboard box,
coils of chalky-brown rubber tube.

I inherited her room, her key.
The walls were papered bright
but the unsayable word
seeped through; some nights
I heard it in the dripping of the tap.

I saw it in my parents' mouths,
how it twisted lips for whispers
before they changed the subject.
I saw it through fingers
screening me from news.

The word has rooted in my head
casting blue shadows.
It has put on flesh,
spawned strong and crazy children
who wake, reach out their claws.

2 *Out-Patients*

Women stripped to the waist,
wrapped in blue,
we are a uniform edition
waiting to be read.

These plain covers suit us:
we're inexplicit,
it's not our style to advertise
our fearful narratives.

My turn. He reads my breasts
like braille, finding the lump
I knew was there. This is
the episode I could see coming –

although he's reassuring,
doesn't think it's sinister
but just to be quite clear...
He's taking over,

he'll be the writer now,
the plot-master,
and I must wait
to read my next instalment.

3 *Diagnosis*

He was good at telling,
gentle, but direct;
he stayed with me
while I recovered breath,
started to collect

stumbling questions. He said
cancer with a small c –
the raw stuff of routine –
yet his manner showed
he knew it couldn't be ordinary for me.

Walking down the road
I shivered like a gong
that's just been struck –
mutilation...what have I done...
my child...how long... –

and noticed how
the vast possible array
of individual speech
is whittled by bad news
to what all frightened people say.

That night, the freak storm.
I listened to trees fall,
stout fences crack,
felt the house shudder as the wind
howled the truest cliché of them all.

4 *In-Patient*

I have inherited another woman's flowers.
She's left no after-scent, fallen hairs,
no echoes of her voice,
no sign of who or how she was

or through which door she made her exit.
Only these bouquets – carnations,
tiger lilies, hothouse roses,
meretricious everlasting flowers.

By day, they form the set in which I play
the patient – one of a long line
of actresses who've played the part
on this small white stage.

It's a script rich in alternatives.
Each reading reveals something new,
so I perform variously – not falsehoods,
just the interpretations I can manage.

At night, the flowers are oracles.
Sometimes they seem to promise a long run;
then frighten me with their bowing heads,
their hint of swan-songs.

5 *Woman in Pink*

The big, beautiful copper-haired
woman in the next bed
is drowning in pink.

She wears pink frills,
pink fluffy cardigan and slippers.
Her 'get well' cards carry pink messages.

Her husband brings pink tissues,
a pink china kitten; he pats her head.
She speaks in a pink powder voice.

Yet she is big and beautiful and coppery.
At night, she cries bitterly,
coughs and coughs from her broad chest.

They've done all they can.
She's taking home bottles of morphine syrup,
its colour indeterminate.

6 *How Are You?*

When he asked me that
what if I'd said,
rather than 'very well',
'dreadful – full of dread'?

Since I have known this,
language has cracked,
meanings have re-arranged;
dream, risk and fact

changed places. Tenses tip,
word-roots are suddenly
important, some grip
on the slippery.

We're on thin linguistic ice
lifelong, but I see through;
I read the sentence
we are all subject to

in the stopped mouths of those
who once were 'I',
full-fleshed, confident
using the verb 'to die'

of plants and pets and parents
until the immense
contingency of things
deleted sense.

They are his future
as well as mine,
but I won't make him look.
I say, 'I'm fine'.

7 *Anna*

Visiting time. Anna rises from her bed,
walks down the ward, slowly,
treading glass. She wears
her hand-sewn patchwork dressing-gown,
cut full, concealing her swollen abdomen.

She smiles at people she passes;
pulls her shoulders back,
making a joke about deportment;
waves a skeletal hand
at Mrs Shah, who speaks no English.

Her little girls sit by her bed
in their school uniforms. Too good,
they're silent as they watch her,
tall in her brave vestment
of patterned tesserae

that once were other garments –
as she was: a patchwork mother
made of innumerable creative acts
which they'll inherit with her robe
and make of them something new.

She stops. We hold our breath.
Gaining time, she whispers to a nurse
then turns, walks back to her children,
smiling. Look, she is telling them,
I'm still familiar. I belong to you.

Class is irrelevant in here.
We're part of a new scale –
mobility is all one way
and the least respected
are envied most.

First, the benigns,
in for a night or two,
nervous, but unappalled;
foolishly glad their bodies
don't behave like that.

Then the exploratories;
can't wait to know, but have to.
Greedy for signs, they swing
from misery to confidence,
or just endure.

The primaries are in
for surgery – what kind? What then?
Shocked, tearful perhaps;
things happening too fast.
Still can't believe it, really.

The reconstructions are survivors,
experienced, detached.
They're bent on being almost normal;
don't want to think
of other possibilities.

Secondaries (treatment)
are often angry – with doctors, fate –
or blame themselves.
They want to tell their stories,
not to feel so alone.

Secondaries (palliative)
are admitted swathed in pain.
They become gentle, grateful,
they've learned to live
one day at a time.

Terminals are royalty,
beyond the rest of us.
They lie in side-rooms
flanked by exhausted relatives,
sans everything.

We learn the social map
fast. Beneath the ordinary chat,
jokes, kindnesses, we're scavengers,
gnawing at each other's histories
for scraps of hope.

9 *Difficult Passages*

'You did not proper practise,'
my cello teacher's sorrowful
mid-European vowels reproached me.
'Many times play through the piece
is not the proper practising –
you must repeat difficult passages
so when you make performance
there is no fear – you know
the music is inside your capacity.'
Her stabbing finger, moist gaze,
sought to plant the lesson in my soul.

I've practised pain for forty years –
all those Chinese burns;
the home-made dynamo we used
to test our tolerance for shocks;
hands wrapped round snowballs;
untreated corns – all pain practice.
Fine – if I can choose the repertoire.
But what if some day I'm required
to play a great pain concerto?
Will that be inside my capacity?

I've hung the washing out
and turn to see
the door slammed shut
by a capricious wind.

Locked out, face to the glass,
I see myself reflected
in the mirror opposite,
framed, slightly menacing.

No need for wuthering
to feel how it might be –
I have that sepia, far-seeing
look of long-dead people.

Perhaps I wouldn't feel dead,
just confused, lost track of time;
could it be years since I turned
with that mouthful of pegs?

And might I now beat on the glass
with jelly fists, my breath
making no cloud in this crisp air,
shout with no sound coming?

Death could seem this accidental –
the play of cells
mad as the freakishness of weather,
the arbitrary shutting out.

Might there be some self left
to look back, register
the shape of the receding house?
And would it feel this cold?

11 *Choosing the Furniture*

The curtains said:
what do you fear more than anything?
Look at it now.

A white room.
I lie and cannot speak,
can not get up.
I stream with pain from every part.
I cry, scream until the sound chokes me.
Someone at the door looks in,
glances at her watch, moves on.
No one comes. No one
will ever come.

The lamp said:
think of what would be most blissful –
what do you see?

A white room
lined with books; a window
looking out on trees and water;
bright rugs, a couch, a huge table
where I sit, words spinning from my fingers.
No one comes; time is limitless,
alone is perfect.
Someone leaves food at the gate –
fruit, bread, little chocolate birds.

The moon laughed:
there is only one room.
You choose the furniture.

12 *I Shall Paint My Nails Red*

because a bit of colour is a public service.

because I am proud of my hands.

because it will remind me I'm a woman.

because I will look like a survivor.

422

because I can admire them in traffic jams.

because my daughter will say ugh.

because my lover will be surprised.

because it is quicker than dyeing my hair.

because it is a ten-minute moratorium.

because it is reversible.

13 *Watching Swallows*

In my fiftieth year,
with my folded chin
that makes my daughter call me Touché Turtle;

in my fiftieth year,
with a brood of half-tamed fears
clinging around my hem,

I sit with my green shiny notebook
and my battered red notebook
and my notebook with the marbled cover,

and I want to feel
revolutions spinning me apart,
re-forming me –

as would be fitting in one's fiftieth year.

Instead, I hum a tune to my own pulse.

Instead, I busy dead flies off the sill
and realign my dictionaries.

Instead, through the window,
I make a sign of solidarity
at swallows, massing along the wires.

Sathyaji

STITCHING THE DARK (2005)

Dusk, and the boathouse keeper
calls the late, scattered boats
from beyond the curve
in the lake; calls them by name,
Hirondelle! Angelique! George Sand!
Are they real or imagined,
those smudges of black
in the shade of the far bank?
Again his call, carrying, returning.

What's in a name? You are –
in the name I called you by;
its weight and shape hard to convey
except – it lent itself to tenderness,
teasing and respect; closeness
and a certain distance.
Now it's a vessel
for the far-flung
only sure reality of you.

Love draws you back.
In saying your name, I see it
boat-shaped and luminous
stitching the dark,
returned from formless drift
about the world. Let me
recall you. I've words enough –
a sheaf of versions. My pen
engraves you differently each time.

Nothing can be held, or hurried.
Wind casts a shiver on the water;
shallows uncertain in withdrawing light.
A phalarope races its image
and is gone; reflected, relinquished,
discarnate as the distant boats
the boathouse keeper calls and calls,
only a name to summon each of them.

Yet, here they come.

(Lac Jemaye, France)

424

Life on Mir

COUNTDOWN (2011)

They took small fish, to observe
the effects of weightlessness in water.

Goldfish, ordinary on earth, were now
miraculous, their glitter precious currency,
their tiny mouths' O and O a greeting.

So that when they died some men wept,
feeling, as if for the first time,
how grave a life is. Any life at all.

Countdown to Midnight

COUNTDOWN (2011)

It's coming in silence, the way an abstraction
takes shape as an image waiting to grow;
it's coming as hope against hope – potential
as infancy, or unmarked snow.

It's a ship of uncertain destination,
a breathing space between promise and dread;
an imperfect cadence, a Chinese whisper,
a codebook no one could hold in their head.

And though the voice of reason grumbles
dates change nothing, and the pledges
the old year offered were paper-thin,
still, to the parliament of wishes –

our blinkered, greedy, quarrelsome
humanity – let New Year come.

6 | KAREN SOLIE

Filmed by Pamela Robertson-Pearce in Newcastle,
13 November 2013

Karen Solie won the Canadian Griffin Prize with only her third collection, *Pigeon*, in 2010, and has quickly established herself as one of the most distinctive and unsettling voices in Canadian poetry, a 'sublime singer of existential bewilderment'. Her poems are X-rays of our delusions and mistaken perceptions, explorations of violence, bad luck, fate, creeping catastrophe, love, desire, and the eros of danger, constantly exposing the fragility of the basis of trust on which modern humanity relies. They are double-edged, tense and tender, an edgy blend of irony and guts, of snarl and praise, of sharp intelligence and quizzical ambiguity.

In Canada, Don McKay has praised her 'fierce writing of quickness and edge that can take on just about anything: the highway, Freud, farm suicides, sturgeon, all manner of flawed and far-off romance – with candour and a trenchant humour that's the cutting edge of intelligence. Not to mention sly skinny music, not to mention sheer metaphorical pounce, moves that accomplish themselves before you realise they're underway.'

Karen Solie was born in Moose Jaw in the province of Saskatchewan, and grew up on the family farm. She initially wanted a career as a vet but dropped that plan to pursue her writing. She has published four collections in Canada.

I first came across her work when she took part in Poetry Parnassus at London's Southbank Centre in 2012, and arranged for Bloodaxe to publish her first UK edition, *The Living Option: Selected Poems*, the following year. In 2013 she returned to the UK to launch the book at Aldeburgh Poetry Festival, followed by readings in Hull, Sheffield, Edinburgh, and Newcastle, where we were able to film her before her NCLA event. All the new poems in the Bloodaxe edition have since been published in North America in a new collection, *The Road In Is Not the Same Road Out* (Anansi, Canada; Farrar, Straus and Giroux, US, 2015).

Sturgeon

SHORT HAUL ENGINE (2001) | THE LIVING OPTION (2013)

Jackfish and walleye circle like clouds as he strains
the silt floor of his pool, a lost lure in his lip,
Five of Diamonds, River Runt, Lazy Ike,
or a simple spoon, feeding
a slow disease of rust through his body's quiet armour.
Kin to caviar, he's an oily mudfish. Inedible.
Indelible. Ancient grunt of sea
in a warm prairie river, prehistory a third eye in his head.
He rests, and time passes as water and sand
through the long throat of him, in a hiss, as thoughts
of food. We take our guilts
to his valley and dump them in,
give him quicksilver to corrode his fins, weed killer,
gas oil mix, wrap him in poison arms.
Our bottom feeder,
sin-eater.

On an afternoon mean as a hook we hauled him
up to his nightmare of us and laughed
at his ugliness, soft sucker mouth opening,
closing on air that must have felt like ground glass,
left him to die with disdain
for what we could not consume.
And when he began to heave and thrash over yards of rock
to the water's edge and, unbelievably, in,
we couldn't hold him though we were teenaged
and bigger than everything. Could not contain
the old current he had for a mind, its pull,
and his body a muscle called river, called spawn.

Early in Winter

SHORT HAUL ENGINE (2001) | THE LIVING OPTION (2013)

The roads are bad and you miss
your old car, an even-tempered '68 Volvo,
those times jerry-rigged cardboard gaskets
and pantyhose fanbelts got you home
through worse weather, the expansiveness
of that gesture. The year's first snow

fell at noon and stuck, a thin light resting
on the firs that drags out the fade
of 4 o'clock and throws a clean sheet
over roadkill, a small blessing of dying
in winter. There is a loveliness to inadequacy
so simply put. I place a hand on your arm,

heavy clothes a door to the warm kitchen
of your body. You are deep inside the driving,
leaving me to consider the beautiful stall
of water frozen in the act of falling
from its pious glacier, to my resolve
to find an opening in this season,
feet cold, heart wagging its little tail.

Thrasher

MODERN AND NORMAL (2005) | THE LIVING OPTION (2013)

Yellow-legs ekes lower at nightfall to a stick nest
brambled in the shade-kill, doing for himself, deft

as a badger in a hammock. Mornings, toeing wracked heights
of the cottonwood, he flaps his brown flag above alkaline

slough beds, over plowlands attesting
to the back and forth of work, their brown degrees

scriven by road allowance cut at right angles through shriven
weeds, fenceposts bracketing brown rut lines slantwise

in relief. In relief at the topmost, he mimics domestic, migrant,
spaniel, spring peepers, quacks, urks, and gurgles akin

to a four-stroke in heavy water. He's slightly

off. None respond. His own call is the vinyl scratch
between tracks, a splice point. He was hatched

that way, ferruginous, a wet transistor
clacking from the egg in which he had lain curled

as an ear with an itch inside. He carries on
like AM radio. Like a prison rodeo. Recounts loser

baseball teams, jerry-riggers, part-timers, those paid in scrip,
anyone who has come out of retirement once

too often. He is playbacks, do-overs, repeats, repeats
the world's clamorous list, makes it his, replete,

and fledges from persistence what he is.

Tractor

PIGEON (2009) | THE LIVING OPTION (2015)

More than a storey high and twice that long,
it looks igneous, the Buhler Versatile 2360,
possessed of the ecology of some hellacious
minor island on which options
are now standard. Cresting the sections
in a corona part dirt, part heat, it appears
risen full-blown from our deeper needs,
aspirating its turbo-cooled air, articulated
and fully compatible. What used to take a week

it does in a day on approximately
a half-mile to the gallon. It cost one hundred
fifty grand. We hope to own it outright by 2017.
Few things wrought by human hands
are more sublime than the Buhler Versatile 2360.

Across the road, a crew erects the floodlit
derricks of a Texan outfit whose presumptions
are consistently vindicated.
The ancient sea bed will be fractured to 1000 feet
by pressuring through a pipe literal tons
of a fluid – the constituents of which
are best left out of this –
to tap the sweet gas where it lies like the side
our bread is buttered on. The earth shakes
terribly then, dear Houston, dear parent
corporation, with its re-broken dead and freshly
killed, the air concussive, cardiac, irregular.
It silences the arguments of every living thing
and our minds in that time are not entirely elsewhere.

But I was speaking of the Buhler Versatile 2360
Phase D! And how well recognised it is
among the classics: Wagner,
Steiger, International Harvester, John Deere, Case,
Minneapolis-Moline, Oliver, White, Allis-Chalmers,
Massey Ferguson, Ford, Rite, Rome.
One could say it manifests fate, forged
like a pearl around the grit of centuries. That,
in a sense, it's always been with us,
the diesel smell of a foregone conclusion.
In times of doubt, we cast our eyes
upon the Buhler Versatile 2360
and are comforted. And when it breaks down, or thinks
itself in gear and won't, for our own good, start,
it takes a guy out from the city at 60 bucks an hour
plus travel and parts, to fix it.

The Road In Is Not the Same as the Road Out

THE ROAD IN IS NOT THE SAME AS THE ROAD OUT (2015) | THE LIVING OPTION (2013)

The perspective is unfamiliar.
We hadn't looked back, driving in,
and lingered too long
at the viewpoint. It was a prime-of-life
experience. Many things we know
by their effects: void in the rock
that the river may advance, void
in the river that the fish may advance,
helicopter in the canyon
like a fly in a jar, a mote in the eye,
a wandering cause. It grew dark,
a shift change and a shift
in protocol. To the surface of the road
a trail rose, then a path to the surface
of the trail. The desert
sent its loose rock up to see.
An inaudible catastrophic orchestra
is tuning, we feel it in the air
impelled before it, as a pressure
on the brain. In the day
separate rays fall so thickly
from their source we cannot perceive
the gaps between them, but night
is absolute, uniform and self-
derived, the formerly irrelevant
brought to bear, the progress
of its native creatures unimpeded.
We have a plan between us, and then we
each have our own. Land of the four
corners, the silent partner, 500 dollars
down, no questions, the rental car
stops at the highway intersection, a filthy
violent storm under the hood. It yields
to traffic from both directions.
It appears it could go either way.

Spiral

THE ROAD IN IS NOT THE SAME AS THE ROAD OUT (2015) | THE LIVING OPTION (2013)

You said a storm makes a mansion of a poor man's house.
I wonder if you did so to make the best of living where
it always blew, the maddening wind that messed up our ions
and made men want to fight. Now you have no house.
There's no need. The cure took the good with the bad.

Who cannot escape his prison but must each day rebuild it?
For a year rather than drink we smoked and went to bingo.
It was like working in a mine, the air quality and incessant
coughing, bag lunches, good luck charms, the intergenerational
drama. It's not my place to say what changed.

You hadn't developed around a midpoint, and fell to the side.
A part remained exposed. Still, you were kind –
unusually so, it seems to me now, for someone with talent.
But loneliness expands to fill the void it creates. To plot against it
was to plot against yourself. You felt the effect of the whole.

When the mind is so altered this resembles death but it is
not death. Then the faint trail ran out and you continued on.
The night you've entered now has no lost wife in it, no daughter,
no friends, betrayal, or fear; it is impartial, without status.
I would like to think it peace, but suspect it isn't anything.

When our friend wrote you'd died I was on Skye,
where the wind in its many directions is directionless
and impossible to put your back to. He said you'd been living
rough for awhile, he wouldn't go to the wake at the bar,
it was too much sadness. That day I'd walked the beach,

picking up shells, their spirals of Archimedes and logarithmic
spirals, principle of proportional similarity that protects
the creature and makes it beautiful. Sandpipers materialised
through tears the wind made, chasing fringes of the rising tide.
At first there were two, then three appeared, but when I began
to pay attention I realised they were everywhere.

7 | PIOTR SOMMER

Filmed by Pamela Robertson-Pearce in Galway, 5 April 2008

Piotr Sommer is one of Poland's leading poets. As an editor and translator, he has been responsible for introducing Polish readers to the work of many modern and contemporary British and American poets. A number of those poets have in turn worked with him on translating his own poems into English, including John Ashbery, Douglas Dunn and D.J. Enright, who were soon joined by other co-translators. The first selection of his work to appear in English with their help was *Things to Translate and other poems*, published by Bloodaxe in 1991. This was followed by an expanded selection, *Continued*, in 2005.

In his introduction to *Continued*, August Kleinzahler writes: 'Sommer's main subject is the "quandary-ness" of "ordinary life": an old dog, the colour and texture of a lemon, a lift in a dilapidated block of flats, the crash of toiletries on a bathroom floor. The art of the poetry – and its art is considerable, singular and memorable – is in the way it matter-of-factly transforms ordinary incident, character, landscape, object and the assorted interactions thereof, into tiny metaphysical and epistemological essays: investigations into the subjects of language, imagination, impermanence, memory, identity. It is a poetry that engages large subjects through its attentiveness to seemingly small or minor events...

'There is a quality of otherness in the poetry, or the suggestion of otherness. Boundaries are continually being crossed. There are sallies and retreats. What at first may seem straightforward is, in fact, rather craftily and carefully assembled and held taut in a web of contingencies. Sommer is very much the poet as double-agent, working both sides of the border and travelling incognito.'

Born in 1948, he has published ten books of poetry in Polish and many translations, and has worked as an editor with Poland's premier literary journal, *Literatura na Świecie* (Literature in the World), since 1976. He has also taught at several universities in the US and was a visiting translator at the University of Warwick in Britain. We were able to film him during his visit to Cúirt International Festival of Literature in Galway in 2008.

The poems read by Piotr Sommer on the film were translated by him with these co-translators: John Ashbery [PS/JA], Edward Carey [PS/JA], D.J. Enright [PS/DJE], Michael Kasper [PS/MK], Mark Slobin [PS/MS], Mark Slobin & W. Martin [PS/MS/WM].

Piosenka pasterska

PIOSENKA PASTERSKA (1999)

Czytaj te parę zdań, jakbym był
obcym, innym
językiem, którym może wciąż jestem
(choć mówię twoimi słowami, posługuję się
twoimi słowami);
którym byłem mówiąc
twoim językiem,
stojąc za tobą i słuchając
bez słowa,
śpiewając
w twoim języku
moją melodię.
Czytaj, jakbyś miał słuchać,
nie rozumieć.

Niedyskrecje

CZYNNIK LIRYCZNY I INNE WIERSZE (1988)

Gdzie jesteśmy? W ironiach
których nikt nie chwyci, krótkotrwałych
i nieakcentowanych, w trywialnych pointach
które kwitują metafizykę niedorzecznym
detalem, w piątku, co wypada
na piątego listopada, w mnemotechnice dni.
Można dać przykład i można to przyjąć
na wiarę, kocią łapę na gardle.

I lubi się jeszcze pewne słowa i te, za przeproszeniem,
składnie, które udają, że coś je z sobą łączy.
W tych międzysensach zawiera się cały człowiek,
włazi tam, gdzie widzi trochę miejsca.

Shepherd's Song

SHEPHERD'S SONG (1999) | CONTINUED (2005)

Read these few sentences as if I were
some stranger, some other
language, which I may still be
(though I speak with your words, make use
of your words);
which I was, speaking
your language,
standing behind you and listening
wordlessly,
singing
in your tongue
my tune.
Read as if you were to listen,
not to understand.

[PS/MK]

Indiscretions

LYRIC FACTOR AND OTHER POEMS (1988) | CONTINUED (2005)

Where are we? In ironies
that no one will grasp, short-lived
and unmarked, in trivial points
which reduce metaphysics to absurd
detail, in Tuesday that falls on
day two of May, in mnemonics of days.
You can give an example or take it
on faith, cat's paw at the throat.

And one also likes certain words and those – pardon me –
syntaxes that pretend that something links them together.
Between these intermeanings the whole man is contained,
squeezing in where he sees a little space.

[PS/DJE]

Pewne drzewo na Powązkach

CZYNNIK LIRYCZNY I INNE WIERSZE (1988)

Całą pamięć zawdzięczamy przedmiotom
co przygarniają nas na życie i
oswajają dotykiem, zapachem
i szelestem. Dlatego tak im trudno
się z nami rozstać: do końca
oprowadzają nas po świecie,
do końca używają nas, zdziwione
naszą obojętnością i niewdzięcznością
tej sławnej prządki Mnemozyne.

Wiersz apolityczny

CZYNNIK LIRYCZNY I INNE WIERSZE (1988)

Silnik przyrody cykał, ćwierkał i chlupotał,
szumiał i dudnił, prawie rósł,
choć rzeczka była płytka,
mała, właściwie potok,

grzało popołudniowe słońce,
nie padał deszcz, a świerszcze
dawały sobie płynne zmiany, świetne technicznie,
bo przerw się nie słyszało, to była jakby

absolutnie wypełniona cisza:
mechanizm grał miarowo
i wcale się nie krztusił
sobą ani nadmiarem głosu, jak gdyby ciągle

obejmowała go gwarancja
którą wystawił diabli
wiedzą kto, bez stempli, bez papierków,
na gębę albo i na wiatr,

a jednak w maszynerii
wszystko dalej grało, falowało,
nie to że równomiernie, bo raz bliżej
a raz dalej, ze wszystkich stron,

A Certain Tree in Powązki Cemetery

LYRIC FACTOR AND OTHER POEMS (1988) | CONTINUED (2005)

All memory we owe to objects
which adopt us for life and
tame us with touch, smell
and rustle. That's why it's so hard
for them to part with us: they guide us
till the end, through the world,
till the end they use us, surprised
by our coolness and the ingratitude
of that famous spinner Mnemosyne.

[PS/JA]

Apolitical Poem

LYRIC FACTOR AND OTHER POEMS (1988) | CONTINUED (2005)

Nature's motor ticked, chirped and bubbled,
hummed and rumbled, almost swelled,
although the river was shallow,
small, in fact a brook,

the late-day sun was warm,
no rain fell, and crickets
changed shifts smoothly, technically perfect –
you couldn't hear the gaps, it was like

some absolutely packed silence:
the mechanism ran on steadily
and didn't choke at all
on itself or on the surfeit of voices as if

still covered by warranty
issued by god knows who,
without stamps, without paperwork –
with a handshake, or even with the wind –

and yet in the machinery
everything played on, rolling
not quite so evenly, now nearer,
now further off, from all sides,

z umiarem lub impetem, jak tam
dogadzało, niby w orkiestrze
której składniki poszczególne, części
pierwsze, to znaczy instrumenty

a może i publiczność:
źdźbła traw, które obejmowałem
wzrokiem, pokrzywy i paprocie,
nie poruszały się, a nawet

stały w miejscu,
jak gdyby albo były martwe albo
ciągle miały czas, albo
cierpliwość.

Nie bój się, nie zginie
CZYNNIK LIRYCZNY I INNE WIERSZE (1988)

Jakże miałbym nie rozumieć, co czujesz
tylko dlatego, że sam nigdy nie zgubiłem
książeczki PKO z oszczędnościami
z całego życia. A jednocześnie
radio jest zapalone i na pustej ulicy
kątem oka widzę przez okno
czterdziestolatka, z którym wczoraj
siedziałem kilka lat
w jednej ławce, spod podłogi
dobiega stukot magla i nawet
na sznurku do bielizny na balkonie
usiadł białobrązowy motyl. Muszę
zrobić małe zakupy, zdążyć na pociąg,
mam w kieszeni tylko kilkadziesiąt
złotych, ale klucze dzwonią
kiedy potrącam je palcami,
ulica robi się ludna, kieszenie
robią się pełne.

moderately or forcefully, as it
pleased, like an orchestra
whose particular components, primary
parts – the instruments

and maybe the audience too,
the blades of grass
my eyes surveyed, nettles and ferns –
didn't move, just

stood there
as if they were either dead or
still had time, or
patience.

[PS/MK]

Don't Worry, It Won't Get Lost

LYRIC FACTOR AND OTHER POEMS (1988) | CONTINUED (2005)

How could I fail to understand how you feel
even if personally I never lost
a PKO bankbook with my life
savings in it. Yet meanwhile
the radio's on, and glancing through the window
I see, on the empty street,
a forty-year-old with whom yesterday
I sat for a few years
on the same school bench, the knocking of the mangle
is heard under the floor, and even
on the balcony clothesline
a brown-and-white butterfly has landed. I have
some shopping to do, a train to catch,
there's only a few dozen złotys
in my pocket, but the keys
jingle when I brush them,
the street is getting peopled, pockets
are filling up.

[PS/MS]

Oddalające się planety jarzębiny

CZYNNIK LIRYCZNY I INNE WIERSZE (1988)

Ciągle jest coś ważniejszego: buteleczki
wypełnione do połowy Cardiamidem z kofeiną,
wciąż żywe, nawet puste
a też żywe, skoro stoją obok
koszyka z pieczywem i Piernika domowego w proszku
i nietkniętego wciąż słoika z Ziołomiodem. Żywe jest
niesprzątnięte mieszkanie –
to nie coś, to życie jest ważniejsze.

Powiększona wątroba
nie musi oznaczać najgorszego.
Mogła się zmęczyć hormonami,
razowym chlebem i kęsem wieprzowiny.

Szuflada w stole
pełna przeróżnych rupieci
przestałaby być żywa
gdyby zrobić w niej porządek.
Gdyby ułożyć książki w szafce,
zdjęcia w albumie, uprać resztę
brudnej bielizny, odmalować pokój –
one by też przestały.

Trzeba jeść, brać lekarstwa, stawiać
przy łóżku miednicę, schodzić z łóżka,
robić sobie herbatę i
wzywać lekarza,
który nie wytrze butów
lecz machinalnie wypisując
receptę, powie: ma pani
ładny obraz.

Rzeczywiście
ładny,
szczególnie po południu,
kiedy nałapie słońca.

(Listopad 1985)

Receding Planets of the Rowan Tree

LYRIC FACTOR AND OTHER POEMS (1988) | CONTINUED (2005)

There's always something more important – little bottles
half-filled with Cardiamid-and-Caffeine,
still alive, even when empty
they're alive, since they stand by
the basket of bread and the Homemade Gingerbread Mix
and the still untouched jar of Herb Honey. The untidied
apartment is alive –
not something, it's life that is more important.

The enlarged liver
doesn't have to mean the worst.
It could have tired itself with hormones,
brown bread and a bit of pork.

The table drawer
full of odds and ends
would no longer be alive
if it were put straight.
If books were ordered in the closet,
the photos in the album, the rest of the dirty clothes
washed, the room repainted –
they too would no longer live.

It's necessary to eat, take medicines, put
the bowl by the bed, get out of bed,
make tea and
call the doctor
who won't wipe his shoes
but mechanically writing out
the prescription, will say: you have
a nice picture there, madam.

As a matter of fact
very nice,
especially in the afternoon,
when it catches the sun.

(November 1985)

[PS/EC]

441

Mały traktat o niesprzeczności

CZYNNIK LIRYCZNY I INNE WIERSZE (1988)

Syn wychodzi przed blok zaczerpnąć powietrza
bo jesień jeszcze ładna i szkoda pogody.
Idzie nad staw badać robale, wraca
i sprawdza wszystko w książkach.

Z okna kuchni patrzę, jak chłopcy grają w nogę.
Otwierają się drzwi i przy otwartych drzwiach
słychać, że winda dzisiaj działa,
domyka się i rusza, ku pożytkowi.

Liść klonu

CZYNNIK LIRYCZNY I INNE WIERSZE (1988)

Liść klonu prześwietlony słońcem
u schyłku lata jest piękny, ale
nieprzesadnie i nawet zwykły
pociąg elektryczny przejeżdżający
o niespełna trzysta metrów dalej
daje muzykę lekką i nienatrętną
a do zapamiętania, ku jakiemuś
pożytkowi, być może, a nawet
pouczeniu (świat jakoś czasem
nie mówi wprost, że wszystko wie
i że ma dobrą pamięć, a już tym bardziej
nie będzie się nią popisywać)

Rano na ziemi

PIOSENKA PASTERSKA (1999)

Rano na ziemi cienki śnieg, a przedtem
tyle ciepła, prawie przedwiośnie.

A Small Treatise on Non-Contradiction

LYRIC FACTOR AND OTHER POEMS (1988) | CONTINUED (2005)

Son goes out of the apartment block to get some air
since the autumn's still pretty, and why waste the weather.
He goes to the pond to study bugs, returns
and checks everything in books.

From the kitchen window I watch the boys kick a ball.
The door opens, and while the door's open
you can hear that the lift works today,
clicks shut and moves on, to be useful.

[PS/MK]

A Maple Leaf

LYRIC FACTOR AND OTHER POEMS (1988) | CONTINUED (2005)

A maple leaf with the sun shining through it
at the end of summer is beautiful, but
not excessively so, and even an ordinary
electric train passing by
nearly three hundred yards away
makes music, light and unobtrusive,
and yet to be remembered, for its own sort of
usefulness perhaps, or even
instructiveness (the world somehow
doesn't quite say it knows everything,
has a good memory and, above all,
won't show it off)

[PS/JA]

Morning on Earth

SHEPHERD'S SONG (1999) | CONTINUED (2005)

Morning on earth, light snow, and just when
it was so warm, practically spring.

443

Ale na termometrze w kuchennym oknie
plus siedem stopni
i w ogóle dużo słońca.
                                    Jest pan
od światła, którego lubię
i nie ma pana od gazu
którego nie cierpię.
I nagle dwaj panowie M. –
za jednym z nich przepadam, drugi
trochę za bardzo prymus.
Wracają, obaj dziewięcioletni.
Mijają krzak jaśminu, co jest
jak duży bukiet z kresek.
                              Pod drzwiami
cieszy się pies, coś się z czymś
nie kłóci.

Ciąg dalszy

PIOSENKA PASTERSKA (1999)

Nic nie będzie tak samo jak było,
nawet cieszyć się z tych samych rzeczy
nie będziemy tak samo. Nasze smutki
będą się różnić między sobą i my będziemy
różnić się między sobą zmartwieniami.

I nic nie będzie tak samo jak było,
absolutnie nic. Proste myśli będą brzmiały
inaczej, nowiej, bo będą prościej i nowiej
powiedziane. Serce będzie umiało się otworzyć i miłość
nie będzie już miłością. Wszystko się zmieni.

Nic nie będzie tak samo jak było,
i to też będzie jakoś nowe, bo przecież
przedtem bywało podobnie: poranek,
reszta dnia, wieczór i noc, a teraz już nie.

But the thermometer in the kitchen window
says seven degrees,
and pretty sunny.
                    Here's
the electric company man I like,
and no sign of the gas man
I can't stand.
And all of a sudden two Misters M. –
one I've fallen for, the other
a bit of a hotshot –
coming back, both nine years old,
just passing the jasmine bush,
a huge bouquet of sticks.
                    Behind the door
the dog's excited, nothing's
at odds with anything.

[PS/MS/WM]

Continued

SHEPHERD'S SONG (1999) | CONTINUED (2005)

Nothing will be the same as it was,
even enjoying the same things
won't be the same. Our sorrows
will differ one from the other and we
will differ one from the other in our worries.

And nothing will be the same as it was,
nothing at all. Simple thoughts will sound
different, newer, since they'll be more simply, more newly
spoken. The heart will know how to open up and love
won't be love anymore. Everything will change.

Nothing will be the same as it was
and that too will be new somehow, since after all,
before, things could be similar: morning,
the rest of the day, evening and night, but not now.

[PS/MK]

8 | ARUNDHATHI SUBRAMANIAM

Filmed by Neil Astley in Mumbai, 3 November 2011

Arundhathi Subramaniam's poems explore life's ambivalences – around human intimacy with its bottlenecks and surprises, living in a Third World megalopolis, myth, the politics of culture and gender, and the persistent trope of the existential journey. They probe contradictory impulses: the desire for adventure and anchorage; expansion and containment; vulnerability and strength; freedom and belonging; withdrawal and engagement; an approach to language as exciting resource and desperate refuge.

She has published two books of poetry in Britain with Bloodaxe, *Where I Live: New & Selected Poems* (2009), which combines selections from her first two Indian collections, *On Cleaning Bookshelves* and *Where I Live*, with new work, and *When God Is a Traveller* (2014), which was shortlisted for the T.S. Eliot Prize.

The later poems included in *Where I Live* are meditations on desire in which the sensual and sacred mingle inextricably. There is a fascination with the skins that separate self from other, self from self, thing from no-thing. These are poems of dark need, of urgency, of desire as derailment, and derailment as possibility.

The poems of *When God Is a Traveller* are full of wonder and precarious elation, about learning to embrace the seemingly disparate landscapes of hermitage and court, the seemingly diverse addresses of mystery and clarity, disruption and stillness – all the roadblocks and rewards on the long dangerous route to recovering what it is to be alive and human. Their recurrent themes are wandering, digging, falling, coming to terms with unsettlement and uncertainty, finiteness and fallibility, exploring intersections between the sacred and the sensual, searching for ways to step in and out of stories, cycles and frames.

She also writes on spirituality and culture, with books including *The Book of Buddha* (Penguin, 2005) and *Sadhguru: More Than a Life* (Penguin, 2010). She edited Pilgrim's India: An Anthology (Penguin, 2011), and co-edited *Confronting Love* (Penguin, 2005), an anthology of Indian love poems in English.

We heard her read for the first time at Poetry International at London's Southbank Centre in 2006, and asked her on the spot if she'd like to be published in Britain by Bloodaxe. Later, I was able to film her in her home city when we shared a stage at Tata Literature Live! Mumbai LitFest in 2011.

How Some Hindus Find Their Personal Gods

(for AS who wonders about ishta devtas)

WHEN GOD IS A TRAVELLER (2014)

It's about learning to trust
the tug
that draws you to a shadowed alcove
undisturbed
by footfall
and butter lamps,

a blue-dark coolness
where you find him
waiting patiently,
that perfect minor deity –

shy, crumbly,
oven-fresh, just a little
wry, content to play a cameo
in everyone's life but your own.

A god who looks
like he could understand
errors in translation,
blizzards on the screen,
gaps in memory,
lapses in attention,

who might even learn by rote
the fury,
the wheeze,
the Pali,
the pidgin,
the gnashing mixer-grinder,
the awkward Remington stutter
of your heart,
who could make them his own.

After that you can settle for none other.

My Friends

WHEN GOD IS A TRAVELLER (2014)

They're sodden, the lot of them,
leafy, with more than a whiff
of damage,
mottled with history,
dark with grime.

God knows I've wanted them different –
less preoccupied, more jaunty,
less handle-with-care,

more airbrushed,
less prone
to impossible dreams, less perishable,

a little more willing
to soak in the sun.

They don't measure up.
They're unpunctual.
They turn suddenly tuberous.

But they matter
for their crooked smiles,
their endless distractions,
their sudden pauses –

signs that they know
how green stems twist

and thicken
as they vanish
into the dark,

making their way
through their own sticky vernacular tissues
of mud,

improvising,
blundering,
improvising –

Winter, Delhi, 1997

ON CLEANING BOOKSHELVES (2001) | WHERE I LIVE: NEW & SELECTED POEMS (2009)

My grandparents in January
on a garden swing
discuss old friends from Rangoon,
the parliamentary session, chrysanthemums,
an electricity bill.

In the shadows, I eavesdrop,
eighth grandchild, peripheral, half-forgotten,
enveloped carelessly
by the great winter shawl of their affection.

Our dissensions are ceremonial.
I growl obligingly
when he speaks of a Hindu nation,
he waves a dismissive hand
when I threaten romance with a Pakistani cricketer.

But there is more that connects us
than speech flavoured with the tartness of old curd
that links me fleetingly to her,
and a blurry outline of nose
that links me to him,
and there is more that connects us
than their daughter who birthed me.

I ask for no more.
Irreplaceable, I belong here
like I never will again,
my credentials never in question,
my tertiary nook in a gnarled family tree
non-negotiable.

And we both know
they will never need me
as much as I, them.
The inequality is comforting.

Madras, November, 1995

ON CLEANING BOOKSHELVES (2001) | WHERE I LIVE: NEW & SELECTED POEMS (2009)

Secret garden, swimming
in the amniotic light of a green afternoon,
where the trees are familiar, the pink musanda,
the thunder's north-eastern baritone and its subtexts,
where much lies buried beneath generations of soil
and the thick sugarcane slush of rain –

a cosmic despair over algebra homework
rising with the aroma of turmeric and damp jasmine,

the silent horror of my grandmother
who watched her husband drive away her cats
through the stern geometry of her kitchen window,

my fourteen-year-old indignations
near dusty bougainvillea tresses
at belonging to a tribe of burnished brahmins
that still likes to believe its skin is curdled vanilla,

and the long amorous wail
of confectioned Tamil film songs
from the transistor of a neighbour's gardener, long dead.

No, I am not sentimental
about the erasure of dynastic memories,
the collapse of ancestral houses,
but it will be difficult to forget
palm leaves in the winter storm,
ribbed, fossilised,
against heaving November skies,
building up their annual heritage of anguish
before the monsoons end.

Home

WHERE I LIVE (INDIA, 2005) | WHERE I LIVE: NEW & SELECTED POEMS (2009)

Give me a home
that isn't mine,
where I can slip in and out of rooms
without a trace,
never worrying
about the plumbing,
the colour of the curtains,
the cacophony of books by the bedside.

A home that I can wear lightly,
where the rooms aren't clogged
with yesterday's conversations,
where the self doesn't bloat
to fill in the crevices.

A home, like this body,
so alien when I try to belong,
so hospitable
when I decide I'm just visiting.

To the Welsh Critic Who Doesn't Find Me Identifiably Indian

WHERE I LIVE (INDIA, 2005) | WHERE I LIVE: NEW & SELECTED POEMS (2009)

You believe you know me,
wide-eyed Eng Lit type
from a sun-scalded colony,
reading my Keats – or is it yours –
while my country detonates
on your television screen.

You imagine you've cracked
my deepest fantasy –
oh, to be in an Edwardian vicarage,
living out my dharma
with every sip of dandelion tea
and dreams of the weekend jumble sale...

451

You may have a point.
I know nothing about silly mid-offs,
I stammer through my Tamil,
and I long for a nirvana
that is hermetic,
odour-free,
bottled in Switzerland,
money-back-guaranteed.

This business about language,
how much of it is mine,
how much yours,
how much from the mind,
how much from the gut,
how much is too little,
how much too much,
how much from the salon,
how much from the slum,
how I say verisimilitude,
how I say Brihadaranyaka,
how I say vaazhapazham –
it's all yours to measure,
the pathology of my breath,
the halitosis of gender,
my homogenised plosives
about as rustic
as a mouth-freshened global village.

Arbiter of identity,
remake me as you will.
Write me a new alphabet of danger,
a new patois to match
the Chola bronze of my skin.
Teach me how to come of age
in a literature you've bark-scratched
into scripture.
Smear my consonants
with cow-dung and turmeric and godhuli.
Pity me, sweating,
rancid, on the other side of the counter.
Stamp my papers,
lease me a new anxiety,
grant me a visa

to the country of my birth.
Teach me how to belong,
the way you do,
on every page of world history.

I Speak for Those with Orange Lunchboxes

WHEN GOD IS A TRAVELLER (2014)

I speak for those
with orange lunch boxes,

who play third tree
in an orchard of eight
in the annual school play,

who aren't headgirls,
games captains, class monitors,

who watch other girls fight for the seesaw
from the far wall across the sand-pit,

who remember everyone's lines
but their own,

who pelt after the school bus
their mother's breakfasts still heaving
in their gut,

who still believe
there'll be exams one day
they'll be ready for,

Those with orange lunch boxes.
I speak for them.

Or Take Mrs Salim Sheikh

WHEN GOD IS A TRAVELLER (2014)

Who ripples hospitably
out of her halwa-pink blouse
    and sari ('Synthetics are so practical
    to wear on trains, na?'). Who invokes
the protocol of Indian railways to ask
for your phone number even before
    the journey begins. Who unwinds
    her life story, well-oiled,
without a single split end.

    She's Hindu,
    a doctor, like her husband.
The Matron warned her
about inter-faith unions,
    but she had no doubts,
not even in '93 when others did.

Her ancestors supplied butter
    to Queen Victoria,
    His grandfather, better still,
was court dewan of Kolhapur.

    'I've been lucky.'
'The gods have been good.'
'I eat and cook non-veg.'
    'Many of my friends are pure brahmin,'
    'My sons are circumcised.'
'My heart is pure.'
'I practise no religion,
    only homeopathy.'

Over lunch she remembers
    the day her mother-in-law died in her arms.
'I bathed her,
and when the body was taken away,
I told my husband
I want to be buried in the kabrastan –
    it's closer to our home than the crematorium.'

Take Mrs Salim Sheikh.

Where the Script Ends

WHEN GOD IS A TRAVELLER (2014)

His shirt is tangerine,
the sky Delft,
the sunshine daffodils.

Even jealousy gleams brighter here
than broccoli
          stir fried.

In this daytime land
the canals speak
an unambiguous tongue.

We look over our shoulders
for a hint
of Venice.

All languages are honest here,
just none honest enough.

At home he speaks a dialect
he's never written in –
not even when his mother died.

And I know what it is to live
in a place where the mind's ink
has many tributaries, fermented enough
to make all songs
seem just a little
untrue.

It doesn't matter
whether he reads my lips
or I his mandarin fine print

because it still makes sense,
the old dream –

woman and man
under a night sky

and for a moment between them,
a single moon.

Prayer

ON CLEANING BOOKSHELVES (2001) | WHERE I LIVE: NEW & SELECTED POEMS (2009)

May things stay the way they are
in the simplest place you know.

May the shuttered windows
keep the air as cool as bottled jasmine.
May you never forget to listen
to the crumpled whisper of sheets
that mould themselves to your sleeping form.
May the pillows always be silvered
with cat-down and the muted percussion
of a lover's breath.
May the murmur of the wall clock
continue to decree that your providence
run ten minutes slow.

May nothing be disturbed
in the simplest place you know
for it is here in the foetal hush
that blueprints dissolve
and poems begin,
and faith spreads like the hum of crickets,
faith in a time
when maps shall fade,
nostalgia cease
and the vigil end.

Filmed at home in Cork by Neil Astley, 16 February 2012

Matthew Sweeney is one of Ireland's leading poets. He has published eleven collections, most recently, *Horse Music* (2013) and *Inquisition Lane* (2015) with Bloodaxe. I was able to film him reading a selection of poems from the manuscript of *Horse Music* when I visited him in Cork in 2012.

Horse Music is as sinister as its dark forebears, but the notes he hits here are lyrical and touching as well as disturbing and disquieting. Confronting him in these imaginative riffs are not just the perplexing animals and folklorish crows familiar from his earlier books, but also magical horses, ghosts, dwarfs and gnomes.

Central to the book are a group of Berlin poems – introducing us to, among things, the birds of Chamissoplatz who warn of coming ecological disaster, or the horses who swim across the Wannsee to pay homage to Heinrich von Kleist in his grave. Many poems in the book range freely across the borders of realism into an alternative realism, while others stay within what Elizabeth Bishop called 'the surrealism of everyday life' – such as a tale about Romanian gypsies removing bit by bit an abandoned car.

As well as his characteristic outlandish adventures and macabre musings, *Horse Music* also includes responses to family deaths – balanced by a poem to a newborn, picturing the strange new world that will unfold for her. That strange world unfolds for us too in the eerie poems of *Horse Music*.

Horse Music won the inaugural Pigott Poetry Prize at Listowel Writers' Week. His other books include three published by Raven Arts Press in Ireland, two from Secker & Warburg, and five from Cape: *The Bridal Suite* (1997), *A Smell of Fish* (2000), *Selected Poems* (2002), *Sanctuary* (2004), and *Black Moon* (2007), which was shortlisted for the T.S. Eliot Prize and for the *Irish Times–Poetry Now Award*.

Born in Lifford, Co. Donegal, Ireland in 1952, Matthew Sweeney moved to London in 1973 and studied at the Polytechnic of North London and the University of Freiburg. After living in Berlin and Timişoara in Romania for some years, he returned to Ireland and now lives in Cork. He was writer-in-residence at University College Cork in 2012-13, and is a member of Aosdána.

Horse Music

HORSE MUSIC (2013)

Hearing of horses speaking Irish on the island
he took a boat out there, paid an islander
daft money to lead him to the westernmost field
where a shy pair of russet ponies stood head-
to head on a hilly mound that jutted out over
the leaping froth of the Atlantic. He pretended
not to notice them, said goodbye to his guide
in Irish picked up from books in southern Spain –
his lifetime's hobby – then sat on his hunkers,
listening hard, but either the horses were quiet
or he needed to get closer. He waited until a
gang of screaking gulls got the horses neighing,
then over he went, soothing them with murmurs,
stroking them, until one said in fluent Irish
to the other 'This hairy fellow could be OK,
but we can't trust him, can't trust any of them.
Two legs? I mean, imagine yourself like that.'
The other whinnied, and hoofed the ground,
then began to sing a song, a wrenching lament
for a red-haired woman, that intensified
when the second horse joined in, so the man
slipped away, head down, back to the harbour.

Fans

HORSE MUSIC (2013)

Seven horses climbed out of the Wannsee
and galloped, dripping, to Kleist's grave.
They neighed and bent their forelegs –
one rapped the stone gently with a hoof.
another came forward to lick the name.
Then, one by one, they felt a weight
drop on their backs, and a jab in the side
poke them into a joyful canter along
the big lake's bank. Such whinnying
had not been heard for centuries, thought

a man walking three barking terriers.
When each horse returned another left
till all seven had felt the rider's weight
then they stood in a ring around the grave
to neigh a soft, high-pitched chorus
before pulling off in strict formation
to trot in a row, heads high, back to where
they'd left the water, wade in again,
watched by a group of shrieking kids, then
swim in an arc towards the farther shore.

The Tunnel

(for Seamus Heaney)
HORSE MUSIC (2013)

Into the tunnel he went,
led by a torch, a tiny
silver torch bought in Crete.

In his pocket was a scalpel
and a folded bag. His mobile
was slotted into his belt.

Earphones brought him Coltrane's
gnarled tones. He wriggled
past a dog's skull, a tennis ball,

a dusty copy of the bible.
An edition of *North* was propped
against the wall. He checked,

it was signed. He slithered on,
his beam now bouncing off mosaic
mirrors on the low ceiling.

As the sax swirled, he hummed
along, sniffing the trapped air,
feeling ahead, as if the light

would miss something vital,
would blank out a sign.
He stuck gum in his mouth.

Chewing, he muscled on, past
a framed photo of bombed Berlin,
a warped tennis racquet, a gun.

A map of Europe appeared on the wall,
then disappeared. A voice rode over
Coltrane, counting to a hundred,

and at the hundred, he emerged
into a red chamber. He stood up
and walked to the seated corpse.

Sunday Morning

HORSE MUSIC (2013)

The Sunday morning bells
are clanging and clanking,
droning and echoing,
and somewhere a dog, a black
cocker spaniel is howling,
and my rotund grandmother
wants me to go to the shop,
before the crowd leaves Mass,
to buy her Woodbines and
Silvermints, and get myself
a Peggy's Leg, so as soon as
the bells die away, Bonzo
and I head up the road,
where his enemy, the goose
is waiting to charge out,
lunging at him, while I
kick at the jabbing neb
and shout, calling the dog
after me, as the farmer
stands in his door and laughs
till we cross to the other side

where the shop should be
but isn't, and the dog
has vanished, and the cash
in my hand is a different
currency, and hundreds of
houses, streets, squares are
all around me, so I run back
down, but the sea is gone,
then the bells start up again.

The Slow Story of No

HORSE MUSIC (2013)

Sing us a gypsy song,
set the accordion going
get the *tuica* flowing,
invite us to sing along,
making it up as we go,
but following you, as you tell
in a Carpathian howl
the slow story of no –

no Mercedes on the grass
next to the bottle bank,
no moustachioed men to thank
for clearing the rusty mess.
No, it happened organically,
like a mouse corpse rotting.
No heads were plotting.
The wheels rolled away.

The doors and windows walked,
the leather seats flew
over the morning dew.
No bystander gawked.
The engine gave a creak
and wrenched itself up
to float like a spaceship
into another week.

And the chassis that remained
let wind blow through it,
let children climb on it,
while old men complained,
and no thin, grey horse
chomped grass, until
his trailer was full –
with nothing, of course,

and no Mercedes on the grass,
the slow story of no.

Booty

HORSE MUSIC (2013)

Going down the hill
in a striped French teeshirt,
I met a thrush who
was bashing a snail
on the road, repeatedly,
while cars whizzed past,
then, as the road levelled,
and the river arrived,
I spied a heron, perched
on a half-submerged
supermarket trolley,
just before the sawn-off
stump of the vandalised
tree, newly peeled,
and sporting a sad face
in sketched black lines,
so I slunk on, to the
market, where I half-lived,
and I asked my butcher
for a cheap French cut.

10 | PIA TAFDRUP

Filmed by Pamela Robertson-Pearce in Ledbury, 7 July 2008

Pia Tafdrup is one of Denmark's leading poets. She has received the Nordic Literature Prize – Scandinavia's most prestigious literary award – and the Swedish Academy's Nordic Prize. She has published three books of poetry with Bloodaxe, all translated by David McDuff. *Queen's Gate* (2001) was a translation of a single volume published in Danish in 1998. This was followed by two books each combining two parts of a quartet written over ten years that centres on the theme of journeying and passage, its individual parts creating a field of tension: *The Whales in Paris* and *Tarkovsky's Horses* (published in English by Bloodaxe in 2010 as *Tarkovsky's Horses and other poems*) and *The Migrant Bird's Compass* and *Salamander Sun* (published in 2015 as *Salamander Sun and other poems*). Each part portrays an element: water, earth, air and fire, each is represented by a creature, and each part has a key figure: the beloved person, the father, the mother and the "I" that recalls its life. The quartet is an attempt to find structure in the midst of chaos.

When we filmed her during her visit to Ledbury Poetry Festival in 2008, only the first two parts of her quartet had been published in Danish, and David McDuff's translations of those were still in manuscript. In the film she talks about their translation process.

Through a sequence of highly sensual poems centred on water in all its forms, Pia Tafdrup creates her own myth in *Queen's Gate* ('the woman's way into the world'), a composite picture of the basic elements of the life-cycle of nature and man, mirrored through a conceptual world that takes the body as its axis.

The poems of *The Whales in Paris* span the moment of conception to eternity. Life is seen as a confrontation with what is bigger than oneself: love, desire and death, primordial forces that are present even in our very modern civilisation.

Tarkovsky's Horses is about loss in a double sense: her father's increasing forgetfulness, his loss of his faculties and then her loss of a father. Disintegration of identity and its inexorable progress are followed through every phase, in a concrete and naked form that draws on the myth of Orpheus and Eurydice.

Min mors hand

DROTTNINGPORTEN 1998

Badar mig i en droppes stilla ljus
och minns hur jag blev till:
en blyerts lagd i handen,
min mors svala hand om min, som var varm.
– Och sen skrev vi
in och ut mellan korallrev,
ett undervattensalfabet av bågar och spetsar,
av snåckspiral, av sjostjårnetaggar,
av fåktande blåckfiskarmar,
av grottvalv och klippformationer.
Bokståver som darrade och fann en våg
i yrsel over det vita.
Ord som flappande plattfisk
som gråvde ner sig i sand
eller vaj ånde havsanemoner med hundratals trådar
i stilla rorelse, alia på en gang.
Meningar som strommande fiskar
som fick fenor och lyfte sig,
fick vingar och rdrde sig rytmiskt
bultande som mitt blod, som blint
slog stjårnor mot hjårtats natthimmel,
då jag såg att hennes hand hade slåppt min,
att jag for långesen skrivit mig ut ur hennes grepp.

Sus

DROTTNINGPORTEN 1998

Det grona, dropparna på skogsbottnen
efter regn, dropparna i mossa och jungfruhår,
det hdga gråset, den våta sommaren,
dår fågeln har rede och råven lya.
Det susar i tråden, susar i huvudet,
det porlar, det brusar, kallt, varmt, kallt,
dropparna tåta i lovverk, det glimtar, blinkar,

My Mother's Hand
QUEEN'S GATE 2001

Bathing in a drop's quiet light
I remember how I came into being:
A pencil stuck in my hand,
my mother's cool hand around mine, it was warm.
– And then we wrote
in and out between coral reefs,
an undersea alphabet of arches and apexes
of snail-shell spirals, of starfish points,
of gesticulating octopus arms,
of cave vaults and rock formations.
Letters that vibrated and found their way,
dizzy over the white.
Words like flat fish that flapped
and dug themselves into the sand
or swaying sea anemones with hundreds of threads
in quiet motion at the same time.
Sentences like streams of fish
that grew fins and rose,
grew wings and moved in a rhythm,
throbbing like my blood, that blindly
beat stars against the heart's night sky,
when I saw that her hand had let mine go,
that I had long since written myself out of her grasp.

Whistling
QUEEN'S GATE 2001

The greenness, the drops on the forest floor
after the rain, the drops in moss and maidenhair,
the tall grass, the wet summer,
where the bird has a nest and the fox a lair.
It whistles in the trees, whistles in my head,
it sparkles, rushes, cold, hot, cold,
the drops tight in the leaf, it gleams, flashes,

når jag ror vid det våta, ruskar grenarna,
sprider det blanka, det vilt glånsande
som valler också från mig, ljustungt.
Jag öppnar munnen, räcker ut tungan,
kånner det våta, det stjärnfärgade,
det susar i tråden, susar i huvudet,
den hoga sommaren, det vildvuxna gråset,
din regnvåta smak, ditt råa, doftande regn,
sjunker till botten i det morkt lågande grona,
i en kil stiger fåglar hogt over tråden.

Kerne

HVALERNE I PARIS [THE WHALES IN PARIS]   2002

Jeg var en nat i august, hinsides planeternes is,
jeg var en hånd, der greb og holdt fast,
jeg var et sneskred, en blodsort væg i brand,
jeg var en skærende passage i min mors hjerte,
hvor hun skulle afgøre,
                           om livet var værd at leve,
jeg var min fars begær, jeg var tilgivelsen,
jeg var pulsen i jorden, de dybeste årer,
jeg var duggen i græsset en råkold morgen,
jeg var blomst og nektarduft,
jeg var en dryppende sødlig smag
af æblet med bitter karneolrød skal,
                           – en kerne,
der uden at synke red på vandet
og blev skyllet i land på en nordvendt kyst
på den seksoghalvtredsindstyvende breddegrad,
jeg var det skjulte, der blev fundet af en lysstråle,
set af en engels øje –
et øje der troede, det fór vild,
dér hvor stranden var salthvid, sandet let som aske,
og bøgeskoven forcerede stejle skrænter
for at reflekteres i vandet,
                           ekko på ekko...
Jeg var en rygende feber i blodet,

when I touch the wetness, shake the branches,
spread the shine, the wild glitter
that pours out of me too, heavy with light.
I open my mouth, stick out my tongue,
feel the wet, the star-coloured,
it whistles in the trees, whistles in my head,
the high summer, the wild grass,
your rain-wet taste, your raw fragrant rain,
I sink to the ground in the dark blazing greenness,
in a wedge birds rise high above the trees.

Kernel

TARKOVSKY'S HORSES AND OTHER POEMS 2010

I was a night in August, on the other side of the planets' ice,
I was a hand that gripped and held fast,
I was an avalanche, a blood-black wall on fire,
I was a strident passage in my mother's heart,
where she had to decide
                            if life was worth living,
I was my father's lust, I was forgiveness,
I was the pulse in the earth, the deepest veins,
I was the dew in the grass one raw, cold morning,
I was flower and nectar scent,
I was a dripping sweetish taste
of the apple with bitter carnelian-red peel,
                                        − a kernel,
that rode on the water without sinking
and was washed ashore on a north-facing coast
on the fifty-sixth parallel,
I was the hidden, found by a beam of light,
seen by an angel's eye —
an eye that thought itself lost,
where the shore was salt-white, the sand light as ash,
and the beech-wood forced steep slopes
to reflect themselves in the water,
                            echo on echo...
I was a raging fever in the blood,

jeg var en hinde, der bristede, fuglene der bar,
jeg var suset i rummet under kronernes kuppel,
en svirren af lyde, der førte vægtløst ind,
hvor stier viskes ud,
                    og der ikke er vej tilbage,
ind i det skjultes magnetfelt, ind i zonen af sugende mørke,
hvoraf samtlige bogstaver springer
– ud i lyset,
        ud i stilheden for at slå rod
                                i endeløs nutid,
hvor skyggerne bor, og ikke assimileres.

Vi er ikke endagsdyr

HVALERNE I PARIS [THE WHALES IN PARIS]   2002

I mørket vogter månen
konkavt.
Dine øjne er lukkede —
alle har set noget,
men ingen det samme.
Hvad ansigtet skjuler,
                iagttager natten
og døren står åben.
Dine øjne er lukkede —
dit ansigt er nær mit.
En kraft stiger og stiger
fra det øjeblik, vi fødes,
                – og vi er ikke endagsdyr.
Vores hjerne er ikke konstrueret
til at styre vinger,
men til at bygge sprog
og navigere på anden vis:
At tænke er at forsøge
at se på en ny måde, polarklart
– hvilket vil sige
også at fatte begrænsningen.
Dine øjne er lukkede —
din krop er et kast frem
i det safranlysende skær.

I was a membrane that burst, the birds that flew,
I was the murmur in the room beneath the treetops' cupola,
a whirring of sounds that led weightlessly in
where paths are erased,
                    and there is no way back,
into the magnetic field of the hidden, into the zone of sucking darkness,
from which all the alphabet's letters spring
– out into the light,
                    out into the silence to strike root
                                        in endless present,
where the shadows dwell, and do not assimilate.

We Are Not Creatures of a Single Day

TARKOVSKY'S HORSES AND OTHER POEMS 2010

In the darkness the moon keeps watch
concavely.
Your eyes are closed —
everyone has seen something,
but not the same.
What the face conceals,
                    the night notices
and the door stands open.
Your eyes are closed —
your face is near to mine.
A power rises and rises
from the moment we are born,
                    – and we are not creatures of a single day.
Our brains are not constructed
to guide wings
but to build languages
and navigate in a different way:
to think is to try
to see in a new way, with polar clarity
– which also means
to grasp the limitation.
Your eyes are closed —
your body is a leap forward
into that saffron-glowing radiance.

Søvnen har væltet
din hjernes rosettasten;
den viser en skrift,
vi ikke har tydet før...
Vores sted er tiden,
og vi læser,
som ville vi forsøge at huske det,
der endnu ikke er hændt os.
Hvad vi ikke gør,
            tilgives ikke.
Den ene hånd griber hårdt,
den anden beskytter,
en tredje velsigner.
Dine øjne er lukkede —
sjælen tiltrækkes
af det uendelige rum,
bygget af musikkens pauser.
Jeg har dit skrig
            i min mund.

Sleep has overturned
the Rosetta stone of your brain;
it shows a script
we have not deciphered before...
Our place is time,
and we read,
as though we are trying to remember
what has not yet happened to us.
What we do not do
                    is not forgiven.
One hand grips hard,
the other protects,
a third blesses.
Your eyes are closed —
the soul is drawn
by that infinite space,
built from the pauses in the music.
I have your cry
            in my mouth.

Mindst ét sår

TARKOVSKIJS HESTE 2006

– Mindst ét sår har kroppen altid,
sagde min far foran spejlet,
hvor han bandt sin slipseknude,
da jeg første gang så
                blod strømme
fra knæet, hvor jeg havde slået hul.
– Mindst ét sår har kroppen altid,
er den første hele sætning, jeg erindrer
min far rette til mig,
dengang jeg netop var begyndt
at lære verden at kende.
Jeg var fire år
og tog del
      i mit livs
første filosofiske diskussion:
– HVORFOR SKAL MAN DØ?
Min far ånder mørke
spærret inde i sig selv.
– Det gør ondt —
er den sidste sætning, min far
siger til mig
        på sit dødsleje.
Efter en hel dag
uden mulig kommunikation
står denne sætning
klar
som et sår kan skinne.
Eftermiddagens stilhed eksponerer ordene.
Se,
hvor såret lyser.
– Det gør ondt —
         men mellem disse to sætninger
har et liv foldet sig ud,
              helligt, helligt…
For som Theofanes, grækeren,
i Tarkovskijs *Den yderste dom,*
efter alverdens kvaler
        udbryder:
– Alligevel er det så smukt, og nu sner det.

At Least One Wound

TARKOVSKY'S HORSES AND OTHER POEMS 2010

– *The body always has at least one wound*,
my father said in front of the mirror,
where he was tying his tie,
when for the first time I saw
                                        blood streaming
from my knee, which I had grazed.
– *The body always has at least one wound*
is the first whole sentence I remember
my father addressing to me,
in those days when I had just begun
to get to know the world.
I was four years old
and took part
            in my life's
first philosophical discussion:
– WHY DO WE HAVE TO DIE?
My father breathes the darkness
locked inside himself.
– *It hurts* —
is the last sentence my father
says to me
            on his deathbed.
After a whole day
without communication being possible
this sentence stands
clear
as a wound may shine.
The afternoon's silence exposes the words.
Look
how the wound is glowing.
– *It hurts* —
    but between these two sentences
a life has unfolded,
            holy, holy...
For as Theophanes, the Greek,
in Tarkovsky's *Andrei Rublev*,
after all kinds of trouble
            blurts out:
– *It's so pretty, though, and now it's snowing.*

473

Godnat

TARKOVSKIJS HESTE   2006

Min far bliver iført
natskjorte.
Så længe jeg var barn,
dryssede han
stjernestøv og månegrus
ned i mine øjne.
Så længe jeg var barn,
talte jeg som et barn,
tænkte jeg som et barn,
dømte jeg som et barn.
Hver godnathistorie,
        jeg fik,
havde sin egen farve.
Min far fortalte, så en blind
under mørkets klokke
ville kunne se
            en regnbue.
Jeg sov og drømte
det umulige
langt borte fra verdens angst.
Jeg vender mig om,
            vender mig mod ham,
ser i min fars øjne
stjernestøv og månegrus.
Nu kommer natten —
            den lange nat.
Mælkeveje af morfin
suser
gennem hans krop
        med lysets tyngde
            af smertes ophør.

Goodnight

TARKOVSKY'S HORSES AND OTHER POEMS   2010

My father is being dressed
in a nightshirt.
When I was a child
he sprinkled
stardust and moon gravel
down on my eyes,
When I was a child
I spoke as a child,
I understood as a child,
I thought as a child.
Every good night story
                    I received
had its own colour.
My father told them so a blind man
under the bell of darkness
would be able to see
                    a rainbow.
I slept and dreamt
the impossible
far away from the world's anxiety.
I turn around,
        turn towards him,
see in my father's eyes
stardust and moon gravel.
Now the night is coming —
                    the long night.
Milky ways of morphine
murmur
through his body
            with the light's heaviness
                        of pain's cessation.

All poems translated from the Danish by David McDuff

11 | BRIAN TURNER

Filmed by Neil Astley in Ledbury, 4 July 2011

Here, Bullet is a harrowing, first-hand account of the Iraq War by a soldier-poet, published in the US in 2005 and by Bloodaxe in Britain in 2007. Brian Turner writes powerful poetry of witness, exceptional for its beauty, honesty and skill. Like Keith Douglas's poems from the North African desert in the Second World War, Turner's testament from the war in Iraq offers unflinchingly accurate description but no moral judgement, leaving the reader to draw any conclusions.

In *Phantom Noise* (2010) he pumps up the volume as he faces and tries to deal with the traumatic aftermath of war. Flashbacks explode the daily hell of Baghdad into the streets and malls of peaceful California, at the same time sending Turner's imagination reeling back to Iraq. If he thought he had written all he could of his Iraq experiences in *Here, Bullet,* he was mistaken, for what he saw and felt there affected him so profoundly that more poems had to be written, years later, from a place of apparent safety.

Repetitive media reports show little of people's daily experience of the five-year war. In both books we see and feel the devastatingly surreal reality of everyday life and death for soldiers and civilians through the eyes of an eloquent writer who served in the US Army for seven years, and was an infantry team leader for a year in Iraq from November 2003 with the 3rd Stryker Brigade Combat Team, 2nd Infantry Division.

In 1999-2000 he was deployed to Bosnia-Herzegovina with the 10th Mountain Division. Born in 1967, he received an MFA from the University of Oregon and lived abroad in South Korea for a year before joining the army. His memoir *My Life as a Foreign Country* was published by Jonathan Cape in 2014.

Phantom Noise was shortlisted for the T.S. Eliot Prize. Brian Turner has read his work at many festivals in Britain and Ireland. I was able to film him reading poems from both his books during his visit to Ledbury Poetry Festival in 2011.

Here, Bullet

HERE, BULLET (2005/2007)

If a body is what you want,
then here is bone and gristle and flesh.
Here is the clavicle-snapped wish,
the aorta's opened valves, the leap
thought makes at the synaptic gap.
Here is the adrenaline rush you crave,
that inexorable flight, that insane puncture
into heat and blood. And I dare you to finish
what you've started. Because here, Bullet,
here is where I complete the word you bring
hissing through the air, here is where I moan
the barrel's cold esophagus, triggering
my tongue's explosives for the rifling I have
inside of me, each twist of the round
spun deeper, because here, Bullet,
here is where the world ends, every time.

Hwy 1

HERE, BULLET (2005/2007)

> I see a horizon lit with blood,
> And many a starless night.
> A generation comes and another goes
> And the fire keeps burning.
>
> AL-JAWAHIRI

It begins with the Highway of Death,
with an untold number of ghosts
wandering the road at night, searching
for the way home, to Najaf, Kirkuk,
Mosul and Kanni al Saad. It begins here
with a shuffling of feet on the long road north.

477

This is the spice road of old, the caravan trail
of camel dust and heat, where Egyptian limes
and sultani lemons swayed in crates
strapped down by leather, where merchants
traded privet flowers and musk, aloes,
honeycombs and silk brought from the Orient.

Past Marsh Arabs and the Euphrates wheel,
past wild camels and waving children
who marvel at the painted guns, the convoy
pushes on, past the ruins of Babylon and Sumer,
through the land of Gilgamesh where the minarets
sound the muezzin's prayer, resonant and deep.

Cranes roost atop power lines in enormous
bowl-shaped nests of sticks and twigs,
and when a sergeant shoots one from the highway
it pauses, as if amazed that death has found it
here, at 7 A.M. on such a beautiful morning,
before pitching over the side and falling
in a slow unraveling of feathers and wings.

Eulogy

HERE, BULLET (2005/2007)

It happens on a Monday, at 11:20 A.M.,
as tower guards eat sandwiches
and seagulls drift by on the Tigris River.
Prisoners tilt their heads to the west
though burlap sacks and duct tape blind them.
The sound reverberates down concertina coils
the way piano wire thrums when given slack.
And it happens like this, on a blue day of sun,
when Private Miller pulls the trigger
to take brass and fire into his mouth:
the sound lifts the birds up off the water,
a mongoose pauses under the orange trees,

and nothing can stop it now, no matter what
blur of motion surrounds him, no matter what voices
crackle over the radio in static confusion,
because if only for this moment the earth is stilled,
and Private Miller has found what low hush there is
down in the eucalyptus shade, there by the river.

PFC B. Miller
(1980 – March 22, 2004)

16 Iraqi Policemen

HERE, BULLET (2005/2007)

The explosion left a hole in the roadbed
large enough to fit a mid-sized car.
It shattered concrete, twisted metal,
busted storefront windows in sheets
and lifted a BMW chassis up onto a rooftop.

The shocking blood of the men
forms an obscene art: a moustache, alone
on a sidewalk, a blistered hand's gold ring
still shining, while a medic, Doc Lopez,
pauses to catch his breath, to blow it out
hard, so he might cup the left side of a girl's face
in one hand, gently, before bandaging
the half gone missing.

Allah must wander in the crowd
as I do, dazed by the pure concussion
of the blast, among sirens, voices
of the injured, the boots of running soldiers,
not knowing whom to touch first,
for the dead policemen cannot be found,
here a moment before, then vanished.

The Inventory from a Year Sleeping with Bullets

PHANTOM NOISE (2010)

Rifle oil, *check*. Smoke grenades, *check*. Desert boots, *check*. Plates of body armor, *check*. The list ongoing – combat patrols added, 5 Paragraph Op Orders, mission briefs, nights spent staring for heat signatures through the white-hot lens, lasers bore-sighted to the barrels they guide. The conceptual and physical given parallel structure.

A dead infant. A night-crushed car. A farmer slumped over a Toyota steering wheel near an Army checkpoint. A distraught relative staring beyond, pieces of brain on the dashboard. The refusal to render aid. The fresh dark soil over the bodies.

The boredom. The minutes. The hours. Days. Weeks. Months. The moments unbound by time's dominion. The years after.

Torture fragments. A man pissing on the Qu'ran. A man at a rifle range firing a bullet. A bullet carrying the middle vowel of the word *Inshallah*. A combat load of ammunition.

3rd Squad. 1st Platoon. Blackhorse Company. The faces – ones I hated and the ones I loved. Even the ones I don't remember. And all who don't remember me. *Contact. Three O'Clock. 50 meters. Talk the Guns.*

And Seattle at night. Rain drizzling down. First weekend home from war. Sgt. Gould sucking a woman's nipple in the cuddle room at the rave party. Glow sticks in mouths, a language of light. A language I don't recognise. A man in an Energizer bunny suit, on roller-skates, bass pounding the camouflage of tireless eternal Easter followed by a brunette in black leather bustier, thigh-high wet leather PVC boots, her eyes the dark carbon from the barrel's chamber as she pulls a leashed man by the throat. These people. *My people.*

Put it all in the rucksack. Throw the rucksack on your back and call it your *house*. Do a commo check with anyone out there in the bush, listening. Do a commo check back home. Get your shit on straight. *Stay Alert and Stay Alive*. Drink water and conduct your PCIs. We've reached the *Line of Departure*. So lock and load, man. From here on out we are on radio silence.

At Lowe's Home Improvement Center

PHANTOM NOISE (2010)

Standing in aisle 16, the hammer and anchor aisle,
I bust a 50 pound box of double-headed nails
open by accident, their oily bright shanks
and diamond points like firing pins
from M-4s and M-16s.
                    In a steady stream
they pour onto the tile floor, constant as shells
falling south of Baghdad last night, where Bosch
kneeled under the chain guns of helicopters
stationed above, their tracer-fire a synaptic geometry
of light.
          At dawn, when the shelling stops,
hundreds of bandages will not be enough.

ε∿

Bosch is walking down aisle 16 now, in full combat gear,
improbable, worn out from fatigue, a rifle
slung at his side, his left hand guiding
a ten-year-old boy who sees what war is
and will never clear it from his head.

Here, Bosch says, *Take care of him.*
I'm going back in for more.

ε∿

Sheets of plywood drop with the airy breath
of mortars the moment they crack open
in shrapnel. Mower blades are just mower blades
and the Troy-Bilt Self-Propelled Mower doesn't resemble
a Blackhawk or an Apache. In fact, no one seems to notice
the casualty collection center Doc High is marking out
in ceiling fans, aisle 15. Wounded Iraqis with IVs
sit propped against boxes as 92 sample Paradiso fans
hover over in a slow revolution of blades.

The forklift driver over-adjusts, swinging the tines
until they slice open gallons and gallons of paint,

Sienna Dust and Lemon Sorbet and Ship's Harbor Blue
pooling in the aisle where Sgt Rampley walks through —
carrying someone's blown-off arm cradled like an infant,
handing it to me, saying, *Hold this, Turner,*
we might find who it belongs to.

ૐ

Cash registers open and slide shut
with a sound of machine guns being charged.
Dead soldiers are laid out at the registers,
on the black conveyor belts,
and people in line still reach
for their wallets. Should I stand
at the magazine rack, reading
Landscaping with Stone or *The Complete*
Home Improvement Repair Book?
What difference does it make if I choose
tumbled travertine tile, Botticino marble,
or Black Absolute granite. Outside,
palm trees line the asphalt boulevards,
restaurants cool their patrons who will enjoy
fireworks exploding over Bass Lake in July.

ૐ

Aisle number 7 is a corridor of lights.
Each dead Iraqi walks amazed
by Tiffany posts and Bavarian pole lights.
Motion-activated incandescents switch on
as they pass by, reverent sentinels of light,
Fleur De Lis and Luminaire Mural Extérieur
welcoming them to Lowe's Home Improvement Center,
aisle number 7, where I stand in mute shock,
someone's arm cradled in my own.
                              The Iraqi boy beside me
reaches down to slide his fingertip in Retro Colonial Blue,
an interior latex, before writing
T, for *Tourniquet*, on my forehead.

482

12 | CHASE TWICHELL

Filmed at home near Keene in the Adirondacks, upstate New York,
by Pamela Robertson-Pearce, 15 September 2009

Chase Twichell's poetry is marked by a strong identification with the natural world, one that exceeds any with other human beings. There's a dissociation born of a rough childhood, which only the later poems address head-on, though many earlier ones circle around it. Central early concerns are the heartbreak of love between men and women, the ecological decimation of our planet, and the nature of the human mind. Her retrospective *Horses Where the Answers Should Have Been* (2010) shows the evolution of a distinctive voice in American poetry through several collections written over 35 years.

Beginning with *Perdido* (1991), each of her collections has had a distinct centre of gravity, with each poem contributing to a whole larger than the sum of its parts. *Perdido* probes the relationship between love and death. *The Ghost of Eden* (1995) grieves and rails against our poor stewardship of the earth. *The Snow Watcher* (1998) chronicles the early years of her study of Zen Buddhism – a crucial influence on all her later work – and begins to address a central fact of her childhood: early sexual abuse at the hands of a "family friend", and a lifelong battle with depression. *Dog Language* (2005) continues to explore these themes, and also the dementia and death of her father from alcoholism. In the background, questions regarding the human self continue to arise.

The new poems in *Horses Where the Answers Should Have Been* are are much more frontal in their treatment of these evolving, interlocked concerns, forthrightly taking on childhood sexual trauma, mental illness and substance abuse. But the heart of the book is the poems' focus on Twichell's continuing, deepening enquiry into the nature of the self as seen through the eyes of Zen. What is most interesting (and problematic) about these poems is that just as poetry goes where prose cannot, so Zen goes where language cannot. Thus the poems become sparer and sparer as they approach saying what cannot be said.

She introduces and reads poems from different collections which focus on these concerns in the reading, and on her close identification with nature in particular, which she expands upon in an interview excerpt at the end. We filmed her at home in the Adirondacks in her study, until recently her office for Ausable Press, the lively poetry imprint she set up and ran from 1999 to 2009.

Touch-me-not

THE GHOST OF EDEN (1995) | HORSES WHERE THE ANSWERS SHOULD HAVE BEEN (2010)

I have to fight in myself the desire
to put down the pen and go outside
where the tufted, seed-heavy grasses

float on the slow river of August.

When a poem touches on the act of writing,
it breaks the dream. That's why this one
opens as it does – defensive,

already split between wanting to know
where it's going and wanting not to know.

I lie down under the sketchy canopy
of the field with my face close
to the cellar smell of earth

where the white shoots gleam
doubled up in the dew
in their little preserve.

I'd rather watch the bees
work the wildflowers

than follow the cursive tracks
wherever it is they go.
Something, maybe the soul,

says language is a whip that hurts it,

slicing open the still-forming
sky-colored chicory flowers,
leaving the flayed stems to say

what the truth is.
I'd rather listen to the brook,

its words always garbled
just out of earshot.

It's not the words themselves
that scare the soul,
but their unearthly gleam,

the gleam the pallbearers follow
first to the church
and then to the hole in the ground.

One day what has always been true
will no longer be true, just like that.

If this were a poem about my own death,
I'd know how to make the rasp and honey
of the August field take on that meaning,

and I'd rest for a while in the image
of my body married to the black
beloved dirt, the microbes, the rains,

the weed seeds sending out
their slender filaments of root.

But it's not my death that's set
like a steel trap at the end of the poem.
It's the earth's, upon whose body I lie,

and toward whom the ant-trails of ink all lead.

This world has always been widow and widower,
the one we leave bereft

when we slip into the place
without sunlight, without leaves.
Now what has always been true

is no longer true. I want to lie down
and swim in the shade with the trout lilies
to avoid saying it.

The earth as it has always been
is saying its goodbyes. Another world

will overrun the emptiness,

but I love this one.
I let it hold me longer than I mean to,
the feather-leaves of yarrow,

the vetches' frail tendrils,
and the spotted touch-me-nots

that give such an intimate response
if you touch one of the tiny swollen pods –

faintly striped, fat in the middle,
and containing a tense spring,
an unspiraling release

that flings the seeds in all directions.
I touch, and between my fingers

the miniature violence spends itself.

Like the seeds I'm propelled
toward some future field,

which glows from far off
like the idea of plutonium,
immortal and alien.

When I hear the wind taking leave
of the stricken trees – the beeches,
the birches, the red spruce –

or the wet-rag-on-glass sound of the phoebe

in her nest of lichens under the eaves,
when I walk in the ferns' green perfume

or lie with my face among cool roots
and sprouts all intertangled and doomed,

I'm imagining what will happen
to the soul in me,

which feeds on these things,
and which I fear will go on living

after the loved world dies.

City Animals

THE GHOST OF EDEN (1995) | HORSES WHERE THE ANSWERS SHOULD HAVE BEEN (2010)

Just before the tunnel, the train
lurches through a landscape
snatched from a dream. Flame blurts

from high up on the skeletal refinery,
all pipes and tanks. Then a tail of smoke.

The winter twilight looks like fire, too,

smeared above the bleached grasses
of the marsh, and in the shards of water

where an egret the color of newspaper
holds perfectly still, like a small angel

come to study what's wrong with the world.

In the blond reeds, a cat picks her way
from tire to oil drum,

hunting in the petrochemical stink.

Row of nipples, row of sharp ribs.
No fish in the iridescence.
Maybe a sick pigeon, or a mouse.

Across the Hudson,
Manhattan's black geometry begins to spark

as the smut of evening rises in the streets.

Somewhere in it,
a woman in fur with a plastic bag in her hand
follows a dachshund in a purple sweater,

letting him sniff a small square of dirt
studded with cigarette butts.
And in the park a scarred Doberman

drags on his choke chain toward another fight,

but his master yanks him back.
It's like the Buddhist vision of the beasts
in their temporary afterlife, each creature

locked in its own cell of misery,
the horse pulling always uphill
with its terrible load, the whip

flicking bits of skin from its back,
the cornered bear woofing with fear,

the fox's mouth red from the leg in the trap.

Animal islands, without comfort between them.
Which shall inherit the earth?

Not the interlocking kittens frozen in the trash.

Not the dog yapping itself to death
on the twentieth floor. And not the egret,
fishing in the feculent marsh

for the condom and the drowned gun.

No, the earth belongs to the spirits
that haunt the air above the sewer grates,

the dark plumes trailing the highway's
diesel moan, the multitudes
pouring from the smokestacks of the citadel

into the gaseous ocean overhead.

Where will the angel rest itself?
What map will guide it home?

Horse

THE SNOW WATCHER (1998/1999) | HORSES WHERE THE ANSWERS SHOULD HAVE BEEN (2010)

I've never seen a soul detached from its gender,
but I'd like to. I'd like to see my own that way,
free of its female tethers. Maybe it would be like
riding a horse. The rider's the human one,
but everyone looks at the horse.

Decade

THE SNOW WATCHER (1998/1999) | HORSES WHERE THE ANSWERS SHOULD HAVE BEEN (2010)

I had only one prayer, but it spread
like lilies, a single flower duplicating
itself over and over until it was rampant,

uncountable. At ten I lay dreaming
in its crushed green blades.

How did I come by it, strange notion
that the hard stems of rage could be broken,
that the lilies were made of words,

my words? Each one I picked
laid a wish to rest. I mean killed it.

The difference between prayer
and a wish is that a wish knows it will be
a failure even as it sets out,

whereas a prayer is still innocent.
Wishing wants prayer to find that out.

Cocktail Music

DOG LANGUAGE (2005/2006) | HORSES WHERE THE ANSWERS SHOULD HAVE BEEN (2010)

All my life a brook of voices
has run in my ears,
many separate instruments
tuning and playing, tuning.
It's cocktail music,
the sound of my parents
in their thirties,
glass-lined ice bucket loaded
and reloaded but no one tending bar,
little paper napkins, cigarettes,
kids passing hors d'oeuvres.
It's drinking music,
riffle of water over stones,
ice in glasses, rise and fall
of many voices touching –
that music. Husbands grilling meat,
squirting the fire to keep it down,
a joke erupting, bird voices snipping
at something secret by the bar.
It's all the voices collapsed
into one voice,
urgent and muscled like a river,
then lowered, as in a drought,
but never gone. It's the background.
When I lift the shell to my ear,
it's in there.

Savin Rock

HORSES WHERE THE ANSWERS SHOULD HAVE BEEN (2010)

What I know is a slur of memory,
fantasy, research, pure invention,
crime dramas, news, and witnesses
like the girl who liked to get high
and the one who was eventually
returned to her family unharmed.
The rest I made up.

The fathers drank beer in the grandstand,
flattening cans and dropping
the dull coins into the underworld.
It was daylight – we went right under,
down into the slatted dark,
the smell under the bleachers
where lots of men peed,
paper cones and dead balloons,
people jostling and whispering.
Down there were the entrances
to the dark rides, the funhouses:
Death Valley and Laff-in-the-Dark.
Of course that's not true;
they were right on the main boardwalk
under strings of bulbs lit up all night.

Mom says, *To remember something,*
go back to the place where you forgot it.
But the place was torn
down forty years ago; there are motels
there now, where the Ferris wheel
lurched up and over the trees,
over the fathers at their picnic table
close enough to feel the Tilt-A-Whirl's
crude rhythms through the ground.
They make the cars go faster or slower, depending.
After hours the boys loosen up the machines
and take girls for rides.

Hey kid! I flipped a coin in my head
and it came up tails. Want to take a walk?

491

He looked older than our parents.
How old did our parents look?
He was fifty, or thirty. I remember
the smell of whatever he put on his hair,
and the blue nail on his thumb.
He could flip a lit cigarette around
with his lips so the fire was inside.
I rode a little metal car
into Laff-in-the-Dark to dance
with the skeleton (possibly real
since some teeth had fillings)
that flung itself at me from the dark.

A dog watched me from a pickup window.
The World's Biggest Pig lay
beached on its side, heaving.
The tattooed lady had a tattooed baby.
No one ever tattooed a newborn child
for real, did they? The Chinese Dragon
was only an iguana.
The go-kart man asked me if I wanted
a little on the side. I said no.
His friend in the bleachers
blew me a kiss.
In the Maze of Mirrors
I was fatso and skeleton,
skirt blown up by a fan. Not true.
A fan blew a girl's skirt up.
It wasn't me. I was a tomboy. I wore pants.

At the stable, girls in love with horses
visited and groomed and fed them daily.
For girls it was about trust,
being part of a couple,
the horse and the girl,
but for the man in the barn
it was about making girls feel
groomed and visited.
Come on over here. Didn't a guy ever
brush your hair with a currycomb?
I don't believe it! Not once?
Little honeycomb like you?
And kittens, always good bait.

A little dish of spoiled milk.
Do you think they don't pass them around?
They pass them around.
Marked kids get shared,
little pink kid tongues *lick lick licking*
like a puppy! Good dog!
And on the carousel a man appeared
from nowhere to help her on,
hand palm up on the saddle just as she sat,
squirming there until the horse pulled her away.
Little cowgirl, giddy-up!

Thus she became half human half animal,
and remained so her entire life,
now a shepherdess, now a sleek young
she-goat, so lithe and small-hipped,
half tame, little goatskin haunches –
hand-fed on snow cones and cotton candy –
the girl who was eventually
returned to her family unharmed.

Tell me, little shepherdess,
how this bodes for first love:
the centaur pissing outside your tent
in the afterlife, having come down
over the stony pastures to claim you
and feed you trout and fiddleheads
and take you to bed on the high ledges
where the wind holds you down for him.
But he won't be the first.

Sweet-sharp bouquet of darkroom,
holster with toy six-gun,
hot umbrella lamps nudged into place
by his fat pink fingers.
A little maraschino light presides over
negatives strung up like game to dry.
The tomboy's showing her rump,
hard little buttocks under the tender wrapping,
the skin. Little wonton.

13 | PRISCILA UPPAL

Filmed by Pamela Robertson-Pearce in Newcastle, 22 April 2013

Priscila Uppal is a Canadian poet and fiction writer of South Asian descent who has gained an international reputation for her boldly provocative poetry in just a dozen years, since publishing her first collection, *How to Draw Blood from a Stone*, at the age of 23. Noted for their startling imagery, unforgettable characters and visionary lines, her poems are exact and penetrating, yet surreal and deeply moving. Drawing from the scientific to the literary, the medical to the historical, Uppal is as concerned about the inheritance of the past as she is about the tragedies of the present, which makes her both a witness of the terrors and inconsistencies of the past and a messenger of an incomprehensible future.

In 2010 Bloodaxe published her first UK edition, *Successful Tragedies: Poems 1998-2010*, including work from six books published in Canada, including *Ontological Necessities*, which was shortlisted for the Griffin Poetry Prize in 2007, and a recent collection, *Traumatology*. In these poems she meditates over spilt milk with Freud, has sex with Christopher Columbus, issues warnings to gynaecologists, sets up shelters for virgins from Greek myths and organises a protest on Abraham's lawn, and much more… Readers experiencing Uppal for the first time will enter a turbulent but vital landscape, discovering a poet dedicated to uncovering the motivations behind our cruelties and our compassions and determined to explore the absurdity of the world.

We filmed her in Newcastle in the course of a reading tour with Tishani Doshi organised by Bloodaxe which also took them to Grasmere, Edinburgh, Galway (Cúirt), Hull, Sheffield and Liverpool. After introducing and reading five poems from *Successful Tragedies*, she talks about her work, surrealism and Canadian poetry. She has since published a further book with Bloodaxe, *Sabotage* (2015), a collection of poems exploring private and public acts of destruction, disruption and vandalism in the 21st century.

Born in Ottawa in 1974, she is a professor of Humanities and English at York University in Toronto. She was the first-ever poet-in-residence for Canadian Athletes Now during the 2010 Vancouver and 2012 London Olympic and Paralympic Games as well as the Rogers Cup Tennis Tournament in 2011.

If Abraham

PRETENDING TO DIE (2001) | SUCCESSFUL TRAGEDIES (2010)

If Abraham hadn't responded to God's command
how much better the relationship with his son
might have been. No nights of discomfort
in the dark, calling out in his sleep
for good Samaritans, no more fights
at breakfast about the day
it almost happened, no more hiding
the largest and sharpest kitchen knives.

If Abraham hadn't heard another word
and done the deed, how many days before some troupe
of angered parents hunted him down, stood
on his lawn with signs and government officials
broke every unbarred window
in his home, how many years before
the smell came off his hands,
before he could eat meat again.

If Abraham was smart as the men in my neighbourhood
he would have destroyed evidence of his plans,
taken the boy no further than the basement,
and kept the fires burning until
not a soul could have recognised that body.

Sex with Columbus

PRETENDING TO DIE (2001) | SUCCESSFUL TRAGEDIES (2010)

We rode the waves in a month-long stretch
of glorious discovery. My body meeting him
like a welcome error: odd instrument of his
marking round territory.

It was supposed to be a secret between us
and the sea.

Later I heard he bragged to his buddies.
Claimed to be the first, though he wasn't.

Sorry, I Forgot to Clean Up After Myself

ONTOLOGICAL NECESSITIES (2006) | SUCCESSFUL TRAGEDIES (2010)

Sorry, Sirs and Madams, I forgot to clean up after myself
after the unfortunate incidents of the previous century.

How embarrassing; my apologies. I wouldn't advise you
to stroll around here without safety goggles, and I must insist
that you enter at your own risk. You may, however, leave
your umbrella at the door. Just keep your ticket.

We expected, of course, to have this all cleared away by the time
you arrived. The goal was to present you
with blue and green screens, whitewashed counters.

Unforeseen expenses.
Red tape.
So hard to find good help these days.

But, alas, excuses. Perhaps you will appreciate
the difficulties I've faced in providing you a clean slate.
If you step into a hole, Sirs and Madams, accept the loss
of a shoe or two. Stay the course.

Progress is the mother of invention. Here: take my hand.
Yes, that's right. You can return it on the way back.

The Old Debate of Don Quixote vs. Sancho Panza

TRAUMATOLOGY (2010) | SUCCESSFUL TRAGEDIES (2010)

The men in this family
are much stupider than the women, my large-armed uncle says.
But the women all go crazy.

They go crazy because they read books.
They write books.
They learn languages and go to artsy movies.

The men like to work, to do.
We are happy walking for hours into the woods to cut down a tree
or transporting boxes from one garage to another.
As long as there is something to carry, an object to touch
and exchange, we feel less alone in this universe and know our place.
We know how to play beach volleyball,
how to fix cars and airplanes,
how to enjoy the sun on our foreheads in the sweltering heat.

The women in this family
are never happy. Always thinking, thinking, thinking
about this and that, that and this,
they know only thoughts running in circles, circles,
until exhausted and dizzy.
The women are too smart for their own good.
The books worm out holes in their brains.

They are unhappy in every language they learn.
And so maybe the men in this family are smarter than we think.

My Mother Is One Crazy Bitch

TRAUMATOLOGY (2010) | SUCCESSFUL TRAGEDIES (2010)

How do you write that on a postcard?

How will I tell my brother, that yes, yes, I found our mother
after twenty years and she's about as lovely as an electrical storm
when you're naked and tied to the highest tree in the county.

She has tantrums when we wake in the morning,
tantrums when we catch our cabs for the day,
outside the theatre, inside the theatre, after the theatre,
then again on the ride home. She has several more
when I am hiding in the washroom, washing
my underwear in the sink.

You don't love me enough! is her main point of contention.
So, we battle this love thing out as if it were some native Brazilian dish
I am supposed to swallow until my stomach spasms,
until I learn to crave it. But I am a teacher now, not a student.

My mother switches off the television and starts to snore: even at night,
she accosts me, in the middle
of my across-the-ocean nightmares she makes sure
uncredited appearances.

At the checkout desks of my subconscious I am writing postcards
to all dead mothers out there, all dead daughters
who never had a chance to meet in this life. I collect
their tears the way I have been hoping to collect my thoughts.

Unknown grief is sweeter, I write. *Stay on your side off-stage,*
let others stay on theirs. Only then can we indulge
in the luxury of applause.

14 | MARK WALDRON

Filmed by Neil Astley at Ledbury Poetry Festival, 3 July 2016

Mark Waldron's poems may sometimes pretend they're joking but they never really are. And what is it they're not joking about? Death for one thing, and the fact that we don't actually know who we are, and the fact that we don't truly know who our loved ones are, or what art is, or anything else for that matter.

Sometimes it feels as though someone has run off with meaning. It's no longer to be found where we could once expect to find it, perhaps in religion or in nature or in art, and these poems set off in search of it. Their aim is to see if there's a way of looking and a way of using language that can bring some meaning back to the world, because without it, we're lost.

John Stammers wrote that 'Mark Waldron is the most striking and unusual new voice to have emerged in British poetry for some time. His offbeat observations and surreal imaginings are set off by a precise management of tone and mordant sense of humour. There is much black comedy in these poems but at the same time it becomes evident that a deeply humane sensibility is at work. His great gift is to face two ways at once: to our received culture, traditional and popular, and towards odd new ways of imagining ourselves. He brings to bear a sharp ear for the absurd coupled with a sure footed clarity and grace of speech. This enables him to write unforeseeable wordplays and images. In this way, his work captures exactly the uncertain mix of what it is to be a person living today.'

Mark Waldron was born in New York in 1960 and grew up in London. He works in the advertising business and lives in East London with his wife and son. He began writing poetry in his early 40s. He published two collections with Salt, *The Brand New Dark* (2008) and *The Itchy Sea* (2011), and his third collection, *Meanwhile, Trees*, was published by Bloodaxe in 2016.

His live readings are unlike anyone else's, as this video shows.

All My Poems Are Advertisements for Me

MEANWHILE, TREES (2016)

When I was young there was nothing exactly stupid
about the world. In fact, in the good old days

there was the thump and the tug of it, the way it heaved itself
like a stone, yanked so to speak in glory,

the way it fell up, crushed up, and then crushed up again,
getting newer and newer, louder and sweeter,

the way it watched its own face fall between its fingers
as though its face were a handful of gold coins.

I think I might have known the whole drag of everything
going upwards, a tide that pulled me with it.

Actually, I know I did. (You were part of all this by the way.)
And the sky, well, where to begin?

The sky was so adult, not imbecilic or thin or so-so or girlish.
Did I outgrow it?

Did I drink it, shoot it, find a way round it?
Did I get inside it and drive off in it?

Forgive me, but on my way to work this morning,
even though the sun was on fire and the trees were up,

I was in the apocalypse. Death is not what you think it is.
It's actually what I think it is.

The Uncertainty Principle

MEANWHILE, TREES (2016)

I wouldn't swear to it but it seems to me that light owns
the surfaces of things,
dotting them indiscriminately with its capricious particles.

pok! pok! pok!
pok-pok! pok-pok-pok! pok! pok!

Each, a paintball pellet which,
on splatting, contributes to colour-up the ravenous darkness
rendering it fit for purpose.

That purpose being
to be seen.

I admit I memorised whole portions of you
and under various lighting conditions. I made a bit of a project of it.

There were particles everywhere! An embarrassment of riches!

You held out your hands palms-up
and you smiled at me as they rained down on you like dolphins.

I find it very hot the way particles exist so saucily in two places
at once, don't you?

Your nipples, if I might say so, have something of that quality,
upon their quantum hooters.

pok! pok!

I would shut out my black mouth if I could.
Not everything
is explicable. Exemplar: I know what I mean. Or I think I do.

It's hard to see Hamlet as some kind of everyman,

MEANWHILE, TREES (2016)

bellows old Professor Hydrofoil above the sound of his own engine's biscuity shout as he skims across the pale Baltic waters lit with light. The sky is crazy for him, his riveted body, all chrome fuselage, instant abdomen and what looks from here to be a thing like kindliness. He is, in fact, so shiny, so polished by his mother's early love that we can observe ourselves reflected in his tubular skin. We can see our bent smiles which are the floaty grins of children who hold their parents' hands and watch the happy dogs who run through parks, throwing off their ridiculous beards and laughing, laughing, laughing. But wait! Prof Hydro's gone and got all serio'. He's docked himself in a study in an old house in Palookaville. He's donned huge human clothes. He looks out onto a cold wet street with the fallen leaves of trees stuck on it. The arrangement of the threads in his tweed jacket is such that that arrangement's own woollen heart is broken. On the radio is nothing because it's switched off.

The Shoes of a Clown

MEANWHILE, TREES (2016)

Oh, how I'd love to own a pair of those
long-toed clown shoes. I think I would find myself so engaging
in them. I'd put them on, sit down upon a chair, reach out my legs
in front of me, and happily behold my oddly-shod feet. I'd stand
and slap their long lengths on the ground to generate a flapping sound,

a flapping sound like a crack. Like a *Crack! Crack!* And then I'd hurry
up to see you, I would hurry backwards up the stairs to show you
my two new shoes, and you'd turn round and apprehend my self
emerging up from them, a genie drifting from its polished lamp,
a plant sucking at its just watered ground.

The Dead Are Helpless

MEANWHILE, TREES (2016)

You can do exactly what you want to the dead,
you can call them filthy names,
you can poke your uncovered arse at them,
you can stick them in the eye, or spit on them
or better, you could prop one up before you shove
its face backwards, your palm driven hard against
the nose, and still nothing bad will happen to you.

You can drag the dead outside into the street
and there you can piss upon them. You could beat
one even further into death with a brick and
no one can point a finger at you, and if they do
then you can tell them to fuck off and mock their
squeamishness by blubbing like a baby in mimicry
of the feebly sensitive.

(It occurs to me just now that you might also want
to stand a stiff in a doorway, have it held in place
by means of ropes and then with all your extant
vehemence, slam the door against it, hear it greet
the dead's unwincing face just before it bangs against
the jamb.) You can always confound the dead.
You can act as though you're going this way,

and then you can go that way and punch them,
and they'll just stare up at the ceiling with that
emptied look of theirs (emptied as an egg is from
its shell). And the dead have nothing at all to use
against you but your horror at their passivity
which looks sometimes so like the unresisting
sweetness of your own poor martyred soul.

No More Mr Nice Guy

MEANWHILE, TREES (2016)

This then,
what you actually witness here, before your
very eyelids, is an actual blooming waste of time, in action,

in real time. I squid you not, certain shall we say 'people'
with a certain shall we say 'cheek' have had a go at me about
punctuality & punctuation, specifically the use

or otherwise of ampersands & obscenities and rubbish
and whatnot. As well as my peculiar drinking and poking fun
at people with or without disabilities and so on.

Well from now on, from the very next thing I do onwards,
I'm going to do exactly as I blinking well please, which is to be
marvellously wretched & frightened and broken and hidden.

Confessional Poem

MEANWHILE, TREES (2016)

Forgive me: I've been tempted to make use
of dissonance in an effort to resonate;

I've walked all over my principles
in day-glo flip-flops;

I've attempted to schmooze when I should
have been rough and abusive;

In the locked bathroom, I've allowed my id
to goose my poor ego, scarring it mentally;

I've papered over the cracks with more cracks
to obtain a 'crack effect'; I've admired the cut

of my own jib, juddering stiff on a wester;
I've planted weeds in other people's

gardens on purpose; I've pretended my eyes
are windows and got drunk

in a room behind them; I've pretended
everything's just terribly droll and awful.

I *Collaboration*

At 4pm Manning and I sat down to discuss the
poem and his role in it. An imaginary wind buffeted
and rattled the remote French farmhouse window
like some sort of device, like a signifier of something
trenchant and solemn. Manning said he was so
excited about the poem that he was actually *rock-
hard* as he put it, and what about I set it in a hotel
room and sort him out with a Latvian stripper and
half an ounce of good quality gak. And with that,
quite matter-of-factly, he pulled his johnson out
of his zoot suit pants to show me his predicament.
His member (though my gaze, I can assure you,
recoiled from it with more haste than a hand would
from a hot coal) looked something like a monstrous
jewel in the setting of the surrounding grey fabric
of his trousers; or like, perhaps, a misplaced floral
buttonhole that would have seemed less offensive
had it protruded from the suit's lapel. It appeared
to me that its grotesque rudeness buzzed against its,
dare I say it, rather feminine beauty with a metallic
ringing sound, but perhaps that was merely tinnitus
brought on by the stress of the situation. I'd never
known Manning to talk or behave in this way before.
And even though it soon came to me that he'd been
suffering from concussion after being hit full on
the head by a lance in a jousting accident, and even
though within a day or so he'd recover fully and
return to his sensitive, and innately feminist self, I
found that I always felt a little wary in his presence
thereafter, for what I'd heard and seen that afternoon
must surely have lain dormant in him for all the
time I'd known him. And perhaps since then, I
consequently feel a little less secure in the company
of all my friends and acquaintances as well, of
course, as in the company of myself.

Yes I admit that I have ate

MEANWHILE, TREES (2016)

that once cool and heavy egg that would
one day have hatched a clever goose of gold.

I cooked it in a pan until it smelted from a hard
into a runny yolk,

and then I promptly drank the molten yellow,
gulped it down and felt it start to burn away

my tongue and gums and teeth whose residue
then blew away as smoke. I felt it coursing down

my roasting throat, through the squiggle
of my blistered viscera,

all the way beyond my screaming shitter
from which it oozed and swarmed and spread

wet metal excrement about my seared balls
and buttocks, before it slowly made to thicken.

And once I'd died of pain, then some time
afterwards I ate away my flesh and bone:

I sank my corpse in acid till no bit of it remained
but just this shiny winding cast, this meandered

single golden sprue that rises from its golden stand,
and displayed like this so well describes a fool.

First off,

MEANWHILE, TREES (2016)

take note of my bespoke rabbit-folk,
pale, no meat on 'em (a transient enthusiasm)

as they burst from squiggly silos,
nibbling, nibbling, nibbling, liebling. Nibbling.

Then see how my consort bod escorts me
in its tight suit like a goon, and look how I leaf

so slowly through your autonomous scent
in the labyrinthine library of your presence.

This world is like edible earth to me: edible, certainly,
but full in the sense of crammed.

Me, I am but a pin – sharp, slid into it, new; or I'm old,
a blunt socket that receives existence's

three-pronged plug that sucks my polished electricity.
(I fill myself also, as a dog fills its wallop.)

Me, I'm the national anthem of somewhere shaky.
You, you're as neat as a particle.

I don't particularly mean you to touch me exactly.

15 | SUSAN WICKS

Filmed by Pamela Robertson-Pearce at Totleigh Barton, Devon, 19 November 2009

Susan Wicks' poetry transforms the apparently ordinary into something precise, surprising and revelatory. She has published seven collections of poetry, four of them with Bloodaxe, *The Months*, *House of Tongues*, *De-iced* and *Night Toad: New & Selected Poems*, which includes a selection from three earlier books published by Faber, *Singing Underwater*, *Open Diagnosis* and *The Clever Daughter*. She is a novelist, short story writer and translator of French poetry, most notably the work of Valérie Rouzeau.

She was in her mid 40s when Faber published her debut collection, *Singing Under Water*, in 1992, which earned her inclusion in the 1994 New Generation Poets promotion of mostly younger poets. Writing then that 'poetry itself requires us to remain essentially vulnerable', and that writers should be 'prepared to take emotional and aesthetic risks [and] lay ourselves open', she began using her own life as material, with poems relating to marriage, motherhood and bereavement; in *Open Diagnosis* (1994), a sequence on coming to terms with the onset of multiple sclerosis; in *The Clever Daughter* (1996), the aftermath of her mother's death and caring for a grief-stricken father. The new poems included in *Night Toad* (2003) move outwards from the intimacy of personal loss to a wider landscape haunted by disappearance – a French Flanders still scarred by successive wars, the woman penfriend of a prisoner on Death Row, an old woman with dementia lost in the woods.

Her later collections show a continued widening of scope, with escape as the main thread of the poems in *De-iced* (2007), which also has a seriously playful sequence on a fictional painter; and in *House of Tongues* (2011), acceptance and refusal, power and the lack of it, silence and the refusal of silence, plus a series of poems set in the Swedish Hanseatic harbour town of Visby. *The Months* (2016) is a book of poems about time, with a long title-poem as its centrepiece interweaving material from two pregnancies spanning two generations. One of the outstanding collections of recent years, *The Months* should have won the prizes it wasn't even shortlisted for.

Pamela filmed her in 2009 at the Arvon Foundation's centre at Totleigh Barton in Devon where she was co-tutoring a writing course with Moniza Alvi and I was their guest reader. The film mainly covers poems from collections included in *Night Toad*.

Ha Ha Bonk

SINGING UNDERWATER (1992) | NIGHT TOAD (2003)

Love the Big Bad joke for adults,
electric custard, gooseberry in a lift.
Why couldn't he have come up with something better?
Knock, knock, I got tired of asking.
Irish stew in the Name of the Law.

And why did the Burglar saw the legs off his bed?
So we could hear the springs creak more clearly?
I wanted to lie low too. Very low, lying with you.
Lying all the time if I could.
Was it that I had stolen something?

And now it goes Ha ha bonk
all down the passage.
A Man laughing his head off.
If I see it rolling I shall pick it up,
carry its belly-laugh with me on a silver plate.

Buying Fish

OPEN DIAGNOSIS (1994) | NIGHT TOAD (2003)

I am one of you, though you do not
know it. We are all hesitant, we are all
gentle and elderly. Together
we point and stutter. Our string bags wait
for wet parcels, gape to receive
the same slippery gift. Tonight we shall all
search our mouths for bones,
as the fragile skeletons
are picked clean, discarded, wrapped in plastic
to cheat the rough tongues of cats. I am
one of you. Watch me buy a thin fillet
of plaice for my single serving, drop keys, fumble
the change. I can beg as well as you
for a few sprigs of sour parsley. I can look
a whole slab of rainbow
trout straight in the eye.

The Clever Daughter

THE CLEVER DAUGHTER (1996) | NIGHT TOAD (2003)
(after a misericord in Worcester Cathedral)

For six hundred years I have travelled
to meet my father. *Neither walking nor riding,*
I have carried your heartbeat to him
carefully, to the sound of singing,
my right hand growing to horn.

Your head droops in a stain of windows
as we come closer. The man who made us –
hare and girl – will barely recognise
the lines his blade left: six centuries
have fused us to a single figure.

Clothed and unclothed, we shall reach him,
netted at his cold feet. But as he unwraps us,
my cloak-threads snagging and breaking,
I shall release you, your pent flutter
of madness. And we shall see you

run from his hands and vanish,
your new zigzag opening the cornfield
like the path of lovers, the endless journey
shaken from your long ears, my gift to him
given and yet not given.

Persephone

THE CLEVER DAUGHTER (1996) | NIGHT TOAD (2003)

Wanting someone who looked natural,
they cast you as Persephone, not thinking
how at regular intervals you were taken
to visit your own mother
under a flaking sky of cream paint
down the echoing corridor
to the long-stay ward, where trees

froze in the black glass
of winter – how you were no stranger
to the clockwork rhythms of figures
moaning and swaying, the mechanical
hands that moved across faces
or scattered things in odd corners,
the hungry hands that flapped after
with their wings of ragged knitting.
Each time you would leave her and return
to birdsong, the urgent green
through frost, the melting grass, the world
you would give her if she would only
recognise you through the heavy doors
your father closed between you. Each week
you rehearsed your flower-steps
with a basket of paper petals
as your teachers smiled down on you, exclaiming
at your sweet face,
at the way you seemed never to see him coming –
as if each last dance were the first dance,
and every mother won over by so little.

My Father's Handkerchiefs

THE CLEVER DAUGHTER (1996) | NIGHT TOAD (2003)

In a controlled explosion
of dry grief, fragile as skeletons,
trembling in my hand like my daughter's
origami monsters, their worn muslin
stiff with mucus, they let me prise them
open. With a sound like tearing
the crumbs of snot flick out at me,
my father's latest creations
dead. Each week I wash them,
press warmth into the yielding creases
and bring them back – so many
neat flat squares for him
to snort his thick grief into. Each week
I find them again, wreckage

of crippled beasts and flowers
to flutter or creep or scuttle
into my machine
as I try to name them: butterfly,
tortoise, crane, crab, lily,
cygnet, crane, crane, crane, crane.

Night Toad

NIGHT TOAD (2003)

You can hardly see him –
his outline, his cold skin
almost a dead leaf,
blotched brown, dull green,
khaki. He sits so quietly
pumping his quick breath
just at the edge of water
between ruts in the path.

And suddenly he is the centre
of a cone of light
falling from the night sky –
ruts running with liquid fire,
cobwebs imprinted on black,
each grass-blade clear
and separate – until the hiss
of human life removes itself,
the air no longer creaks,
the shaking stops
and he can crawl back
to where he came from.

But what *was* this,
if it was not death?

Pistachios

HOUSE OF TONGUES (2011)

A darkening January afternoon.
I stand at the kitchen window absently eating
pistachios left over from Christmas; outside, a blur
of hydrangea as I slide
the edge of my nail between the curved wings of a shell.
They say sex is a kind of dying.

At a certain time of life –
you never know exactly when
or where or how fast – sex leaves.
It's like a tide
slowly leaving a beach, imperceptibly exposing
rocks like bony fingers, hidden tongues of sand
and sometimes the rank on improbable rank
of mussels close as bristles –
millions of them, blue-black,
crowding the surface – like the teeth of combs
or petrified fur
that teases the soles of your bare feet
raw – a whole glittering expanse
of blue-black points, and, hidden inside,
that throb of flesh. As the tide recedes
a million brittle mouths lean shut.

A skeleton hydrangea bowls across the dusk,
shivers. I crack another shell open,
feeling saliva spurt
at the green thought
of pistachios, salt on my lips, shells light as paper.

Cycling to See the Fish-ladder

HOUSE OF TONGUES (2011)

Do they riffle their translucent fins
between the rungs to inch up?
Or do they effortlessly rise
as if through someone's sleep
to do what people do
with ladders – search and replace
a frost-cracked tile, or shake a tree
into a waiting skirt? Each trunk I pedal past
swells and shrills with cicadas before it fades.

But when, blinded by sweat, I finally arrive
the ladder's shut
by a Red Alert. *Merci
de votre compréhension.* I straddle my bike
and read what power means
to fish and spawning-grounds. I think I understand:
a glitch and the dream floats belly-up,
the waters of the Garonne
log-jammed and stinking. There's only the sky's

unbroken blue, the tree's small pool of shadow,
a woman's leaning bike. Nothing you can pull out
in a shining shaft, no wooden feet
to dent the mud,
no uprights you can steady against death.

16 | ROBERT WRIGLEY

Filmed by Neil Astley in Norwich, 12 November 2013

Robert Wrigley is a poet of America's northern Rocky Mountains. Over three decades his poetry's pervading concerns have been rural Western landscapes and humankind's place within the natural world. His most recent poems have presented a portrait of a nation, one that is a singular part of a singular planet, with an exuberant and frequently exasperating culture. In such a country, the glimpse of a horse under a full moon can be a defining moment, full of grace and a new, if not always comfortable, awareness. So it is with a saved lock of a lover's hair, the memory of a vanished glacier, or a childhood friend disappeared in war. Elegiac and lyrical, playful and angry, his poetry offers a vision that is fierce, unflinching, and clear.

Philip Levine wrote that 'Wrigley has become someone else, someone who has wandered into a ferocious cave of the natural world and suddenly sees his life, and ours as well, in bold and undreamed of colours. It's almost as though a veil has been lifted from his eyes, and the glorious and terrifying truths have been revealed in poems that are at once majestic and terrifying.'

Born in 1951 in East St Louis, Illinois, he was drafted in 1971, but later discharged as a conscientious objector. The first in his family to graduate from college, and the first male for generations to escape work in a coal mine, he now teaches on the MFA program at the University of Idaho. He lives in the woods on Moscow Mountain, Idaho, with his wife, writer Kim Barnes.

His first book to be published in the UK, *The Church of Omnivorous Light: Selected Poems* (Bloodaxe Books, 2013), draws on several collections published in the US, including *Beautiful Country* (2010), *Earthly Meditations: New and Selected Poems* (2006), *Lives of the Animals* (2003), *Reign of Snakes* (1999) and *In the Bank of Beautiful Sins* (1995). It was launched at Aldeburgh Poetry Festival, followed by readings in Hull, Newcastle, and Norwich, where I tried to film him in the basement of the Butchery, Helen Ivory and Martin Figura's home, but on seeing the subterranean footage decided that a black and white treatment was necessary, one which is nevertheless in keeping with Bob's author photographs, which are always Old West monochrome.

Moonlight: Chickens on the Road

MOON IN A MASON JAR (1986) | THE CHURCH OF OMNIVOROUS LIGHT (2013)

Called out of dream by the pitch and screech,
I awoke to see my mother's hair
set free of its pincurls, springing out
into the still and hurtling air
above the front seat and just as suddenly gone.
The space around us twisted,
and in the instant before the crash
I heard the bubbling of the chickens,
the homely racket they make at all speeds,
signifying calm, resignation, oblivion.

And I listened. All through the slash
and clatter, the rake of steel, shatter of glass,
I listened, and what came
was a blizzard moan in the wind, a wail
of wreckage, severed hoses and lives,
a storm of loose feathers, and in the final
whirl approximating calm, the cluck
and fracas of the birds. I crawled
on hands and knees where a window should
have been and rose uneven

in November dusk. Wind blew
a snow of down, and rows of it quivered along
the shoulder. One thin stream of blood
oozed, flocked in feathers.
This was in the Ozarks, on a road curving miles
around Missouri, and as far as I could
see, no light flickered through the timber,
no mail box leaned the flag
of itself toward pavement, no cars
seemed ever likely to come along.

So I walked, circled the darkening disaster
my life had come to, and cried.
I cried for my family there,
knotted in the snarl of metal and glass;
for the farmer, looking dead, half in
and half out of his windshield; and for myself,

516

ambling barefoot through the jeweled debris,
glass slitting little blood-stars in my soles,
my arm hung loose at the elbow
and whispering its prophecies of pain.

Around and around the tilted car
and steaming truck, around the heap
of exploded crates, the smears and small hunks
of chicken and straw. Through
an hour of loneliness and fear
I walked, in the almost black of Ozark night,
the moon just now burning into Missouri.
Behind me, the chickens followed my lead,
some fully upright, pecking

the dim pavement for suet or seed,
some half-hobbled by their wounds, worthless wings
fluttering in the effort. The faintest
light turned their feathers phosphorescent,
and as I watched they came on, as though they believed
me some savior, some highwayman
or commando come to save them the last night
of their clucking lives. This, they must have
believed, was the end they'd always heard of,
this the rendering more efficient than the axe,

the execution more anonymous than
a wringing arm. I walked on, no longer crying,
and soon the amiable and distracted chattering came
again, a sound like chuckling, or the backward such
of hard laughter. And we walked
to the cadence their clucking called,
a small boy towing a cloud around a scene
of death, coming round and round
like a dream, or a mountain road,
like a pincurl, like pulse, like life.

Heart Attack

MOON IN A MASON JAR (1986) | THE CHURCH OF OMNIVOROUS LIGHT (2013)

Throwing his small, blond son
into the air, he begins to feel it,
a slow-motion quivering, some part
broken loose and throbbing with its own pulse,
like the cock's involuntary leaping
toward whatever shadow looms in front.

It is below his left shoulder-blade,
a blip regular as radar, and he thinks of wings
and flight, his son's straight soar and fall
out of and into his high-held hands.
He is amused by the quick change
on the boy's little face: from the joy

of release and catch, to the near terror
at apex. It is the same with every throw.
And every throw comes without
his knowing. Nor his son's. Again
and again, the rise and fall, like breathing,
again the joy and fear, squeal and laughter,

until the world becomes a swarm of shapes
around him, and his arms
go leaden and prickled, and he knows
the sound is no longer laughter
but wheezing, knows he holds his son
in his arms and has not let him fly

upward for many long moments now.
He is on his knees, as his son stands,
supporting him, the look in the child's face
something the man has seen before:
not fear, not joy, not even misunderstanding,
but the quick knowledge sons

must come to, at some age
when everything else is put aside –
the knowledge of death, the stench
of mortality – that fraction of an instant
even a child can know, when
his father does not mean to leave, but goes.

518

County

BEAUTIFUL COUNTRY (2010) | THE CHURCH OF OMNIVOROUS LIGHT (2013)

County of innumerable nowheres, half its dogs
underfed and of indeterminate breed. County
of the deep fryer and staples in glass against mice,
county of horned gods and billed hats. Sweat county,
shiver county. The hallowed outhouse
upholstered in wooly carpet, the sack of lime,
time out of time, county of country music.

Insufficient snowplows county, county
of the blasted doe all winter in a drift, dust sift
and feather duster county, county of the quo
all status is attached to. Of batches and bitchdogs
howling, of rowels and boots, of soot wash,
of the chimney sweep's red beard,
of the songless radio preaching to no one in the shed.

County of the deadly road, of the shoat pig roasted
in a pit. County of molasses, hobo coffee,
and sugarless soft-drink, county of the methamphetamine
picture window, of the padlock and massive hasp.
County of tools and dewormers. Curry comb
and salt block, black pepper gravy, red-eye venison,
blood sausage, county of Bud Light girl posters.

Treblehook county, chum county, bear bait
and dead wolf county. County of the coyote pelt
nailed to the barn door. Bruised woman county,
of men missing one or more fingers, single-finger
wave county. Pistol alongside the cash register.
Pitch-dense firewood county, county of the fearful
and fearless, of the distant mysterious school.

Target-poor county, Walmart holyland,
malodorous pulp mill and paper plate county.
County of the hundred yard drive to the post office,
oddly familiar faces among the wanted posters,
four hour drive from the county seat county,
unadopted highway, county of no return.
County of August always somewhere burning.

Beercan bejeweled barrow pit county, hardly
one bullet-unpunctuated county road sign county.
County of the ATV and ancient Indian trail
into the high mountains. Get your bull or buck
county. On-the-way-to-somewhere-else,
doe-see-doe, hundred frozen casseroles
after the funeral, go to heaven county,

blister and blister rust county, Jahweh trailerhouse
county, unassisted living, county
of the Gospels and the Penthouse under the bed.
County of tenderness and terror, of almost
universal skepticism, Jesus country county.
County of the cell tower stipend, everywhere
and anywhere, boneyard county, county

a day's drive from the end of the open road.
Softshell Baptist county. Pentecostal pancake county.
County of illusions and of hard facts. Rock
and broken shock, rock and roll aught-six
save your shell casing. County of not quite breath-taking
vistas, of the for sale sign, of timothy and brome,
spring and autumn slaughter county, meat county, home.

Mouth

THE CHURCH OF OMNIVOROUS LIGHT (2013)

When she bought the thrift shop ventriloquist's dummy,
she said, Who could resist him? and it was true,
a little man who'd sit on your lap
and say the things your lips should not.
And they were expensive, these things, custom
made, she believed, though that was what
at last began to bother her about him:
the coiffed black hair, the pencil mustache,
his diminutive, excellent tuxedo,
like a dollhouse playboy or a maitre d' nose high
to the place setting. It wasn't so much
how he looked drolly on as she made love
with a larger if less wooden man, but that
she'd sometimes think to sit him on her bare thigh
afterward as he reviewed his competitor's performance.
And it wasn't that her hand inside him made her,
or him, or them, cruel exactly, or even unkind,
though there were sighs she could fake
and words he would not. It wasn't even the lover
who took him by the throat and tossed him face first
back on his corner chair and then took her again,
and harder, nor that as he did she imagined
the fleshly man the dummy, the taste
of his sweat the dummy's sweat, the smell
of his dangerous rage the source of the words
only the dummy could utter. No. It was,
she insisted, the mouth nothing ever entered
but from within, and how she could open that mouth
all the way and tilt back the empty head of him
and laugh, and laugh, from the gut, from the heart,
which was nothing more or less than her fist.

A Lock of Her Hair

BEAUTIFUL COUNTRY (2010) | THE CHURCH OF OMNIVOROUS LIGHT (2013)

As a hoodoo-voodoo, get-you-back-to-me tool,
this hank's thankless task is vast,
a head down to the ground impossibility, possibly,
since what I'm thinking of is your toe pad pinknesses too,
your soup hots and round-and-rounds, the fine
and perfect poundage of you on my paws, the very cause
and problem I moan for and bemoan
the absence of. For Love, above the head
this reddish coil once lavishly wore, there's an air so far away
it's sad for me to even think the same sun's rays play
where it was and do to you what I would do
if I were there or you were here. Still, some thrills
remembered do resemble thrills, one hopes, and the ropes
of it that gently fell around me bound me so well
no hell of miles can defile this dream I dream. I mean
the anyway DNA I can find of you. I mean the home
of bones and blood that holds the whole of you
and which this fizzed-up missive means to conjure, missy,
my world in a curl, girl, this man oh man half man I am
when you're gone.

INDEX OF TITLES

This index only covers poem titles in English

DVD FORMAT

Since our primary readership is the UK, our films have been converted to PAL format. Whether you can play our DVDs will depend upon what kind of DVD player you have, or whether you watch DVDs on a PC. If you live in Britain, you should have no problem.

PAL/SECAM is the TV format used in Britain and most of Europe, most of Africa, China, India, Australia, New Zealand, Israel, North Korea, and other countries. NTSC is the TV format used in Canada, Japan, Mexico, Philippines, Taiwan, the United States, and other countries.

DVD players sold in Britain and Europe will play PAL DVDs (and most will play NTSC DVDs also).

However, most players sold in the US only play NTSC DVDs (but some recent models will play both PAL and NTSC DVDs). A very small number of NTSC players sold in the US (such as Apex and SMC) can convert PAL to NTSC. But most NTSC TVs don't work with PAL video.

If you live in the US, it is unlikely that you will be able to play our DVDs using a DVD player. However, if you can play DVDs on your computer, you should have no problems.

Most DVD PC software and hardware can play both NTSC and PAL video. Some PCs can only display the converted video on the computer monitor, but others can output it as a video signal for a TV.

In an ideal world we'd produce our DVD-book with DVDs in either format and give overseas readers the choice, but unfortunately that would be much too costly. If the manufacturers had agreed upon a standard worldwide format 20 years ago, no one would have this problem now.